BREAKING FREE

BREAKING FREE

A Memoir of Love and Revolution

SUSAN EISENHOWER

FARRAR

STRAUS

GIROUX

New York

LIBRARY OF CONGRESS CATALOGING-IN-PUBLICATION DATA
Eisenhower, Susan.
Breaking free: a memoir of love and revolution / Susan
Eisenhower. —1st ed.
p.   cm.
1. United States—Relations—Soviet Union. 2. Soviet Union—
Relations—United States. 3. Eisenhower, Susan. 4. Sagdeev, R. Z.
5. Physicists—Soviet Union—Biography. 6. Sovietologists—United
States—Biography.   I. Title.
E183.8.S65E38   1995   303.48′247073′0922—dc20 [B]   94-46563 CIP

To Roald

Acknowledgments

I owe a great debt of gratitude to Ron Goldfarb, my agent. It was in conversation with him that the idea for this book was born. He was unstinting in his encouragement, and without his unwavering support this book might never have been written.

I am also deeply grateful to the entire staff of Farrar, Straus and Giroux, whose professionalism and dedication were evident from the outset. Most important, I extend my sincere thanks and appreciation to my editor, Elisabeth Sifton, for her unflagging interest in this project. She brought skill, sensitivity, and considerable experience to the book, and I, as well as the story, was the beneficiary. Special thanks go to my copyeditor, Lynn Warshow, and to my publicist, Ida Veltri. My thanks also go to her assistant, Luba Ostashevsky, who was an enormous help in coordinating all the various aspects of the book during its production.

I would like to acknowledge my family members for their input and moral support: especially my mother, who read the manuscript at an early stage; my daughters, Caroline, who also read an earlier draft and made many excellent suggestions, and Laura and Amy for their encouragement during the creative process; my sister Anne, for her attentive ear; and my father, for his wise counsel.

Special appreciation also goes to two others who read my manuscript at different stages: Heather Parrish, of the Center for Post-Soviet Studies, who helped check facts and coordinate with the publisher; and John Andrews, a long-time friend. Not only did John read my manuscript and offer invaluable comments, but his confidence in the outcome was as undimming in this process as it was during the turbulent years described in this book.

Finally, I would like to extend my special appreciation to Roald. In working on his own memoirs, *The Making of a Soviet Scientist*, he understood that the political dimension of his experience in the last days of the Soviet Union could be told honestly only with the overlay of our personal story. He was convinced, and it is my hope, that *Breaking Free* will give life to those tumultuous years and that it will offer some understanding of Russia's difficult transition ahead.

S.E.

Contents

PART THREE   1989

PART FOUR   1990

BREAKING FREE

Prologue

If all the records told the same tale—then the lie passed into history and became truth. "Who controls the past," ran the Party slogan, "controls the future: who controls the present controls the past" . . . Whatever was true now was true from everlasting to everlasting. It was quite simple. All that was needed was an unending series of victories over your own memory.

—GEORGE ORWELL, *1984*

The Soviets always enjoyed saying, "The future is bright, but the past is unpredictable." Although it is clearly a matter of degree, rewriting history is also part of the American political landscape. Perhaps that is why my grandfather Dwight D. Eisenhower inserted a time capsule into the wall of my grandparents' home in Gettysburg, not to be opened until the year 2052. No one knows the contents, but his intention may have been to preserve his own unadulterated account of the large historical events that he witnessed and helped to shape.

When I first heard of it more than a decade ago, I was intrigued by his gesture, even if I didn't quite understand its underlying significance. As a student of history, Granddad must have recognized that collective and individual self-interests invariably, over time, refashion events—concocting legends, myths, and icons that are politically or ideologically self-serving.

As someone who watched the second Russian revolution unfold at close hand, I, too, have seen this process at work. Even though less than a decade has elapsed since Soviet Communism was discredited and the Soviet Union collapsed, it is hard sometimes for me to recognize the events, the developments, and the personalities of that period—as they are being depicted. Already people who were involved, centrally or peripherally, in the momentous last days of the Cold War and the Soviet empire have created better historic roles for themselves, or have taken credit for developments that were beyond the influence of any one force. The notion that one man, Mikhail Gorbachev, single-handedly "freed" the Soviet people is one such fallacy.

It was my rare privilege to see, with my own eyes, the awakening of an entire nation as its people created change one small step at a time. Given the nature of Soviet cultural and political history, the strides that were taken by those outside the regime required a special kind of bravery, a courage that was particularly moving to observe, as the outcome of these world-changing events was by no means assured. A deep sense of national humiliation, which eventually brought Russia's neo-fascists to public and parliamentary prominence, was incubating. While these anti-Western, anti-reform forces were waiting for their chance, the outcome of history was teetering in the balance.

Although I was not a "player" in a direct sense during those years of tremendous turmoil, I fell in love with a man who was: Roald Sagdeev, a radical reformer and an early Gorbachev adviser. As the U.S.S.R.'s top space scientist and director of its Space Research Institute, he had close ties to the Soviet military-industrial complex—one of the most reactionary and secretive of all Soviet industrial sectors. During the years 1987–91, Roald's personal safety and the future of our relationship were constantly in question. Because of this, I found myself not only a mesmerized observer but someone with an enormous stake in the outcome of events. These were uncertain and dangerous times, and from the perspective of Soviet history and the outcomes of earlier crackdowns in Czechoslovakia, Chile, and China, Roald and I were living on the edge.

Looking back on it now that I am married to Roald—from the distance of a few years and six thousand miles—it sometimes seems hard to believe that we took the risks we did. But I am faithfully reminded of them by the diary I kept—and it is upon that written record that I have based this book.

Not everyone will agree with the characterizations I have drawn here, but I have tried to depict people and events as I saw and felt them at the time. What follows, then, is my own little time capsule, an intimate offering of this highly public and epoch-making period. It is not a scholarly book of analysis—I have written my share of those assessments elsewhere. It is, rather, a memoir of love in a time of revolution, when my friendship and eventual marriage to Roald gave me not only a roller-coaster seat from which to watch the events but also a vantage point that would change the way I see his country and my own.

PART ONE

The ideal set up by the Party was something huge, terrible, glittering —a world of steel and concrete, of monstrous machines and terrifying weapons—a nation of warriors and fanatics, marching forward in perfect unity, all thinking the same thoughts and shouting the same slogans, perpetually working, fighting, triumphing, persecuting—three hundred million people all with the same face. The reality was decaying dingy cities, where underfed people shuffled to and fro in leaky shoes, in patched-up nineteenth century houses that always smelt of cabbage and bad lavatories.

—GEORGE ORWELL, *1984*

1 : *An Unlikely Road to Russia*

I came of age on my fortieth birthday, December 31, 1991. That evening
my husband, Roald, and I drank a toast to me and to the New Year. But
we also raised our glasses to the demise of Communism and the collapse
of the Soviet empire. Life for us would now truly begin—safe, it seemed,
from the long hand of Roald's enemies and other reactionary forces. When
the red flag went down permanently over the Kremlin that December, it
also signified the end of my own personal journey, a fortuitous one that
had taken me from the sheltered American scene into the jaws of a
revolution—an experience that defined, forever, my view of the world.

From my earliest years, the notion of fate always fascinated me. When
I was young, I would play little games like, If my mother hadn't married
my father, who would I be? This question always gripped me. I understood,
even before I was ten years old, that if my mother had married another
man I would not have been the granddaughter of the thirty-fourth President
of the United States, and consequently the overwhelming identity that
people associate with me would have been absent from my life completely.
So if she had married someone other than my father, I would have been
wholly different than I am. Given the critical significance of my parents'
union in my life, I could not help being exceedingly conscious of the fragile
chain of events that brought them together.

Maybe I carried that realization with me into later life. In the 1970s,
some of my friends and colleagues scornfully criticized me for not having
a "life strategy"—a notion that was popular then among trendy young
professionals who seemed to think it was possible to make a detached plan

for the future of one's life at some early point and then simply "implement" it. I was guilty as charged. By the time I had reached my early thirties, I was only too aware of the power that chance meetings and small off-the-cuff decisions have on making us who we turn out to be. My life had already taken some unexpected turns.

I had a protected and happy upbringing, surrounded by loving parents and grandparents. We were a tightly knit family, especially since my father, John, was Ike and Mamie's second and only surviving child. Close proximity and the peculiarities of my grandfather's position drew our generations together. I flourished in this environment and was given rein to find my place in it. The third of four children and my family's second daughter, I grew up with a reputation of being strong-minded, if not strong-willed. Daddy would jokingly say, with a hint of admiration: "Sue is seldom right, but never in doubt." A gentle tease that was easily made about an outspoken yet unrebellious daughter.

Freewheeling debates were a function of our family life, but they were not part of our lives outside this small inner circle. As part of a visible political family, we had an unspoken rule that beyond what my mother, Barbara, would call (to my embarrassment) "the bosom of the family," we were to keep our opinions to ourselves. This family-imposed censorship was a natural outgrowth of a sincere desire to protect the President. All of us understood that we were, in a sense, his real ambassadors.

Public scrutiny was an unpleasant, if inevitable, fact of life. While both my parents played their roles with considerable success, our fishbowl existence was a strain on my shy and somewhat introverted father. The best years of his life were not his own, and this constituted an irreparable loss that I think he still sometimes feels. I could not gauge him well during my youth; although he was affectionate, he seemed somewhat preoccupied and distant. My mother, however, was gregarious and energetic, and the double role she played, full-time mother by day and daughter-in-law of the President by night, was one she mastered to perfection.

Faced with the challenge the White House poses to normal family life, my parents struggled to dampen the effect my grandfather's presidency might have on us kids. This was especially difficult to do with the Secret Service, which was assigned to watch over my siblings and me. My parents refused protection, but the Lindbergh kidnapping was a lingering worry. So the

"Diaper Detail," as they were known, followed my brother and sisters and me everywhere: onto the playground, around the neighborhood, and to our friends' houses. They even sat outside our classroom doors.

I distinctly remember one incident that took place when I was in first grade. After a fight with my brother—and what I thought was my mother's unsatisfactory intervention—I decided that I was going to run away from home. Angrily I stomped up to my room to pack my most treasured belongings before leaving the house for good. The family's complete disregard for this dramatic moment bothered me and made me even more determined. The entire family looked on as I stormed out of the house. My mother seemed quite unperturbed—and for good reason. Following slowly behind me in a black sedan were two Secret Service agents, conveying on their walkie-talkies my exact whereabouts. The odyssey lasted a little more than one full block. Frustrated and humiliated, I returned home.

I started adulthood as many women did in the late 1960s and early 1970s: with college, early marriage, children. I never imagined that I would end up as a single parent or a career woman. But divorce and the financial responsibility for three young daughters, Caroline, Laura, and Amy, necessitated that I embark on a serious career in the late 1970s. I started work, first in journalism for an upstate New York newspaper chain, then in public affairs and marketing communications for several companies in Rochester and then in Washington, D.C.

Less than ten years later, a temporary professional assignment again decisively altered my life and changed the person I was likely to become. In 1986, for perhaps sentimental reasons, I took a leave of absence from my company, The Eisenhower Group, Inc., to serve as an interim president of the newly established Eisenhower World Affairs Institute, named in my grandfather's memory. The organization needed a marketing and programmatic boost, and I very much wanted it to succeed. I agreed to give it a few years.

I had never intended to get into the foreign policy or Soviet field; I had little incentive to do so. Very few women were in it, and outside of government, job opportunities were scarce. Apart from a general interest in European and Russian history, I had no other connection with Soviet affairs except as a person with a few indelible childhood memories. But it is possible that my family associations predisposed me for what was to come—although neither my grandfather nor my father could ever have imagined that one day their offspring would fall in love with and eventually marry a Soviet official.

I was born in 1951 in Fort Knox, Kentucky, where my father, a regular army officer, was then attending the Armored School. My grandparents were in France at the time. Despite vehement Soviet objections to the newly formed Western alliance, in early 1951 President Truman had sent Granddad to Europe as the first commander of NATO forces. It was a dangerous mission. The Soviet Union took the position that the establishment of NATO constituted "an act of war," and my father later told me that the Communist Party, which was well entrenched in France, had created such a bad atmosphere there that he had actually feared for my grandparents' safety when they left America for Paris. Riots with as many as 100,000 people racked the city, and my grandparents' arrival was greeted with placards and graffiti everywhere saying "Death to the Americans" and "Ike Go Home."

Just seven months after my birth, my father was sent to Korea. He left from Chicago only days after my grandfather won the Republican nomination for the presidency. In November 1952, Granddad was elected thirty-fourth President of the United States. Within two months of his inauguration, Joseph Stalin, Soviet dictator and international outlaw, died. Granddad understood immediately that his passing could create an "opening" in East–West relations. In his memoirs he wrote: "The new leadership, no matter how strong its links with the Stalin era, was not completely bound . . . to the ways of a dead man. The future was theirs to make."

Although my father was by then on assignment to the Pentagon and was later detailed to the White House, I was oblivious of the historic developments taking place in U.S.–Soviet relations, from the first postwar summit meeting in Geneva in 1955 to the signing of the first General Exchanges Agreement in 1958, which established formal U.S.–Soviet interaction across a wide range of professional and artistic lines. It wasn't until years later that I even heard of other Eisenhower initiatives such as Atoms for Peace, my grandfather's proposal to find ways to use atomic energy for international benefit, and Open Skies, his idea of mutual U.S.–Soviet aerial inspection and verification of nuclear stockpiles. My awareness of the U.S.–Soviet standoff began with the arrival of Soviet Premier Nikita Khrushchev in the United States, an encounter I still vividly remember.

During the 1959 Camp David summit meeting, Granddad suggested to

Khrushchev that they take an excursion to the Eisenhower farm in Gettysburg, Pennsylvania. My mother was asked to round up the kids—my siblings, David, Anne, and Mary, and me—from our home adjacent to the farm. In a state of high anticipation, we awaited the helicopter as it lowered itself onto my grandparents' front lawn.

The meeting took place on the sunporch, my grandparents' favorite sitting room. According to my father, Khrushchev "assumed the role of beneficent grandfather," and we, Ike's grandchildren, preened with delight at the attention Khrushchev paid us. During the conversation, the Soviet premier suggested to Granddad that he bring us with him on his forthcoming visit to the Soviet Union. We squirmed in our chairs with excitement at the suggestion. Later, our parents told us there was no way we'd be allowed to go on such a trip: they always worried about the adverse effect publicity could have on our upbringing, but I also had the feeling they thought our presence in the Soviet Union would be used for Soviet propaganda purposes. They were probably wise to be cautious. My siblings and I were preadolescent, and given to youthful surges of enthusiasm. We demonstrated as much when Khrushchev pinned a red star on each of us at the end of the meeting, much to the quiet displeasure of the other adults. After the helicopter lifted off its grassy pad and we were back in the car headed for home, my mother said sharply, "Give me those pins!" Collecting them from us all, she impetuously threw them out the car window. "Don't be too impressed by this man. He is not our friend," she told us gravely. "Khrushchev represents a totalitarian regime that has no respect for human individual life. He said he would bury us. He said: *Ike's grandchildren!*"

My father was no less emphatic. Admonishing my brother, David, for his excitement, Daddy told him sternly that if Khrushchev or the Soviet Union ever invaded the United States, "guess which family would be the first to be shot!"

The memory of Khrushchev lingered for us all, and I began to make a connection between scares about things such as "radiation-contaminated snow" and that friendly little man we had met on the porch at the farm. There were the standard and utterly useless air-raid drills at school, and my parents, like many others, made inquiries about the possibility of building a bomb shelter. They were told that our basement would be of absolutely no use as a shelter in the event of a nuclear war, but like many other young couples around the country, they stocked up on dried and canned food, just in case.

My grandparents' Secret Service men recommended that a bomb shelter actually be built on the farm. Although there was pressure on Granddad to agree, he grimly rejected it. His reasoning was simple: if we had a bomb shelter and were capable, even theoretically, of surviving, how could we morally save ourselves and not the other townspeople, who would also be looking for protection?

Such considerations did not seem academic. I remember the night we sat around the television set and watched President Kennedy address the nation about the Cuban missile crisis. My father, by this time an army reserve officer, listened carefully to the speech, then somberly told us kids that he might be called into active service. Although the significance of the confrontation between Washington and Moscow was too much for us to comprehend fully then, it presented the terrible prospect that Daddy would be embroiled in another real and terrible war.

Between such crises, the Cold War simply loomed. I don't remember specific family discussions on the subject, but anti-Communism came naturally to us and patriotism was something we felt deeply, though we did not wear it on our sleeves. Granddad believed that apart from Communism's obvious atrocities, it robbed people of their uniqueness and denied them the opportunity for self-reliance and personal initiative. He also genuinely believed in man's relationship with the Almighty, and he disdained the Communist state's rejection of God.

Although he hated what the Soviet regime represented, he understood the difference between the totalitarian-authoritarian leadership and its people. In his memoirs, published in 1964, he wrote: "When the day comes that the Communist people are as well-informed as those of free nations, then dissatisfaction, unrest and resentment among hundreds of millions of people will eventually bring about either reforms in their government or the violent destruction of Communist dictatorships."

Such commonsense views about the Soviet Union's future were not widespread at the time. And even though I must have internalized his beliefs, as a young person I also absorbed much of the fear or suspicion of *anything* Soviet or Russian that was pervasive in American society.

During the summer of 1968 I found a job working as a tour guide at Freedom's Foundation at Valley Forge. There I ushered drop-in tourists around the grounds and spoke to them about America's valued institutions that were imperiled by Soviet Communism all over the world. That was the summer the Soviet Union invaded Czechoslovakia—proof, it seemed, that the danger of Soviet power was real and ever-present, and a threat to our "American way of life."

.   .   .

Twenty-five years after Khrushchev issued an invitation for my siblings and me to come to his country, I made my first trip to the U.S.S.R. It was a trip a friend and colleague predicted would change my life. In 1986, John Wallach, foreign editor of Hearst Newspapers, had an idea. He wanted to hold a Chautauqua town meeting in the Soviet Union. The Chautauqua Institution, in upstate New York, had held a small exchange with the Soviets the year before, but now, after the 1985 summit meeting between President Reagan and the reform-minded Mikhail Gorbachev, the time seemed right to take such a debate to the Soviet Union. He thought the Eisenhower Institute should be involved.

The idea was to bring U.S. government figures and well-known opinion leaders together with their Soviet counterparts to debate a number of issues before an audience of a thousand people or more, including two hundred American citizens who would travel with us. Written and verbal questions would be posed to the speakers; entertainers from both countries would also perform in the evenings. The Soviet authorities had never permitted such an open public forum in their country. So we were sailing in uncharted waters.

Relations between the two nations seemed intractable, the arms race continued unabated, and Star Wars technology loomed on the horizon. Although the new Soviet leader had come to power with rhetoric about openness and reform, Soviet state behavior had shown little change. The "evil empire," as Ronald Reagan had dubbed it, had legions of Jewish refuseniks unable to emigrate, and its military forces were fully engaged in Afghanistan. The Soviet government's willingness to permit an open public forum under these circumstances was an intriguing signal.

I persuaded the directors of the Eisenhower Institute to adopt the project in partnership with the Chautauqua Institution. As appealing as the open forum sounded, however, raising money for it was not an easy prospect. Despite my enthusiasm, most people I approached said our plans sounded too risky. "Anything could happen between then and now," they said. Others were just plain doubtful that the conference would accomplish anything. "All you'll get is propaganda, and the audience or 'citizens' they choose will be hand-picked." The naysayers no doubt felt vindicated on April 26 when an explosion and fire at the Chernobyl nuclear power plant was reported. It took Gorbachev two weeks to come forward and address the disaster publicly. His conspicuous silence dealt a serious blow to his credibility as the initiator of *glasnost,* or "openness," in Soviet society.

If it had been difficult to raise money for what we called our Journey in Open Diplomacy before, the Chernobyl disaster now cast a deadly pall on our plans. Deeply concerned that the Institute's first effort might fail, I put all my energy into identifying potential donors and persuading them that the United States had a unique opportunity, through this project, to speak directly to the Soviet people. Eventually the Institute met its goal.

On August 30, only weeks before our delegation was to depart for the Soviet Union, another crisis struck: *U.S. News and World Report* correspondent Nicholas Daniloff was arrested in Moscow for allegedly spying. The American government maintained that the Soviets were retaliating for the American arrest of Gennady Zakharov, an alleged Soviet spy who had worked for the Soviet UN delegation in New York. The Soviets, however, held firm that Daniloff had been collecting secret information on the war in Afghanistan and on other sensitive issues that he had been planning to pass along to U.S. intelligence. There had been other such detentions in the past, but the timing of these two arrests seemed ominous, particularly as the United States and the Soviet Union were moving toward another summit meeting, by then in the advanced planning stages. Secretary of State George Shultz accused Moscow of resorting to "hostage taking as an instrument of policy,"* and there was considerable speculation that certain forces in both countries did not want a superpower summit.

The Daniloff incident was all that was needed to prompt a number of our conference delegates to cancel their participation, particularly those with more conservative views, such as Ambassador Jeanne Kirkpatrick. I was upset that these delegates, indeed the United States government, saw the abandonment of this project as a way to punish the Soviets. Frustrated by the logic, I wondered why they couldn't see that American interests would only be damaged by passing up the opportunity to express our views in an open forum.

My colleagues and I were under a great deal of pressure because of the uncertainty of the situation. While negotiations for Daniloff's release were going on at the highest level, our project, which cost hundreds of thousands of dollars to fund and countless hours to organize, was also being held hostage in the superpower struggle.

---

* It was even implied that the decision to take Daniloff must have involved Gorbachev himself. *Newsweek,* September 15, 1986, p. 38.

Then, as if by a miracle, the United States and the Soviet Union announced that Nick Daniloff had been transferred from Lefortovo prison to home arrest at the American Embassy in Moscow. With the go-ahead from the U.S. administration, we declared that enough progress had been made to proceed with our Journey in Open Diplomacy. With heightened skepticism of the Soviet Union, however, we took off in our chartered plane for the U.S.S.R. and the first open policy debate in Soviet history.

Given the rhetoric on the American side during the Cold War, I was unprepared for what I saw and felt when I arrived in the Soviet Union. Like other Americans, I had known that the Soviet economy was in trouble and that the Soviet system had failed to produce for its people. But our bus ride through the forlorn streets of Leningrad on the morning of our arrival was a profound shock for me. Nothing had prepared me for *how much* it had failed. The glory of Peter the Great's city was covered in dust and decay, a wreck of crumbling façades, rusting streetcars, and empty shops. This was the Communism we were frightened of? This was what the U.S. government still touted as a threat to the American way of life?

If the physical sight of Leningrad was a shock, there was no psychic letup during the long hours of the conference itself, which was held in a sleepy little resort town called Yurmala, only miles from Riga, Latvia. The week was painfully tense, as mutual accusations were hurled from every corner. The American government's plan for a Strategic Defense Initiative and the Daniloff affair brought mutual vindictiveness to such an absurd level that one of the American citizens chided the debaters on both sides for sounding like quarrelsome little boys, locked in an eternal game of one-up-manship.

After the conference, our delegation went to Moscow, where the full force of Soviet oppression could be felt. It was in the atmosphere: on the street, in the hotel, in the food, in the faces. Moscow was large and forbidding, and so was the government hotel we were assigned to there. Built during the Stalin period, the Sovietskaya Hotel was run under the watchful eye of the receptionists and the "hall ladies," whose presence felt like that of reproachful boarding-school hall proctors. Ostensibly there to handle guests' small needs, such as tea and telephone calls, they left no doubt, even in the minds of newcomers, that they monitored everyone's movements in the hotel—and probably a lot more. While the other conference participants had been put in pocket-handkerchief-sized rooms, I was embarrassed and honestly rather unnerved by the huge suite I had been given. I didn't like being singled out, and I was certain that my digs had been wired for sound.

Many of us also got a pungent taste of the daily fare of repression that most Soviets were served up. One person in our group complained that his address book had been tampered with, that several pages of numbers had been torn from it. Others said they had been followed to meetings they were having with refuseniks. Another, under great stress from the apparent surveillance, stayed in his room during almost the entire time we were in Moscow.

Our 250-person delegation was reunited on the plane ride back to Washington. After the chartered 747 took off from Sheremetyvo Airport, one person after another got onto the public-address system of the airplane to issue words of thanks and small impressions. A number of them, still numb from the tension and the bilateral bickering, offered toasts to America and freedom and democracy. After an hour and a half in the air, the pilot announced that we had left Soviet airspace. Sensing the mood of the delegation, he added, "God bless America." With that, the passengers broke into rapturous applause.

I sat glumly, unable to share my colleagues' and friends' patriotic outpourings. America wasn't the issue. Freedom wasn't the issue. The objective of our visit had been to increase understanding and to open the process of debate in the U.S.S.R. During the conference hadn't we chided the Soviets for their excessive expressions of national chauvinism? Hadn't we tried to make a breakthrough beyond superpower point scoring and one-upmanship? There was no reason to feel competitive or superior; no need to try to win converts. I was upset that my American colleagues couldn't see what I felt so deeply and saw so clearly with my eyes. The Soviet regime couldn't meet the most basic needs of its people. Although the state provided the minimum, I could see little that held out any hope for the future of the Soviet state, at least within the pat Leninist formulas.

Instead of applauding, I tried to suppress the profound sadness I felt: for the Soviet people, who had so little to show for their suffering and sacrifice; and for us, who spent so much of our national wealth and energy competing with an empty ideology.

I hated to hear them clap.

.   .   .

It was clear that to be involved in U.S.–Soviet relations was at best un-comfortable and at worst risky. The Daniloff case had apparently proved that one false step could create an opening for forces—on either side—to exploit a situation for some unknown but hostile political end. Still and all, what I had seen during those days only intrigued me. The contradictory and enigmatic quality of life in the Soviet Union whetted my appetite for a deeper involvement in the field. And it was not without its challenges.

After that first trip to the U.S.S.R., I took part in many discussions with my colleagues on the question of whether or not we had a "patriotic ob-ligation" to keep the United States government briefed about our experi-ences in the Soviet Union. With the Kremlin's new leader in power, and with unanswered questions about the seriousness of Gorbachev's stated intentions, the information stakes, in a sense, were higher than ever.

Most of my colleagues drew a line between sharing general political impressions with the CIA and conveying specific information on the per-sonalities with whom they came into contact. I thought that distinction made sense, but it didn't seem relevant to me. As I had never been in government service, I saw no reason to volunteer information of any kind. Besides, I thought, I couldn't learn anything that our well-funded CIA presumably didn't know already.

After my first trip, it seemed a little odd to me that no one got in touch to interview me, since I had much better contact with high-ranking Soviets than many of my friends and colleagues who were frequently visited and asked questions about their encounters. After several other trips, I guessed I wasn't being interviewed because they already knew what I was doing. My phones at the office were probably bugged. We had severe problems with static on the lines, much like the phones at the Soviet Embassy, and when I hadn't been in the Soviet Union for a while, the barely audible high-pitched sound I could hear on the line would stop.

Not long after the Reykjavík summit meeting between Reagan and Gor-bachev in 1986, I was approached by a very close friend of mine. "I have been talking to the CIA on occasion after my trips to the Soviet Union. You know, just briefing them about my impressions," he said. "They asked me if you would be willing to talk to a young woman from the Agency."

"Me?"

"She wants to ask you some questions."

"About what?" I asked.

"About a few people you know at the Soviet Embassy," he said. "They are specifically interested in what you know about one man there. Perhaps you could even arrange an introduction for her. She'd be working under an assumed name, of course. She will call herself Patty."

I hesitated. "I can't really help," I said. "If I did consent to talk to her I would always worry about my safety in the Soviet Union. I doubt there's a narrow and concise definition for spying, certainly not when they want to deny you something. Remember Nick Daniloff?" But then I added rather foolishly, "But you can have her call me and I'll tell her myself the reasons I don't want to cooperate."

I was actually frightened, not only by what had been proposed, but by what I had said. Something told me that I should talk with the agent directly, so that U.S. officials would not think me uncooperative in a way that might come back to haunt me. I had no idea of what these intelligence agencies were up to, but certainly the popular press left me with the impression that our security services could be pretty ruthless. I didn't know what conclusions they might draw if I refused to help them. But in no time at all I regretted that I had left the door open for such an encounter. I didn't know how the technology worked, but I couldn't be sure that the Soviets wouldn't find out if I made voice contact with an undercover agent. Even a simple exchange of phone calls could be misunderstood, I decided. Better not to take the phone call at all.

As soon as "Patty" started to call my office, I told my secretary to tell her I was out. After ignoring several more phone calls, I hoped I had made it clear that I would not exchange even a word with her.

What I couldn't know at the time was how important it would be in the coming years that I had "nothing in my past" that could be construed negatively by the people who controlled my husband-to-be's future. Yet with no inkling of my future course, I was unhappy as a matter of general principle that my friend had put me in this awkward position. I also felt some resentment toward the shortsighted intelligence people who tried to compromise me. It had been clear from my first trip to the Soviet Union that I had been treated with real respect there. Because of my family's associations with the country, particularly during World War II, I think I enjoyed personal bonds with many of my Soviet colleagues that might otherwise have taken years to develop. (As a matter of fact, one of my Russian friends, slightly the worse for vodka, told me one evening that if my name had not been Eisenhower, they would have assumed I was working for the CIA.) The thought that the intelligence community, and especially my friend, would think nothing of potentially violating these relationships for some cheap information about Soviet Embassy personnel made me fume.

Later, when I saw my friend again, I said, "Someone has to be regarded with trust in this crazy U.S.–Soviet relationship. If everyone is mobilized to play out the silly game, nothing will ever change."

In general, Washington had deep misgivings about nongovernmental involvement in the Soviet Union—outside of simple cultural exchanges. The prevalent attitude was that the vital, complicated, and dangerous work of dealing with Soviets should be left up to the pros. Given the Soviet Union's apparent agenda, I, too, recognized the potential for missteps.

In early 1987, I received a telex from Evgeny Primakov, now director of the Russian Foreign Intelligence Service, then the director of the U.S.S.R.'s Institute of International Relations and World Economy. It was an invitation to attend the International Forum for a Non-Nuclear World and the Survival of Humanity. Despite the pretentious name, the invitation intrigued me, especially since Gorbachev was scheduled to address the gathering. I was interested in seeing him in the flesh, yet I was wary about going to Moscow to discuss a nuclear-free world. The Reykjavík summit, only months before, had been a disaster, and Western suspicion about the Soviet Union's behavior was at an all-time high.

Reagan and Gorbachev had come within a whisker of agreeing to eliminate all strategic nuclear rockets. The issue that had doomed their talks at Reykjavík was the question of what level of activity the Anti-Ballistic Missile Treaty permitted. Gorbachev insisted that the treaty restrict study in this area to laboratory research; the United States wanted a broader interpretation to permit exploration of SDI technology. When it became clear that this disagreement could not be resolved, the talks emotionally broke down.

There was a feeling among some Washingtonians that the Soviets had tried to take advantage of Reagan's apparent lack of preparation for the talks, that Gorbachev had almost "pulled a fast one." Nearly everyone agreed that the U.S. government now faced a much faster and sharper player on the Soviet side and that vigilance was required now more than ever.

Before deciding on what to do about my invitation, I called the State Department and USIA and asked them for advice. The government's displeasure about this forthcoming conference was obvious from the start, even though the people I talked to admitted they knew almost nothing about it. Petulantly noncommittal, they gave no advice at all. "The United States *is* a free country," one person grudgingly reminded me.

Apprehension was not confined to the government. Virtually all my friends and family reminded me that I was especially vulnerable. "Exercise extreme caution, and don't travel alone," they warned me.

Weighing all the advice I received, I thought that taking a staff member with me might be prudent. To arrange this I telephoned someone I will call Sergei Ivanov, a First Secretary of the Soviet Embassy. His job, among other things, was to oversee the development and implementation of Soviet exchange programs with the United States. He suggested that we get together for lunch.

Several days later, at a small table in the back of the dining room at the Jefferson Hotel, I met Ivanov. He was a short, balding man who smoked incessantly. Full of humor and irony, he could be very good company. After a brief exchange, I asked Ivanov if he could help me get an invitation to the conference for a staff member.

He paused for a minute, expelling cigarette smoke as he spoke. "If you want to take a staff member with you, telex Primakov and ask him to invite someone on your staff. For you, Susan, they would do anything, just ask!"

Then his demeanor changed a little, and leaning forward, he added: "I do hope, someday, however, that you will travel back and forth to the Soviet Union so much that you'll feel more comfortable about going there. I am sure the time will come when you'll trust us enough to go alone."

Without waiting for my astonished response he continued, "You know, when I was about to make my first visit alone to the United States, many people advised me against it. They said, 'Sergei, you are taking a risk. If you go by yourself to the United States certain people might try to take advantage of you. They might use your presence for propaganda purposes. They might even set you up with a woman.' "

Then his voice dropped and he exclaimed, "I'm still waiting!"

This did not do that much to reassure me, since I was personally aware that U.S. intelligence would have been only too happy to set up him or anyone else at the Soviet Embassy with a woman. But there was a much larger point, which I understood immediately. Taking a staff member with me would fool no one. If I planned to stay in this business, I decided, I would have to demonstrate that I could handle myself and that I was not frightened of my Soviet colleagues. I had come perilously close to conveying my vulnerability on this occasion, and in doing so, I realized, I could jeopardize my standing, maybe even my safety.

After lunch I returned to my office and told my staff I would be going to the Soviet Union alone. I could always walk out if I didn't like the political rhetoric, and I would take special care to avoid questionable circumstances.

I spoke with my sister Anne later that evening. She was dumbstruck that I was going to Moscow by myself. Despite her protests, I hotly defended my decision.

My mother was equally skeptical. The night before my departure she came to my home for dinner. Anxiously she pressed me for some of the details.

"Tell me about your trip tomorrow," she said. "Where are you going to stay?"

"I don't know at the moment," I said cheerfully, "I expect they will tell me when I arrive." I braced myself for Mother's reaction.

"You don't know where you are staying?" she asked, startled.

I tried to assure her that it was a big conference and probably my hotel would be full of conference participants. I begged her not to worry.

"Whom will we call if we need to reach you? Who is picking you up at the airport?"

"I don't know that either," I confessed. "But they have my itinerary and I know someone will be there to meet me."

"Well, I guess you know what you're doing," my mother doubtfully conceded. "But be sure to call us when you get home. When do you return?"

"I don't know that either. They only issued me a one-way ticket."*

Despite the trepidation that was expressed to me by virtually everyone I spoke to, I completed the arrangements for the trip—and the monumental packing job that went with it. For some reason it seemed particularly hard for me to leave my children this time. Perhaps I conveyed my apprehension to them. During the hours that passed before my departure, the girls were making an unusual amount of commotion and my two younger daughters, Laura and Amy, were at each other's throats. When the taxi finally arrived, we all tearfully said goodbye.

---

* When the Soviet side provided transportation for such a trip, they always issued only one-way tickets. That way they would have to pay for only one leg of the journey in hard currency. As I discovered in this case, on my arrival they immediately gave me my return ticket, which they had paid for in rubles.

I fretted all the way to the airport. When I got to the main terminal, I decided to send the children a letter, which I figured they'd get the following day. I bought a greeting card and wrote on the inside:

February 8, 1987

Girls,
Here I am at National Airport, waiting for my delayed plane to arrive. I was intending to write you in any case to tell you how much I love you and to let you know that I admire the three of you enormously.

You are special human beings—for many reasons—but also because you are willing to share me unselfishly with so many other people.

I want you to know that in an indirect way I am going to the U.S.S.R. for you. I foster the deepest hope that the Eisenhower Institute can and will play a major role in easing the tensions between the United States and the Soviet Union. If we can forge some ties of trust, the world you inherit will be a considerably safer place in which to live.

I will carry the three of you with me in Moscow.

I love you darlings,
Mom

While I was worried about what message my presence in Moscow would convey, as soon as I arrived I understood that for most people at this gathering *being seen* was a primary reason for being there. Although the political-science working group, of which I was a part, dealt with some very substantive and complicated issues, the conference in general struck me more as a circus than as a serious gathering to discuss global issues. On February 17 *The Washington Post* published an article entitled "Soviets Seeing Stars: Celebrities Confer at Moscow Peace Forum." The lead paragraph set the tone:

It was a big weekend for stargazing in the Soviet capital. Yoko Ono was in one hotel. John Kenneth Galbraith in another. Norman Mailer had dinner with Gore Vidal, and some people were saying that Graham Greene may have gone to see Kim Philby.

Despite the appearance of friendship and cooperation in this interaction between the Soviets and their American guests, I sensed that both sides were only too happy to use the other to advance their own agendas. It struck me that these relationships represented another kind of point scoring. On the U.S. side the American political left used the gathering as a way to thumb its nose at the American right for failing to predict the advent of

Gorbachev. On the Soviet side, the conference was used as a public display of broad international support for "socialism with a human face." Those of us uninterested in these tired old political games waited to see if a rumored policy announcement by Gorbachev would be forthcoming. After all, wasn't that the reason the Soviets had brought a thousand people from all over the world to Moscow at their expense?

As it turned out, those of us looking for special significance in Gorbachev's speech were disappointed. The only initiative he announced was one to establish an international foundation that would study and support work on the issues of greatest concern to the global community, such as the arms race and environmental degradation. I remember thinking at the time that a foundation for these purposes was an odd thing to be proposed by the General Secretary of the Communist Party, the party legendarily guilty of opposing arms cutbacks and disregarding ecological concerns.*

What I couldn't know at the time was that this very foundation would pave the way for a major life change for me, and I had already unknowingly embarked on it.

* Almost two weeks after the forum, Gorbachev announced that he would break the deadlock in the arms-control talks by separating discussions on medium-range missiles from those on missile and space-based weapons. This ultimately opened the way for agreement on intermediate nuclear forces.

2 : A Walk in the Woods

The evening sun cast its long shadows across the clipped green lawn. A barbecue pit had been set up at the side of a huge multicolored tent. As a country-and-Western band played "Your Cheatin' Heart," official U.S. and Soviet delegates greeted one another, then lined up behind spits of beef and trays of buttered corn.

Many of the participants from the year before had now returned in the summer of 1987 for another open-forum conference, this one in Chautauqua, New York. The gathering had some of the quality of a class reunion. People mingled; they seemed glad to see each other.

I had nearly begged off going because of some health problems. During the previous two months I had been recovering from major lower-back disc problems, which I had developed just after leaving Moscow, where I had been on Eisenhower Institute business in June. So to go to the Chautauqua conference meant that I had to drag myself from bed. I knew the Americans were committed to the process, but I hoped that my effort to get there would lend support to the Soviets for their continued interest in what was often a painful process. In the intervening year, they had seemingly embraced the open forum we had pioneered.* And now Valentina Tereschkova, a former cosmonaut and the Soviet chairwoman, was bringing nearly two hundred of the most prominent figures in the Soviet Union to America for the 1987 conference.

---

* Success in 1986 terms was defined by one of the Soviet organizers when he noted that after the Yurmala conference no one lost his job.

Deputy Foreign Minister Vladimir Petrovsky, whom I had not seen since the previous conference, greeted me warmly. We found ourselves two seats together at one of the dinner tables and started to catch up. We had exchanged letters during the year about an exhibition of American Impressionist paintings at the Whitney Museum in New York, and we picked up the threads of our mutual interest.

Deep in conversation, I did not notice when a member of the Soviet delegation approached our table. Gazing up, I saw a rumpled, professorial-looking man rest his arm on Petrovsky's shoulder. His reddish-brown hair was unkempt, and through his slightly tinted glasses his bright blue eyes sparkled. "I would like to introduce myself," he said. "My name is Roald Sagdeev and I direct the Space Research Institute."

We had never met before, but I had heard about Sagdeev. In fact, he was a legend in conference circles, known for being quick, funny, and often the iconoclast. Many people regarded him as one of the Soviet Union's most effective spokesmen, particularly on arms control, largely because he lacked the "polished mouthpiece" image and projected a natural credibility. Precisely for that reason, some were wary of him. I had heard a number of Americans say that his anti-Star Wars stance was damaging to "the SDI cause," because of his apparent sincerity, not to mention his reputation as a world-class scientist. Add to that, he could communicate directly in impressive English—the product of many years of interaction with the West.

"I would like to talk to you when you have a moment," he said. People at the table were beginning to disperse, so I excused myself and stood up to speak with him.

"Tell me, please, did you know your grandfather well?" he asked.

Slightly taller than he, I leaned forward to catch his words.

"Yes," I responded, "I was lucky to know him very well."

The band was blaring; it was difficult to hear.

"You look like him," he added, raising his voice somewhat.

"May I take that as a compliment?" I responded, slightly embarrassed.

"Of course!" he boomed merrily.

It was hard to concentrate on the conversation, with the noise and the milling crowd. People nodded to us as they walked by, but Sagdeev did not divert his gaze.

"I wanted to ask you," he said, looking at me intently, "do you think he was serious when he formulated the concept of the 'military-industrial complex'? Do you think he really thought America had one?"

The military-industrial complex seemed to be the one thing every Soviet *had* to mention when they first met me. It was a favorite anti-American propaganda theme. The regime frequently used the famous warning in my grandfather's Farewell Address to show the Soviet people that even a U.S. President had acknowledged that American big business drove the arms race. Here we go again, I thought.

"I think he was perfectly serious," I said. "And we are looking forward to the day when the Soviet government will admit that your country has a military-industrial complex, too." I was hoping my voice did not betray the slight impatience and irritation I felt at being on *that* topic again.

To my utter surprise, Sagdeev smiled broadly. He seemed to like my response.

"Oh, we have one all right. I know who they are, and they shamelessly chase contracts, too."

I was stunned. It was an admission that would have been frowned on by the regime, especially coming from an arms-control official.

But surprise at his candor was nothing compared to what I felt when, without warning, he then asked me to dance.

I was in a terrible quandary. This was an unthinkable request, but I was afraid to insult him. With little choice, I awkwardly agreed. As we made our way onto the otherwise empty dance floor, I felt immensely uncomfortable and *very* exposed. All I could see was the vast expanse in front of me.

We danced for a moment or two in uneasy silence. Just a pitch above the music, he began: "I have had a lot of exposure to the military-industrial complex through my work with the space program." Despite the difficulty of hearing, I could scarcely believe my ears. He seemed so open about it, shouting just above the din of the music.

Our spin on the dance floor created a shock wave of incredulity and amusement among the other guests. Slowly, however, a few others began to join us. As soon as the dance floor filled up, I politely took my leave. My back was killing me, so I had a good excuse to sit things out for a while. Finding a table, I sat down for a rest.

The next thing I knew, the band started to play "When the Saints Go Marching In," and to my surprise I saw Sagdeev, boyishly exuberant, mount the stage, grab the microphone from the lead singer, and begin to belt out a Louis Armstrong imitation: "I want to be in that number . . ."

People clapped and cheered, and an American sitting next to me leaned over and said, "Who's that?"

"I don't know" is all I remember murmuring.

Sagdeev was on a campaign in those days. Between the plenary sessions, he spent his spare minutes busily recruiting participants to a conference he was hosting in October—a few months hence—to mark the thirtieth anniversary of the launching of Sputnik. From that first evening, it was clear he was determined to talk me into being one of them. He insisted we have lunch together to discuss the matter.

Punctually at 12:15 the next day, Sagdeev and I met in the lobby of the Athenaeum Hotel. His voice was still hoarse from all his singing the night before. The dining room, a spartan but sprawling gathering spot, was crowded and noisy. Sagdeev asked the waitress for a quiet table. She cast a quick look around and then led us to an alcove with a window overlooking Chautauqua Lake. "This is a nice table," she said. "It was Thomas Edison's favorite." A plaque hung on the wall confirming her words.

Sagdeev enjoyed the fact that not only had we managed the privacy of the alcove for our discussion but we were also sitting at the table of the great inventor. He dwelled on his luck for a moment and then launched into the reason for our meeting. He reiterated his invitation to me and said proudly that the Space Future Forum would play host to the best brains in the international space community. It would be the first time the Soviet Union publicly focused on space science and international cooperation in such a way.

"That sounds very laudable," I said politely. "But I am sure that I am not alone in feeling uncomfortable about the choice of dates." Sputnik had been one of the most notorious symbols of Cold War competition. "Why not choose the anniversary of Apollo-Soyuz for such a gathering?" I added.

Without being even slightly ruffled, Sagdeev responded that Apollo-Soyuz had been essentially a manned space event and that he wanted to emphasize the use of space for unmanned scientific exploration. His eyes danced. "The anniversary of Sputnik is what you might call a formal excuse for the gathering," he said. "It was much easier to get these guys to agree to our budget since we scheduled the conference on the anniversary. You know how it works."

I had never heard Soviet authorities referred to as "these guys," for a start, and I certainly had never encountered a Soviet official who was so frank about the reasons for featuring an anniversary. Perfect for propaganda exploitation!

Leaning forward in a conspiratorial way, Sagdeev reiterated the importance of my accepting his invitation. There was a big battle under way in the Soviet Union over the use of resources for manned or unmanned space activities, he explained, and the U.S.S.R. needed to re-evaluate its priorities and objectives. To do this, he said, "we need help from the international community."

A Soviet saying that they needed the international community to help them reassign their priorities in space exploration?

Sagdeev went on to explain that the space empire in the Soviet Union had been untouched by *perestroika*. Soviet space ministries, all closed enterprises, had always done their work behind a wall of secrecy. So much so that these top-secret installations in the U.S.S.R. did not have names at that time. They were given numbers, thus their nickname: "mailboxes."

"An international group might be able to impress Gorbachev and make him support the *good* projects," he emphasized.

Sagdeev's own openness was contagious, so I interjected that a forum on the future use of space could well end up being very controversial—particularly in Moscow. It might be used as a propaganda vehicle for marshaling anti-SDI sentiments, I told him. Although I was not a proponent of SDI myself, I did not like the idea that Americans might fall into such a blatant trap.

"There have been attempts to politicize the conference," he confessed, "but it's no longer a worry. I think I can say that I have already liberated the forum from being a hostage of military-space interests. You might say that I have managed to 'de-couple' the forum from the SDI issue." He smiled at his own clever play on arms-control jargon.

I could not help wondering: Who is this man and what does he *really* want?

Despite his disarming approach, and my own nagging skepticism, I felt I had to decline his invitation. Sputnik had posed a very difficult problem for the Eisenhower administration. I could see the headlines now: IKE'S KIN CELEBRATES SPUTNIK IN MOSCOW.

Sagdeev, however, would not take no for an answer. At the end of lunch he wanted to set a time when we could talk about it again. With some hesitation I got out my agenda and looked to see when I might be free. We decided that we'd go for a walk after lunch the next day.

"Where are you going now?" I asked him.

"I am chairing a panel on space cooperation. They are holding a round table in a church not far from here. Maybe it's not accidental," he quipped. "Space has probably become a religion here, too."

The next day we met on the porch of the Athenaeum Hotel and discussed where to go on our walk. Unfolding a map, Sagdeev decided on a rather lengthy route.

"Did you go to the plenary session today?" I asked, making an effort to break the ice.

"I did, and I have to tell you that I just can't get over the audience's reaction. You heard them. The Americans were booing the U.S. government official who spoke harshly about Soviet behavior." Then he added, "Imagine, booing the speaker when his complaints are perfectly justified!"

I paused, unsure of how to react to this apparently anti-Soviet remark coming from a member of the Communist Party and a member of the Supreme Soviet.

He shrugged. "Anyway, I've never much liked these kinds of people-to-people conferences. To tell you the truth, I only came because the organizers agreed to pay my airplane ticket to the United States."

"About *your* conference—" I started.

"Oh, that will be quite different," he interjected.

I wasn't so sure.

My presence in Moscow, I told him, might be misconstrued by people who would think it against American interests to concede the successes of the Soviet space program, and in my position as president of the Eisenhower Institute, I had to think about how my participation would look.

There was a silence for a moment or two. I felt curiously anxious about what his reaction would be. Then I heard myself adding, "But I will make you a deal. If you can convince the most conservative man on my board of directors to come with me, I will accept your invitation."

This suggestion seemed to please Sagdeev a great deal. We tentatively set a date for him to come to the Institute in Washington to meet on this topic before his departure for the Soviet Union. I thought that Karl Harr, the board member I had in mind, would be a perfect traveling companion. As president of the Aerospace Industries Association, Harr represented not only a very conservative constituency but also the American group that would be most sensitive to any Soviet propaganda. Karl, having been a member of the Eisenhower administration—with some responsibilities for the establishment of NASA—would also provide political protection if I were attacked as an easily bamboozled granddaughter.

"If that isn't enough," Sagdeev said with gentle humor, "maybe I could ask someone on my staff to write a short piece for *Pravda* complaining that you are an anti-Communist American conservative. If you were ever criticized for going to the conference, you could always pull out the article to prove that you really aren't a Communist sympathizer at all!'"

I pretended to ignore his joke and replied dryly, "Okay, you just make your case to Karl Harr. If he will come, so will I."

My proposal seemed to satisfy Sagdeev thoroughly. He was now in an expansive mood. With a long walk still ahead of us, he began to tell me about events inside the Soviet Union. As in our earlier interactions, I was frequently floored by his assessment of what was going on.

Sagdeev painted a picture of the Soviet Union that I had never heard from a Soviet citizen before. He passionately talked about the "rot" in his society and how the Soviets had "sold out the future to hold up a façade." During our nearly two-hour walk, he covered every imaginable topic from the military-industrial complex and the Soviet leadership to the importance of openness for doing productive science. He told me about his early work in the U.S.S.R.'s controlled nuclear-fusion program and later as the head of the "civilian" space program. Intensively he spoke about the importance of change and even discussed the need to dismiss incompetent workers, which would create some unemployment. In 1987, the man was speaking heresy, an almost alarming departure from the usual group-speak.

We walked along a long tree-lined path that followed, for some distance, the shoreline of Chautauqua Lake. As we rounded the glistening blue water, Sagdeev recounted in the most personal terms his struggle with the Soviet bureaucracy and the deep desire he had nurtured, for more than a decade, to be a free scientist again. He described the emotional depression he had experienced at losing touch with his creative side and confessed that he had tried and failed to resign from his directorship to go back to science.

"We don't have a culture for resigning in my country." He shrugged. "I tried to leave, but a great deal of pressure was put on me. We were just on the eve of Gorbachev, so I decided to stay for patriotic reasons, to help with the new processes."

The way Sagdeev described his internal conflict, the hint of regret—even sorrow—in his voice, made me feel as a priest must when listening to a person bare his soul in the confessional. That I was hearing such things from a high-ranking Soviet official made me light-headed with confusion. Sagdeev seemed to have some instinctive trust in me, but it was not something I could understand. Soviet officials were usually extremely cautious with foreigners.

"I think one of the most important developments in our country is happening right now," he told me soberly. "The older generation has the chance to rehabilitate themselves in the eyes of their children."

He described the ambivalent feelings he had had for his father's career —as an early member of the Communist Party and a government apparatchik. He even hinted that his own son had been disappointed in *his* failure to avoid joining the Party.

"It requires great courage to be repentant," Sagdeev added.

"It's funny you should say that," I said. "Although you are talking about the internal situation in the Soviet Union, there's a somewhat similar phenomenon going on in my country. I sense a growing recognition among young people that those who made decisions before them saddled their generation with policies that will be very difficult to recover from. I am thinking about the uncontrollable arms race, the budget deficits, the environment—I could go on."

I was rather surprised and embarrassed that I had said this. I had always kept my political opinions to myself, particularly where the Soviets were concerned. Although these were only very general remarks, I felt awkward. It was strange, I thought, that Sagdeev seemed much more comfortable being critical of his system than I was in speaking about mine.

"It's overwhelming, really, when you think about it," he agreed. "We are leaving such a legacy to our children, it's hard sometimes to be optimistic about the future. I started to think about this for the first time during the Cuban missile crisis. Remember the tension then? We were looking at the potential for mass annihilation. And today we have a thousand times more nuclear weapons than in 1962."

"Maybe we have just become numbed to the danger," I said.

"Maybe. During the Cuban missile crisis I was working in Novosibirsk.* We would listen to the Voice of America, especially during this crisis. I remember one night they broadcast President Kennedy's address. He said

---

* A scientific installation in Siberia. Sagdeev was the head of the Plasma Theory Laboratory at the Institute of Nuclear Physics at Akademgorodok, "Academic City."

that America loves peace, but America loves freedom even more. It was a very strong statement. Somehow we thought that any night we could expect war to break out. We felt we were on the verge of catastrophe.

"During this time I woke up from a deep sleep and opened my eyes," he continued. "I saw a bright fireball in the sky, at a very low altitude. In fractions of seconds I saw it. You know, when you wake up suddenly sometimes you can't react adequately for a few moments. What I saw, of course, was the sunrise—nothing else. Mankind was living in such terror then that the dream came to me a number of times. But finally I was left free of the terrifying experience. I think that reflects an important phenomenon. As you say, mankind has grown tired of expecting catastrophe. We have simply, somehow, learned to live in this crazy world."

I told him I had had a similar experience, although not one that recurred. It was during the period of escalating rhetoric between our countries when the Korean Air Lines 007 airliner was shot down over Soviet air space and the Soviet Union was called the "evil empire." I remembered leaving home in Washington one morning to go to my office. "Just as I got to my car, I had an overwhelming flash—though it was quite momentary—that there was going to be some terrible nuclear disaster that day and I would be separated from my children, utterly unable to be with them at the end. The feeling was so strong that I went back into the house and kissed them all and told them I loved them. I found some silly pretext to do so, of course."

And then I added, "I don't think a person ever really gets over such a flash."

Both of us were clearly conscious of the personal turn the conversation had taken. After a few seconds of awkward silence, Sagdeev stopped and consulted the map again.

We were nearing the end of the path and coming to a clearing that looked like the grounds to one of the building complexes. We located our position on the map and headed for the place where our afternoon sessions were going to be held, exchanging instead forced lighthearted banter.

On parting we agreed I would contact him as soon as I knew when Karl could meet him. I was leaving Chautauqua the next day, and Sagdeev, too, was separating from the Soviet group to visit his old friend Carl Sagan at Cornell.

For the rest of the afternoon I could not shake the spell of our intense conversation. My head was swimming. While American relations with the Soviet Union had improved a great deal over the previous year, conversations were usually quite stiff, and still within a mutually recognized safety zone. There was something about Sagdeev's demeanor and the way he talked that deeply unsettled me. His openness and humor belied everything I knew about Soviet social behavior.

But our encounter also stirred something else in me. Sagdeev reminded me of a notion that had been deeply inculcated in me in my youth: that the people of an authoritarian state can summon their free will, just as the people of a free nation can lose their liberty by abrogating their democratic responsibilities.

I noted in my diary that the most moving event of the conference had been "my walk in the woods with Sagdeev."

3 : A View inside the Struggle

I will never really know what was on Sagdeev's mind and why my presence at his Space Forum meant so much to him. He seemed to set some special store in my participation that I couldn't assess. An inner voice urged extreme caution.

I had no particular intention to have any Soviet take me into his confidence. I simply wanted a nice safe distance from which to watch developments in the U.S.S.R. Perhaps that internal voice told me that going to the Space Forum would threaten my proximity to these unfolding events.

When Monday afternoon arrived, I was in a state of high anticipation about the meeting I had set up between Sagdeev and Karl Harr. Harr, a portly, retirement-age lobbyist, was reliably blunt, and I knew that he would tell me exactly what he thought about the idea of going to the Space Forum in Moscow. He was what I called a "happy cold warrior"—a man proud of his long-standing anti-Communist views. I had told Sagdeev as much, which may have accounted for his nervousness when he arrived at the office a few days after the Chautauqua conference. As he met my staff, he was polite, even friendly, but I could sense that he was distracted and somewhat edgy.

I showed him into my office and offered him the most comfortable seat in the room, a large grandfather wing chair. Once he sat down, the chair seemed to magnify his discomfort. I brought him a cup of tea.

A few minutes later Karl joined us. A man not much taller than Sagdeev, Karl had an impish quality that seemed to relish the whole encounter. We chatted for a few minutes, then I recapped the purpose of our meeting. Any decision to go to the Space Forum could be made only by Karl and me together, I reiterated. I then turned to Sagdeev.

After a slight squirm in his chair, he began: "Dr. Harr, in some respects my country is like your country. We have good guys and we have bad guys. I am one of the good guys and I need your help. I know that Susan has doubts about coming to this conference, but it is very important that both of you come in order to support our efforts for promoting real space science."

I was momentarily at a loss for words, but Karl wasted no time in delivering his rejoinder. "That may well be so," he said rather coldly, "but it's not my job to make you look good."

An hour later, the three of us had agreed that Karl and I would attend the Space Future Forum. Karl was eager to go to Moscow in the midst of all the changes and see things for himself, but I also think that Roald had impressed him more than he would have wanted to admit at the time.

As soon as Sagdeev had closed the door behind him, Karl and I broke out into laughter. "I have never seen anything like that before!" Karl said, shaking his head. "Didn't you love his opening line?"

"Are you sure you want to do this, Karl?" I asked.

"So we go to Moscow, Susan. If we don't like what we see, we can always walk out and come home."

A trip to the Soviet Union during this time turned out to be very convenient for me. I was in negotiation with one of the Institute's counterparts, so any spare time in Moscow could be put to good use. Indeed, to maximize the time there—at Soviet expense—I decided to go to Moscow several days before the conference began. Karl planned to come a few days later. I sent the Space Research Institute a telex advising them that I would be traveling by myself and arriving early, but I was worried because I never got a confirmation from the conference's coordinating committee.

My concerns, it turned out, were not ill founded. When I reached Sheremetyvo Airport in Moscow, no one was there to greet me. After waiting a few minutes for someone to take me to the VIP lounge, as had been the practice in the past, I gave up and made my way down to the public customs hall.

It took some time for my bags to come off the belt. While I was waiting, I scrutinized the other passengers, looking for someone who might be a Westerner. I saw two older men standing in the corner who I thought might be Americans, and my guess was correct. They volunteered to give me a ride to the Academy Hotel, where they were being met by their scientific colleagues. I hoped that from that hotel I could locate the offices of the forum's organizing committee.

When my two bags appeared on the belt, I lined up to go through customs inspection. As they went through the X-ray device, I could see that the contents of the larger one were being evaluated. The blood drained from my face as I remembered that I had brought a video for General Nicolai Chervov, the Soviet General Staff's arms-control expert. During the Chautauqua conference we had discussed the prospects for nuclear accident, and I had said that I would bring him a recent movie I thought he might find interesting. I could just see the skeletal outline of the video spools on the screen monitor when I suddenly remembered that foreigners were absolutely prohibited from bringing them into the Soviet Union—particularly videos that might have political content.

The conveyor belt stopped abruptly. The uniformed customs officer, a severe-looking young man, eyed me sternly and asked, "Do you have a videocassette in your suitcase?"

How could I say anything but yes? Its outline could be seen by everyone.

I nodded.

"What is on it?" he asked coldly.

"A movie," I replied.

"What is the name of the movie?"

I could feel myself sinking. My mouth was getting dry, and I was having difficulty forming the words *War Games*.

The customs official disappeared into another room at the back of the customs hall. He did not return for about twenty minutes. During this time my mind raced through all the stories I had heard about Soviet customs. I could dimly recall complaints during the Chautauqua–Eisenhower conference in Latvia. One participant, bringing religious material and Bibles into the U.S.S.R., had been harassed by customs officials and then had all his material confiscated. Other people had been detained for questioning about pamphlets in their suitcases. These offenses were probably recorded somewhere and would, most likely, make getting future entry visas difficult.

I had been foolishly absentminded to make this blunder. I had known from my own reading that no real liberalization of such procedures had taken place. *

I vowed to myself that after I got through customs I would never be so stupid again.

"What is its intended purpose?" the tall haughty officer asked me when he finally returned.

"I was going to give it to a friend of mine," I said, deciding not to lie.

"Is he a Soviet citizen?"

"Yes."

"And what is his name?"

I replied rather meekly, "I would rather not say, but he is one of the members of your military establishment whom I saw in the United States recently. He requested the film."

This was a hint to the officer that the recipient was cleared for travel. Getting permission to leave the Soviet Union was rigorous, and only people who had been thoroughly screened could travel abroad.

The customs official disappeared again for another ten minutes.

I was in a state of growing concern that my two new American scientist friends would give up and leave the airport. They had already completed customs and left the hall.

The officer appeared again suddenly.

"Miss Eisenhower, you may go . . . take your bags," he prompted with his hand. I didn't ask him about the video and he said nothing more. "By the way," he added, with a sudden flash of smile, "we want your people to know that we are pleased that the INF agreement† has been reached in Washington between Minister Shevardnadze and Secretary Shultz. It is very good news."

The scientists were waiting for me at the curb. After I had explained my ordeal, we set off for downtown Moscow, where the driver dropped us at the Academicheskaya (Academy) Hotel, located in the shadow of a huge statue of Lenin, just off Oktyabrskaya Square. Run by the Academy of Sciences, the hotel was the guest house for visiting scientists and I was

* As late as September 15, 1991—four years later—*Newsweek* ran an article on the KGB in which they noted that state security forces were calling for an "uncompromising" campaign against such dangers as videocassette recorders, which, they claimed, are "used by some people [in the West] to spread ideas alien to us, the cult of violence, force and amorality."
† The treaty on Intermediate Nuclear Forces.

hoping that there might be an organizing committee for the Space Forum there, with lists of the participants and their hotel and room assignments. My guess turned out to be correct.

On the second floor, behind a glass door half draped in musty curtain, an office of telephones, ashtrays, and idle women met us. I addressed a stout middle-aged woman sitting behind a makeshift desk. When I told her of my dilemma she shrugged, obviously unable to think what to do with me. Stolidly she sat, alternating between the telephone and long list searches.

After some minutes of watching her demonstration of futility, I decided to try a new tack. "Academician Sagdeev personally extended this invitation. If you can find him I am sure he will clear up this difficulty." The woman eyed me skeptically.

I sat in an armchair to wait while she made more telephone calls. To my surprise, after a few minutes I was summoned.

Sagdeev was on the other end of the line, delighted, it seemed, to hear the sound of my voice. "Susan!" he said exuberantly, "you're in Moscow!" Then he apologized for not meeting me personally at the airport. There had been a mixup, he explained. My telex had not been received and they were expecting me on Monday.

"Not to worry," he added reassuringly. "I will be there in fifteen minutes to pick you up. You are staying at the Rossiya Hotel, just on the edge of Red Square. It is not far."

I went downstairs to wait. About twenty minutes later the glass doors suddenly opened and Sagdeev came charging through the lobby with a broad smile on his face.

"Susan, welcome to Moscow!" He planted a kiss firmly on my right cheek and simultaneously gathered my bags, which he carried to his chauffeur-driven car. He apologized again for not "properly" meeting me. The receptionist and one of the organizers from upstairs watched all this and nodded goodbye to me with new respect.

Participating in the Space Future Forum had been a big enough step for me, but the evening of my arrival Sagdeev asked me to be on its Initiating Committee. Anticipating my resistance he suggested that Karl Harr also participate. Between this nagging worry and jet lag, I slept only a few hours during the night. I finally dropped off near morning and then awoke to find that I had overslept. I had less than a half hour to dress before being picked up by Sagdeev to go to the Space Research Institute.

Sagdeev and his driver, Ivan, were waiting for me when I came out of the building on the north ramp of the Rossiya Hotel. Ivan, a handsome Ukrainian with a luscious thick dark beard, drove through the streets of Moscow with real panache. Nevertheless, it took more than half an hour to get to the institute, known by its acronym as IKI. Located in an outer section of Moscow, it was surrounded by other research institutes in science, economy, and international relations. Built in the early 1970s, the long rectangular building, with peeling paint and dusty corners, did little to give away the institute's technical reputation. Since Apollo-Soyuz, IKI was known in the West as the headquarters of the Soviet civilian space program. But there was really no equivalent to NASA in the Soviet Union, and the Space Research Institute was roughly more equivalent to the Jet Propulsion Lab in Pasadena, California. As I would later discover, the whole space empire was run by the Soviet military, and Sagdeev's institute was the only small civilian territory within its realm.

Sagdeev took me up a flight of steps, down what seemed to be an endless corridor, past a model of Sputnik, a marble bust of Lenin, and a number of informal photographic displays of rockets being launched. At what seemed like the end of the building, we came to the director's suite of offices. In Sagdeev's study a sizable desk was stacked high with piles of scientific journals and papers. Behind it were two bookcases bursting with books and souvenirs. Above it all, the predictable portrait of Lenin.

Even though it was Sunday morning, several of Sagdeev's senior staff were waiting in his office, and I was immediately invited to sit down with them at the conference table, near a window that overlooked a covered winter garden. The table was dominated by a scale model of one of Mars's moons, Phobos. As we talked, they told me that the institute was less than a year away from sending a sophisticated mission to this moon, with the international participation of fourteen countries. They hoped that the project would reveal the secrets of Mars's origins.

Each staff member was formally introduced, along with a brief description of his role at the institute. Then, to my dismay, a man with a video camera on his shoulder came in and started taping our meeting. I was startled by this and felt immediately ill at ease. I simply couldn't imagine why they would be taping this, and what they would use it for.

As we continued around the table with the introductions, the last man to speak was Georgi Managadze, a Georgian experimental physicist whom Sagdeev had brought to IKI from the Kurchatov Institute of Nuclear Energy. The graying Georgian, with a dashing thick mustache, enthusiastically described the laser technology that he had been developing for the sample analysis of the soil of Phobos.

With obvious delight Sagdeev interjected, "Georgi must be proud. The experiment he is working on is the one that prompted Paul Nitze* to suggest that IKI might be violating the ABM treaty."

"Well, are you?" I asked. My voice was firm, but in fact I felt rather dizzy. Why was I being told this with a videotape rolling?

"It all depends on how you interpret the treaty," Sagdeev replied playfully.

The subject was dropped, but later in the day, Managadze, still beaming from the exchange, pulled out a newspaper article that reported Nitze's accusation.

After coffee, the five of us left the director's office for a tour of the institute. I was growing ever more concerned about the presence of the cameraman, especially since the first stop was the very laboratory that had produced Managadze's laser device. Managadze and Sagdeev enthusiastically gave me an overview of his progress.

For more than an hour, Sagdeev threw open the doors, it seemed, to every room in the institute. I saw computers, I saw a prototype of a spacecraft in the midst of the testing process, and I was even given a demonstration of the image-processing equipment they would be using on the data sent back from space. I was almost embarrassed by what I was seeing. Given the state of U.S.–Soviet relations at the time, it was like watching a strip-tease, a forbidden peek-a-boo.

Before I was set to leave, Sagdeev pulled me aside and raised the question of the Initiating Committee again. "If there is anything you don't like about the decisions we are making, or the way the forum is being organized, you can tell me and we will make the necessary changes. You must trust me. We won't do anything that will embarrass you or your country."

Every night Sagdeev planned some activity for Karl and me. Both of us felt slightly awkward that the host of the conference lavished such attention on us. One evening he gave a dinner for us at a newly opened cooperative

---

* Ronald Reagan's ambassador-at-large, a leading American expert in arms control, specifically on the ABM treaty and the INF treaty.

restaurant, and on several other occasions he took us to his colleagues' homes, where we were overwhelmed with tables of food, toasts, and after-dinner singing. Karl and I were captivated, taken with the warmth of Soviet hospitality and the simplicity of the fun.

At first I didn't think too much about Sagdeev's attention. On other trips to the Soviet Union I had received similar high-level treatment. But as the days wore on, he talked to me more and more about the political conditions surrounding his life—and his perspective on the troubled Soviet system. I was humbled, if nervous, that he seemed to trust me so implicitly. And the mounting intensity of his confidences gave me the impression that he was conscious of the passing nature of our friendship and was trying to absorb as much of it as he could—before it vanished.

One evening after dinner, as Sagdeev was returning me to my hotel, I confessed to him that I was suffering from real fatigue. Since my arrival in Moscow I had been unable to sleep properly. I felt overstimulated and still on alert. Not only that, being away from Washington had given me the chance to think about some of my difficulties back in the United States with the Institute and its staff. I hinted to Sagdeev that I was unable to rid myself of office worries, even this far from home. I was seriously thinking, I confessed, of firing one of my employees.

He listened to me carefully, and then said sympathetically that he knew the feeling. "But you have to know that nothing you are dealing with at home could be as bad as it is here." In the most sobering detail, he described for me the problems of a full-employment society, and the difficulties of operating in an environment where your enemies can use ideology and the Party to settle workplace scores.

"In the end," he told me wistfully, "you are left with a few people who are good because they are driven to be good—inside themselves. I am stuck with some people on my staff who are openly hostile toward me, who are what I call my 'dedicated enemies.' I can't get rid of them, no matter how much they poison the work of the institute." Of his fifteen hundred employees, he added, he'd take only twenty if he were to start over from the beginning.

IKI, as I knew from my Western colleagues, was regarded as probably the best-run institute in the Academy of Sciences. It was also regarded as unusually efficient and innovative. So if, in the ideal world, Sagdeev would take only twenty people from it with him, it was quite a statement, perhaps even a sensitive one.

We rode in silence for the next few minutes. I felt some awkwardness, perhaps because of what he had just conveyed or possibly because of the quiet. There was an unspoken intensity between us that made silence uncomfortable. But it was also nearly impossible for me to reconcile all the different things I had seen and heard since coming to Moscow. I looked out of the dirty car windows and watched the cityscape pass by.

When we reached Dzerzhinsky Square I knew we were nearing my hotel. The towering figure of Felix Dzerzhinsky stood in front of a building of burnished amber. It was the most notorious address in Moscow. In the basement of its Lubyanka prison tens of thousands of people had been shot, tortured, or brutally interrogated on their way to the Siberian gulag. This was the home of the KGB.

"Isn't it ironic," Sagdeev said softly, breaking the silence, "the two principal buildings on this square are the KGB headquarters and Detsky Mir, the largest children's department store. What a sacrilege that next to the place where children's toys are bought the nation's parents and grandparents were sent to their fate." He seemed weary as he spoke. The streetlamps reflected a grayish light on his somber features. Perhaps it was the hour, or the pull of some thoughts, that absorbed him.

When we reached my hotel, he slowly turned to me and took my hand. "You bring an energy and a vitality to every gathering you grace." Then he gave my hand a small squeeze.

"No matter what you do, no matter what happens," he said seriously, "promise that you will always be my very dear friend."

Unable to return his gaze, I whispered spontaneously, "You can be assured of that."

The next morning, after completing a diary entry, I obviously changed my mind about what I had written. The bottom of the page in my notebook is torn off. I must have worried that its contents could spell trouble if they were ever seen by a third party. All that remains of the entry that day is a simple passage:

> I had difficulty getting to sleep last night. I don't know why, but I thought about everything that has ever been on my mind. I even prayed that all that danced in my head would disappear and let me be at peace . . .

If the growing friendship between Roald and me was adding to my tiredness, apparently I was not alone. When I saw Sagdeev later that day —before the start of the Initiating Committee—I could see in his eyes that he, too, was exhausted.

He sat wearily behind his desk, dwarfed, it seemed, by the towering piles of papers and books.

"I confess that I arranged for you to arrive at the institute before the others," he said somberly. He looked down, avoiding my eyes. "I was unable to sleep last night. My mind thought of every possibility of how we might collaborate. I kept wondering what would be feasible. And then I thought of it."

I silently waited for him to go on.

"I think we should write a book together," he said, looking up. "It could be a book on U.S.–Soviet relations, for instance: lost opportunities. It might have two parallel lines. On one page I could offer my contribution from the Soviet standpoint; on the other page you could offer yours and the American viewpoint." He went on to discuss the idea at greater length, warming more and more to the notion.

Before I had a chance to respond, the intercom rang and his secretary told him the other guests had arrived.

"Please think about it," he said, rising from his chair.

"I will."

"Oh good," he said, his face lightening, "that makes me feel *much* better."

The conference room next door was full of people. Sagdeev made all the introductions. The Initiating Committee, comprised mostly of scientists who had worked with him during the International Mission to Halley's Comet, were there to preview a film that was going to be used to open the plenary session of the Space Forum the next day. In twelve minutes it was to tell the story of the first thirty years of the space age.

Sagdeev insisted that everyone be satisfied with its contents. As the lights dimmed and the room became dark, Sagdeev sat back in his chair and the video began to roll.

After the first several frames it was clear that "new thinking" was the basis on which the story of Sputnik and the space age was to be told, at least at this conference. As the draft version began describing, in grandiose terms, Russia's talent for aviation and rocketry, as exemplified by the "great genius" Konstantin Tsiolkovsky, Sagdeev shouted, "Cut, cut."

"This is overkill," he snapped at the producer. "Simply explain what Tsiolkovsky did. We can make up our own minds about whether or not he was a 'great genius.' Keep it simple."

The next day, when the video was in final form, Sagdeev's edits had created a video clip of overly generous proportions. I wondered at the time if he would get in trouble for the fact that the only flag pictured in the entire twelve minutes was the Stars and Stripes, staked on the moon's surface. Even though I had been unwilling to admit it earlier, it was now very clear to me that Sagdeev had no intention of playing superpower games at his Space Forum. On the contrary. Later, when some of us Westerners got into a huddle, we expressed our concern that from the standpoint of Soviet political reality Sagdeev might have been bending backward too far to give the limelight and credit to the other space-faring nations.

Concern about Sagdeev's welfare appeared to reflect the great affection his colleagues had for him. They seemed to fuss and worry about him in a way that they did not about each other. I came to understand that they recognized him as a most unusual person, even rarer for surviving and maintaining his integrity in the Soviet system. His willingness to take risks set him apart. From a Western standpoint, it made him a desirable professional counterpart, even if none of us had any illusions that his traits were typical or appreciated in the Soviet Union.

Perhaps at the time I should have been astute enough to see the video clip as a metaphor for Sagdeev's problems in his own milieu. His film was as unconventional in the U.S.S.R. as Sagdeev himself. He was what the Soviets would call a "white crow" in the estimation of his colleagues in the Soviet military-industrial complex. He had always shown a tendency toward "cosmopolitanism" and other forms of troublemaking. This was underscored by his support for his friend and colleague Andrei Sakharov, one of the few other scientists who, like Sagdeev, had been elected as full Academicians well before their fortieth birthdays. In 1975 the Academy leadership had forced its members to sign a letter condemning Sakharov and his political activities. I was impressed to hear that Roald had been one of the brave few who had not signed the letter, though he had paid a price for it.

Complicating all this, my colleagues told me, was the extraordinary fact that Sagdeev himself was not a Russian but a Tatar, of Muslim origin. This was significant, they explained, because Tatars were a conquered ethnic minority, with only slightly higher standing, in the view of many Russian chauvinists, than the Jews. Sagdeev, a brilliant physicist, had been singled out early on for his scientific capability, becoming the first Tatar to be elected to the Soviet Academy of Sciences. His ethnic background, however, would always be a strike against him, making him more vulnerable to accusations of misbehavior or disloyalty.

Now, surrounded by Western scientists, I, too, wondered how Sagdeev's "new thinking" would be received in conservative Soviet circles. His colleagues seemed to have a deep desire to protect him, and suddenly so did I.

I was surprised by Sagdeev's sudden departure one evening, just before the close of the forum. He seemed subdued and serious when he told me he had to leave the city unexpectedly for the night. At the same time, he mentioned that the Initiating Committee would probably be invited to meet Gorbachev, and we might be notified at only a moment's notice about the time and place. "Please make sure my office knows where you can be reached at all times."

The next day the forum ended, and that evening I saw Sagdeev at a reception given by *Nature* magazine. After a collegial kiss on the cheek, he whispered, "We have to talk." As the guests began to leave, he very nearly ordered me to walk with him for a while. Perplexed, I suggested a stroll around Red Square, but he insisted that we go to Lenin Hills, the scenic bluff overlooking the city.

Twenty minutes later, Ivan parked our car on the side of the road, and Roald and I got out and walked across a large terrace to a railing. Behind us loomed the huge Moscow State University, a mammoth hulk of Stalinist architecture. Before us lay the city, whose lights seemed to extend as far as the eye could see. The night was bracing and clear. Both of us inhaled deeply as we looked out over the view beneath us.

"You seem low," I said. "In fact, I noticed it yesterday, too."

"Maybe."

"Is something the matter?"

"I am missing you already." His words hung in the chilly air.

"I am glad I came to the conference," I said quickly. "I think it was quite a success."

"I think so. But I have to tell you that I am deeply ashamed that my government did not pay proper respect to the space-science community. I'm sorry Gorbachev did not meet with our group. We had the best brains in the world here. And space is one of the areas where so much emphasis has been placed on the Soviet Union's accomplishments. How could he overlook that?"

Many things about Gorbachev had been inexplicable that summer. The General Secretary had spent almost two months in the Crimea, out of public view for the longest time since his accession to power. Rumors that he was ill had flown all over the city, and eventually the world. Then, at the end of September, he reappeared in Moscow with no apparent explanation for his absence.

According to Sagdeev, Gorbachev's long stay in the Crimea had created some unexpected difficulties in trying to reach him about the Space Forum. Aides had put Sagdeev off until Gorbachev's return to the capital, but then they had told him that everyone had been trying to approach the General Secretary and his schedule was already overcommitted. The chances were slim, they had said, that Gorbachev would meet with *any* foreigners any time soon.

Sagdeev recounted this to me with bitter irony. Both of us had seen on *Vremya*, the evening television news broadcast program, that Gorbachev had met the day before with a group of French schoolchildren.

"I called his aides every day," Sagdeev said. "Finally, I said that the forum is closing. The only chance for a meeting would be if Gorbachev would receive the Initiating Committee after the conference is over. On Wednesday there was a hint that he might be available. You remember, I asked you to stay in touch with my office."

Sagdeev had left Moscow to go to his dacha, he told me, where he had written Gorbachev a letter that he delivered personally to the Central Committee that morning. Roald paused and said, "It was a very strong letter."

We began to walk along the railing, the whole length of the bluff. The city lights twinkled below us and a slight breeze had begun to pick up.

Gorbachev read the letter, then had asked Alexander Yakovlev, his close ally in the Politburo, to meet the forum's Initiating Committee. Sagdeev and Yakovlev had spoken many times about the logistics, and everything had been set for 3:00 p.m. Then two hours before, Yakovlev called IKI again and canceled. Apparently Gorbachev had reread Sagdeev's letter and decided that the group was so important that a meeting with Yakovlev would have "undermined the importance of the gathering." Next time, Gorbachev promised, he would meet the group himself.

"Can you imagine?" Sagdeev said with evident frustration. "The whole point is that it was a unique gathering. When will everyone be in Moscow again for such a purpose? Never again, of course!"

I ventured my own interpretation: perhaps Gorbachev had regarded the international aspect of the conference as too controversial. What would international cooperation do for the Soviet side? Space was one of the things the Soviets did best, and it brought international prestige. Why would they want to dilute the glory by putting foreigners on their missions (though they did precisely that with Sagdeev's own Vega mission to Halley's Comet)?

Sagdeev rejected my assertion. "Let's keep the two issues distinct," he said firmly. "Gorbachev should have participated because it's part of 'new thinking,' because the Space Forum was in Moscow, and because the best brains in the world were here to mark a Soviet space achievement. That *is* a form of international recognition and prestige for my country."

As we walked, Roald speculated that perhaps the military-industrial sector of the space program had downplayed the importance of the forum and had influenced Gorbachev's final decision. He surmised that the "complex" felt threatened by his conference. And, I thought to myself, probably threatened by Sagdeev, too.

"International science requires openness. And, Susan, no matter what they say about *glasnost*, I don't live in an open society," he said passionately.

This was particularly so in the Soviet space program, where secrecy is the guardian of reputations in case of failure, he told me. Projects that are open from the very beginning—as they have to be when done internationally—put their organizers at risk. It is impossible to hide failure.

When mistakes are made in the Soviet space program, "unless there are casualties," Sagdeev lamented, "the general rule is that a commission is formed, and they produce a lot of ambiguous papers and conclusions, but the truth never comes out.

"But, Susan," he emphasized, "this must end. Times *have* to change. Without an open discussion of failures and past mistakes, it's impossible to make improvements and avoid such things in the future."

I mulled over everything he was saying, trying to gauge what Gorbachev's rejection had actually meant to Sagdeev personally and politically. I couldn't fully assess the significance this had for him, but I assumed that Gorbachev's refusal to meet with his group played into the hands of the very people Roald was trying to fight. In a country where the "tsar" was still the arbiter of each man's future, I could sense that the General Secretary's attitude had disturbed him a great deal. The gravity of the situation was evident in his face.

The next evening Roald insisted on hosting a farewell dinner for me at the Hunters' Restaurant outside Moscow. Before I left Sagdeev's office for the last time, just before dinner, he spoke to Olga, his invaluable secretary. She picked up the telephone and within a few minutes a young man arrived at the door with a videocassette in his hand. Sagdeev took it from him and thanked him.

"This is for you," he said, turning to me. "It is a souvenir of your visit to IKI and the forum. It is a video of you here with us in Moscow. I had them put it into NTSC—the U.S. television format—so you can use it on your home television VCR." Then he wrote on the box: "From Russia with Love. R."

I realized the moment Sagdeev handed me the video that this was the film the cameraman had made on my first day at the institute. Inwardly I felt ashamed that I had assumed the worst motives for the work, but how could I have ever imagined Sagdeev's real reasons for having it made?

"I hope you won't forget us," he said simply.

The next morning Sagdeev and his driver, Ivan, picked me up for the airport at 6:30. It was still dark outside, but one could just sense the morning light on the eastern horizon. Fog shrouded the Kremlin.

Sagdeev brought my bags downstairs, and he and Ivan loaded my luggage into the trunk of the black Volga. With little time to spare, we set off down the empty Moscow streets for the airport.

After five minutes on the road, Sagdeev broke the silence with some words to Ivan in Russian. The driver took the next turn, which brought us out onto a smaller road. We pulled up near a large cylindrical building around which kiosks and dilapidated trucks stood. Sagdeev jumped out without explanation.

I sat in the car for several minutes, and then suddenly he emerged from the building with his arms full of carnations. "Here," he said, "these are for you." A tinge of emotion caught in my throat.

Sagdeev had been so open with me, and so thoughtful. On the verge of important political battles, he had reached out to me and I had responded, if only tentatively. He had called it our "Roman Holiday."

With my briefcase in hand and the bouquet of carnations tucked under my arm, I boarded the plane for home.

4 : The Mysterious Dr. Sagdeev

It took my participation in the Space Forum to comprehend fully what the "zero sum game" between the United States and the Soviet Union really meant. I now understood, in a firsthand way, that the Cold War and the space race was predicated on the concept that one side's gain was another side's loss.

The Americans had sent the lowest-level delegation of all the space-faring nations to Sagdeev's forum. Then, on the last day of the conference, Tom Rona, deputy to President Reagan's Science Adviser, rose to announce that the United States was going to hold a conference in mid-1988 on "Space and the Human Community." Even with my relative naïveté then, I understood that this was an American effort not to be overshadowed by what was perceived by all the participants as a highly successful Soviet conference. It was clear to everyone that the timing of Rona's proposal was a last-minute effort to steal a little of the Space Forum's thunder. No one was surprised that Rona's conference was never organized or held.

Time magazine ran a cover story on October 7, pegged to the anniversary of the Sputnik launch, entitled "Soviets Take the Lead." I anxiously purchased a copy to see how Sagdeev had been characterized by my countrymen:

The Soviet space program had several notable early successes, including Sputnik 1, the first pictures from the dark side of the moon in 1959 and the first man in space, Yuri Gagarin, in 1961. But its planetary space program did not really take off until shortly after the appointment in 1973 of a 40-year-old scientist named Roald Z. Sagdeyev, as head of IKI. From the outset Sagdeyev started to shake things up. He took physicists out of their labs and put them on the production lines to watch their experiments being built. Says Georgi Managadze, chief of IKI's active space experiments lab: "Sagdeyev follows every stage of manufacturing and testing."

The new director took some unprecedented and risky steps. He brought talented Jewish scientists into the Institute. He began building a corp of young scientists selected on their scientific value rather than the political standing of the scientists. He fought for access to computers. Most important, and politically the riskiest, he introduced a potent mixture of democracy into the space program. "Before Sagdeyev," says Louis Friedman, Executive Director of the Planetary Society, "the Soviet space program was closed. Now they talk about their plans. They even argue in public. He has materially changed the way they do major projects." Declares Thomas Donahue, chairman of the National Academy of Sciences' space science board: "He introduced glasnost into the space-science program years before Gorbachev." Sagdeyev's era might have been short-lived except for one thing: it produced results.

Indeed, space experts in the United States and Europe are now conceding publicly what they would have found laughable a decade ago: although the Soviets lag far behind in electronic gadgetry, they have surged past the U.S. in almost all areas of space exploration. If unchallenged, Moscow is likely to become the world's dominant power in space by the 21st century. Says Heinz Koelle, a West German space technology professor and former director of future projects at NASA's Marshall Space Flight Center: "American pre-eminence in space simply no longer exists." Warns James Oberg, an expert on the Soviet space program: "If the Soviets can aggressively exploit this operational advantage, they can make us eat dust for a long time to come."

It was ironic, I thought when I finished, that after years of complaining that the Soviets were not being *more* forthcoming and open, examples of world-class conduct were seen as threats—or viewed with alarm. In the Soviet context, we still regarded such qualities as openness, honesty, and uncomplicated desire for cooperation as Kremlin ploys. * We weren't at the stage yet to see these genuine qualities, when they occurred, as a sign that the Soviet monolith was fracturing, a trend that would be a positive development for the security of the United States. Perhaps that's because such

* The author of the *Time* article told me, in 1988, that he thought Sagdeev was "too good to be true."

behavior was far from uniform—still by far the exception, not the rule.

On the bluff of Lenin Hills, I had been given a glimpse of the intense effort to make that positive change widespread. Roald had hinted at the power struggle going on in the U.S.S.R.—the battle being waged for the heart and the mind of Mikhail Gorbachev between Soviet vested interests and progressive liberal thinkers. It was apparent that whoever "won" Gorbachev would determine the future of the Soviet Union.

My trip to the U.S.S.R. had also given me an extraordinary insight into one of the leading members of their establishment, and within weeks I was convinced that it had been noticed. Not long after my return, I got a telephone call from one of the forum's American participants, a scientist known to be working on applied SDI research. I had met him only briefly during that week in Moscow, so I was puzzled when he called and asked me to lunch. Somewhat unsettled by this invitation, I suggested that we have breakfast instead, thinking that I could determine what he wanted in a shorter period of time. We met at 8:00 at the Sheraton-Carlton Hotel, just across the street from my office.

John, as I will call him, was thin and lanky. He was quiet, but you could tell that there was considerable substance just below the surface of his inexpressive face. We greeted one another with small pleasantries and anecdotes about our Moscow experiences. John's conversation artfully combined personal candor and observation with off-the-cuff remarks about many of the Soviets I knew—"Oh, he's KGB, with a file a mile long." I soon felt that my initial reservations were not unfounded. I had the impression that John was someone who worked for or had close associations with the CIA. And yes, he was interested in my impressions of Roald Sagdeev.

I offered some lighthearted stories about Sagdeev—anecdotes anyone at the conference could have told—and waited anxiously for breakfast to draw to a close. When it was over, I shuddered slightly at the close encounter. That night I wrote about John in my journal: "I found him most enigmatic. I don't know what he *really* wanted or why he never looked me in the eye."

Waiting for me on my return from Moscow were the various institutional and personnel problems I had told Sagdeev I was struggling with. I found these kinds of workplace issues by far the most difficult part of my job. As I was preparing to fire a staff member, I often thought back to my discussion with Sagdeev. Although my diary entry on this subject was purposely dry and unemotive, reading between the lines I can still conjure up the feelings I invested in these simple words:

He works under extremely high-pressured circumstances . . . He too was talking as if he would like to return to science—perhaps a reaction to his rejection from Gorbachev . . . Although I did not get into the source of my concerns, we talked on a number of occasions about the singular responsibility of heading an organization . . . I miss talking to him.

To my surprise, several days later Sagdeev telephoned me from Japan, where he had gone just after the Moscow forum for a scientific conference. The connection was not very good, and the unexpectedness of his call gave me very little time to prepare for saying anything beyond empty small talk. Six days later a postcard arrived:

Susan,
That was an unbelievable thrill, indeed, to hear your voice so clearly. On the backside you see the volcano (Mt. Zao) wich [sic] is just a few miles from my hotel. I can see it through my window.
The place is very peaceful and quiet after the Moscow Forum. I am left here with my science (at last) and memories of You.
Yours Roald
P.S. Next week I'll be in Kioto for a different meeting and I'll try to write a longer message.

In the next several weeks I received another postcard and two more telephone calls. Roald was planning to come to the United States in the middle of November and I arranged to give a dinner party in his honor so that he could see some of his old friends and meet a few people who were also deeply involved in some of the same issues.*

Then, unexpectedly, I got a telephone call from a lawyer I had met at the Space Forum. "Have you seen the news?" he said gravely. "Our friend Roald Sagdeev has been implicated in a case of illegal high-technology transfer. They have just taken a guy named Charles McVey into custody,

---

* Ambassador Gerard Smith, the SALT negotiator and a friend of mine (and former member of the Eisenhower administration), had expressed an interest in meeting Sagdeev on one of his forthcoming trips. Both men had followed one another's work.

and he says he met with Sagdeev. According to reports, IKI bought embargoed American computers."

I was stunned, literally speechless. I had not seen anything in the newspapers in Washington, so I asked my friend to send me what he had. Although I maintained my composure on the phone, I was deeply disquieted about all I'd heard.

Several days later the clippings arrived. Under the heading "Four Charged in Computer Sales Scheme," the article started out ominously: "Four men, one of them already charged with smuggling technology to the Soviet Union, were indicted Tuesday on charges of trying to sell information that allegedly would have helped the Soviets develop a military supercomputer." The article went on to say that the case was linked to "a potential Soviet 'Star Wars' program" and that federal agents had "infiltrated" the $4 million "scheme."

It was another ten days before American officials backed off the claims that "the head of the Soviet space agency had been involved." But for a week, a number of forum participants called me to see if I had any information. I felt they simply wanted to talk about the news report and work through, in their own minds, their feelings about it. One participant bitterly commented that such a purchase would have been a betrayal of us by Sagdeev.

I could understand my colleagues' deep feelings of disappointment, if the news stories were true, but I reminded them that Sagdeev was a Soviet citizen who was part of a ruthless establishment that had its own imperatives. I didn't think we should take anything done on a high political level as a personal betrayal, because we were not involved in these events and he had not made *us* any promises. Still, I was extremely unsettled by the accusations, and thinking back to our open discussions in Moscow, I felt an even greater sense of confusion. But a voice inside me said that when the moment was right, Sagdeev would tell me about the incident, and that his account would be an honest one.

On Wednesday afternoon, November 18, Sagdeev called me as he had promised. His airplane had landed at National Airport and we agreed that as soon as he got settled at the Madison Hotel, he would telephone again and we would meet. Ever since his arrival in the United States the previous week, he had called regularly, filling me in on gossip or news, using any excuse to ring.

During one of our talks, I had asked him if he was aware of the press reports about Charles McVey and an illegal sale of computers to IKI. Before I could say more, he interrupted: "I am going to be in Washington soon. I would rather not talk to you about this over the telephone."

The night of Sagdeev's arrival we all had dinner together with Carl Sagan and his wife, Annie Druyan. At the end of a pleasant evening, Sagdeev turned to me seriously.

"I am giving a press conference tomorrow. It is an important thing for me. I asked the Soviet Embassy to arrange it. I think it is necessary to be direct about a number of issues that have come up recently. I hope you will come." He said no more.

The next day I arrived at the National Press Club ten minutes or so after the meeting had started. I found a seat at the back of the crowded room. Sagdeev was in the middle of his opening remarks.

". . . right now, while I'm here, there is an important technical group from NASA in Moscow in my institute, which is already proof that we have constructive cooperation . . ."* He completed a full description of the Phobos mission. And then the questions came.

QUESTION: Dave Lynch, *Defense Week*. President Reagan recently repeated his charge that the Soviets have their own SDI but won't admit it. What can you tell us about the scope of Soviet strategic defense research? Is the President correct when he says that the Soviets have spent more money and have more people working in that area than the United States does?

SAGDEEV: I am working in a completely peaceful civilian area, so I can guess only indirectly as a legislator, having some access to discussions. Conceptually there is no strategic defense against ballistic missiles in our country. There is some work which, according to claims, is done within the existing ABM treaty . . . An assessment, in which I participated, on the potential strategic implications of SDI, which was approved by our government, shows that in no case we should follow the American path with strategic defense. The most unstable, extremely vulnerable situation would be if both sides would eventually possess such defensive shields

---

* All quotations in my account from this press conference are taken from a transcript provided by the National Press Club.

in space. I think the report, which I haven't seen but which I read about in the newspapers, was issued recently by the Pentagon . . . as a kind of farewell postcard from Mr. Weinberger.* [Laughter]

Questions and answers about summit issues and space exploration went on in this fashion for another twenty minutes. And then Brian Brumley asked for the floor.

QUESTION: Brian Brumley, Associated Press. You mentioned a few months ago U.S. concerns about technology transfer . . . The U.S. places export restrictions on various types of technology items. Your name was mentioned by federal investigators in a case in California. Four people are now under arrest . . . Could you explain to us how it was you think your name was involved? It states that you had a meeting with a certain Charles McVey. Did you meet him?

SAGDEEV: You know, I think the process that is going on in California is going according to American law. In our country, we have our own legislation and our own law. And we are very much looking forward to cooperating with the United States on how to prevent nuclear war and how to prevent the spread of AIDS. But it is probably too premature to have cooperation in preventing the export of computers to the Soviet Union. And until now, we have not gotten an invitation to join COCOM . . .

QUESTION: [still Brumley] Did you in fact meet with Mr. McVey, or was that meeting . . .

SAGDEEV: Look, I would not like to comment on this issue more.

The press conference lasted no more than another five minutes, but Sagdeev was still flushed from his exchange with Brumley when I saw him at its conclusion. I wanted to stay and talk to him, but I had another meeting myself.

We said goodbye and I walked back to my office deep in thought, consumed by everything I had heard and by things that hadn't been said. I would see Sagdeev many times in the coming weeks and wonder why he'd said nothing more on the subject of Charles McVey.

---

* Caspar Weinberger had just announced his intention to leave as Secretary of Defense. He was replaced by Frank Carlucci.

5 : The Dazzling Summit

Washington was getting ready for another summit meeting and Sagdeev was still in the city. Despite this, I had to make an urgent visit to Moscow to try to clarify some critical elements of the Eisenhower Institute's new project.

After the first Chautauqua Conference in the Soviet Union, the Institute had decided, in light of the near-disaster of the Daniloff affair, to look into the function that ongoing exchange programs fulfilled in bilateral U.S.–U.S.S.R. relations. This we would do in connection with the thirtieth anniversary of the first postwar bilateral treaty, the General Exchanges Agreement of 1958.* Our plans included a dinner in the State Department's Benjamin Franklin rooms; a four-day conference in Gettysburg, Pennsylvania; the opening of a photography exhibit we had compiled on U.S.–Soviet exchanges; and a day full of briefings for members of Congress on Capitol Hill. All this to take place in January 1988, just two months away.

Two nights before my departure, I took Roald to dinner in downtown Washington. He came by himself, so I assumed he had sneaked out without his customary bodyguard or embassy "escort." Our evening at Joe & Mo's, a Washington steak house, was the first time we had ever been alone together. The uneasiness I felt was dispelled almost immediately when Roald handed me his menu and asked me to order for him. "It's intimidating. I don't know how to cope with pluralism in eating," he said.

---

* Nineteen fifty-eight must have been quite a year. There were many anniversaries and events pegged to them—though I must say I believe we started planning our program before IKI decided on a Sputnik conference.

That night we seemed to cover every imaginable topic from Roald's early childhood to my own last five years as a single parent. Roald, the oldest of four boys, had been born in Moscow, but his father, a professor of mathematics, had moved the family back to Kazan,* capital of their native Tatarstan, when Roald was four. During these years his father suffered from severe bouts of depression—an illness that ironically may well have saved his life. While he bounced in and out of the hospital, many of his comrades in the Communist Party were arrested in the purges.

Sagdeev confessed that he could never really reconcile himself to his father's Communism. On the anniversary of his fifty years in the Party, his father had been given the privilege of using one of the special food stores for the Party elite. "So that is why the Revolution was fought," Roald had said to him bitterly.

I was surprised by this story, and I wondered about the tension between them. But Sagdeev spoke emotionally about the years when he had accompanied his father to the university to visit scientific laboratories, which had piqued his interest in mathematics and science. "What a joy it was to discover the ease with which I could solve mathematical problems," he said. He also had a talent with the chess board—a skill he brought to tournament level.

From Kazan, Sagdeev went to Moscow State University, as a student of physics—in the same year as one of the university's more famous students, Mikhail Gorbachev.

The stories Roald told me were of far-off places, incidents and lives shaped by completely different historical and cultural forces from the ones I knew. But pride in family was something that we shared. Sagdeev pulled a folder from his coat pocket and produced photographs of his grown daughter and son. He also had pictures of his son's pre-school children. I knew that Roald was married, but he showed me no photograph of his wife, and I did not ask him about her.

Sagdeev moved the topic to me. Regretfully I had no pictures, but I told him about my three daughters and the circumstances that had brought us from Rochester, New York, to Washington. It was a complicated story, but I thought that I would share it openly with him.

I had been married twice, I told him. My first husband was an Englishman whom I had dated while I was in Europe at the American College in Paris. We married and lived in London for nearly six years before we came

---

* A city six hundred miles east of Moscow, on the Volga River.

to the United States—to Rochester—in 1975. My two older daughters were preschoolers and it had not been an easy adjustment for us. Culture shock and the social and political turmoil in America during those dissatisfied times helped to doom my well-meaning, if uncommunicative, marriage. How I had wanted a safe harbor then! Perhaps because of the breakup of my marriage, I married again on the rebound, a move that later devastatingly ended in divorce as well. Within a few years my first husband became a Catholic priest, leaving me with the sole responsibility for our children. I stayed in Rochester (what I called "the scene of the accident") for another year, and then decided to come to Washington with my three daughters. Job prospects, I thought, would be better in the nation's capital. I worked in the Washington office of Burson-Marsteller, a big public-relations firm, before starting my own company.

Sagdeev was moved, he confessed, by the role I was playing as bread-winner and mother to three growing girls. I was amused at the indignation he expressed about my ex-husbands, who had left me with far more than the lion's share of the parental and financial burden. "I could never have done such a thing," he asserted.

The following evening, still reeling from our hours of talk over that long, intimate dinner, I nervously greeted my dinner guests at my home in Bethesda. Roald came with a few presents for me: a bottle of Italian perfume and an exquisite silver fountain pen. He was in high spirits, full of humor and sparkle. He captivated my guests who had never met him before and charmed even those who were old friends. I enjoyed watching him out of the corner of my eye, and he was amused to watch me watch him.

After coffee, Sagdeev was emboldened to decline Karl Harr's offer to drive him back to his hotel in the city.

"I have something serious I have to discuss with you," he said after the last of the guests had gone.

I sat down on the long white living-room couch, bracing myself for what appeared to be a very important exchange.

"I was given an honorarium for a speech I made on my last trip to the United States. It's two thousand dollars. I want you to use it to buy two computers for your older girls. They need to start learning to use them. Please, I want you to take it."

What an extraordinary, if unacceptable, offer! I gently told him that I appreciated the thought, but I couldn't take money from him, even for the children. He was, I reminded myself, not only an acquaintance but a Soviet official. Despite his protests, I was adamant.

Then I added softly, "Perhaps your offer came from our talk last night. You shouldn't worry about us. The girls and I are really fine. You needn't worry, we are making ends meet."

Both of us remarked that the previous evening we had talked for more than seven hours straight and still it felt as if we had just started. This sentiment, given voice, was powerful and frightening. And once said, it gave reality and life to what had previously existed only in our individual minds.

For the very first time, we spoke openly about our developing friendship. Roald confessed that he had been completely captivated by me at Chautauqua, but that it was not until the Space Forum that he had realized how deeply attached to me he had become. "I can't explain it," he said. "I feel closer to you than I have ever felt to anyone else."

If I had had any of those same feelings, I had put them far from my mind—as best I could. His words terrified me. We were not ordinary people in ordinary circumstances. In fact, we were two highly visible people from two countries that had spent trillions of dollars defending themselves against one another. And in Sagdeev's case, he was an important official in a sensitive government sector.

I could see that it would be up to me to keep the brakes on our continued friendship. It had to be maintained strictly and platonically, I told him. I could see all the potential dangers. To allow it to become more would threaten our control and our wisdom. Under all the circumstances, that would be not only damaging to us both but possibly downright dangerous. Roald conceded the problems, but as he spoke he continued to couch his words in future terms. He did not seem deterred.

Late that night, when I drove Roald back to his hotel, he reached for my hand and held it between both of his. When we arrived at the Madison Hotel, he kissed my cheek and bade me farewell.

Two days later I arrived in Moscow. The city was covered in patches of snow and ice, a hint that the winter season was at hand.

There to negotiate the last details of our forthcoming project, I had not been anxious to go on this trip. Roald had shown me such a different side to Moscow on my last visit that I had almost dreaded the thought of going there without him. Still, I had some consolations. My oldest daughter,

Caroline, was with me, and she had the opportunity to see at first hand what my work was about. I also needed time away from the office to do some serious thinking. For the last few months I had been in a terrible state, trying to figure out if I should stay at the Institute.

When I had taken the job as president, it was assumed that I would give the organization a few years. However, the Eisenhower Centennial in 1990 was looming, and organizing the events now looked likely to become part of my current responsibilities. In fact, the directors put a high priority on these commemorations. I had gotten the board to agree to hire a director to organize them, but as time went on, it was clear that I'd have to be involved at virtually every step. I was uncomfortable about this, because I didn't think it was appropriate for a family member to play such a prominent part in organizing these events. I also worried that these activities would take me away from the part of my work that was focused on the Soviet Union.

Also, leaving the Institute might enable me to take some big financial strides. I was going to have to pay for Caroline's college tuition in a matter of only a few years, and Laura would be right behind her.

At least the time in Moscow gave me a chance to draw a breath and look around, to evaluate what being involved in U.S.–Soviet relations really meant to me. I had grown in the job and become a good negotiator. It was something I wanted to continue to develop.

Almost as soon as I arrived in the city and negotiations started, I could sense traces of what was called "Yeltsin humiliation." Boris Yeltsin, the outspoken Moscow City Communist Party chief and candidate member of the Politburo, had been "disgraced" for a "politically erroneous" speech he had delivered at a recent Central Committee meeting. According to reports, his "mistake" had been to charge that *perestroika* was moving too slowly —the most direct attack he could make on Gorbachev. This "error" assured him of his sacking from the Central Committee and Politburo, and of his eventual removal as Party chief of Moscow.

While the news was accepted in the West without too much fuss, it was painfully felt in Moscow. The newspapers were not permitted to print Yeltsin's speech, so *samizdat* copies, self-published and self-circulated, were secretly distributed throughout the city. To the intelligentsia's distress, all the old methods had been used to discredit Yeltsin: a coerced public apology, pages and pages of newspaper denunciations, and the firings. Gorbachev's role in these events put everyone on alert. And though many had placed their hopes in him, skepticism about *perestroika* now returned. To many Soviet intellectuals, Yeltsin's punishment was proof that Gorbachev was, underneath it all, just "like all the rest of them."*

Ministers and deputy ministers who had been making relatively free-wheeling decisions before this took Yeltsin's ouster as a warning that mavericks might lose their jobs. They had been given the signal, and caution permeated everything, as was evident in my own negotiations.

We had been in thorny discussions for at least six months about trying to put together a joint Soviet-American performance at the Kennedy Center following the State Department dinner. We had discovered that the National Symphony Orchestra would be in rehearsal in Washington during January, and I thought it would be very powerful to have the NSO's conductor, Mstislav Rostropovich, perform with one or more Soviet musicians. Rostropovich had been stripped of his Soviet citizenship during the Brezhnev era, and the great cellist and conductor was now an American citizen. Though relations between him and the Soviet authorities were poor to nonexistent, I thought that such a concert would give Soviet recognition of his status as an *American* conductor. Conversations with Rostropovich's staff had been encouraging.

I had intentionally avoided talking to Rostropovich directly about his possible participation. I felt that it was essential I get Soviet permission first. I did not want Rostropovich to be further humiliated by another Soviet rejection. But with the way things were going in Moscow, it looked as if that permission was not going to be forthcoming, and I wasn't going to give into Soviet demands that the concert proceed without Rostropovich's participation. Caroline, who had been invited into the negotiations by the Deputy Minister of Culture, was asked to sit on the Soviet side of the table. As I expressed my firm resolve, I was amused to watch her shoot me looks—her eyes growing larger and larger. I wrote in my journal:

> Today we were hard at it. The Ministry of Culture was tough. The whole issue of Rostropovich is being handled differently than it was six weeks ago. I can tell that the Yeltsin affair has had its impact . . . The decision to let Rostropovich play a role in our project must clearly now be made at the highest levels. No one else will take the responsibility. Not now.

---

* Fred Coleman confirmed this attitude in an article in *Newsweek* on November 30, 1987, which discussed how Gorbachev, as General Secretary of the Communist Party, controlled *Pravda*.

Despite our efforts, I was destined to go back to the United States empty-handed. The Ministry of Culture did not give its approval.

Roald had asked me to telephone him as soon as I got back to Washington. So, around 8:30 p.m., after my long, tiring journey from Moscow, I phoned his hotel. He had been waiting in his room, ready to convey good news. During the week I was away, he had been contacted by Ambassador Yuri Dubinin, who told him that he was under instructions to stay in Washington to serve as adviser to Gorbachev during the summit. It was clear we had much to discuss so we agreed to meet the next day.

Promptly at 3:00 the following afternoon, Sagdeev came to my office. After hearing about my meetings in Moscow and my failure to get approval for my concert, he suggested he could talk to Nicolai Shishlin, Alexander Yakovlev's closest aide, to see if there was a mutually convenient time for the three of us to get together. Yakovlev was one of the most progressive men on the Politburo and he had great influence with Gorbachev: if anyone could get my concert request straight to the top, it was Shishlin, who not only served as Yakovlev's close adviser but was also a frequent speech writer for Gorbachev himself.

After a few back-and-forth phone calls, the three of us had dinner that evening at a restaurant, not far from my office, on K Street.

Shishlin, whom I had known since the first Chautauqua Conference, was an approachable and friendly man. He was a journalist by background, though he was currently working as a staff member of the Communist Party. He radiated a kind of integrity, as well as warmth. When asked if something was possible, Shishlin always liked to say, "Why not?" But his words never struck one as being disingenuous, only hopeful.

After I explained all the ins and outs of the negotiations I had had in Moscow, Shishlin suggested that I write a letter to Yakovlev directly. He promised to deliver it personally and to call me with some kind of decision before the end of the summit meeting. I was most grateful to him.

Several days later, I invited Sagdeev and Shishlin for dinner at my home. We were joined by Andrei Kokoshin, with whom Roald and I had spent my last evening in Moscow at the end of the Space Forum. Kokoshin, a man about my age, had already made a name for himself as a successful interlocutor between the Academy of Sciences and the military industry.*

---

* Kokoshin is currently Russia's First Deputy Minister of Defense.

The dinner-table conversation that evening was dominated by summit talk: of SDI, of a possible Mars venture, of the prospects for improving U.S.–Soviet relations. Lost opportunities seemed to be on everyone's mind. Not surprisingly, the U-2 incident came up, and the subsequent cancellation of the 1960 Paris summit and Eisenhower's prospective trip to the U.S.S.R. I was not sure what the Soviet line had been about the whole incident or what these men thought had been the reason for the U-2 program in the first place. I suggested that it had been adopted as a unilateral "Open Skies" effort to monitor nuclear weaponry, and that it had also enabled the Eisenhower administration to keep defense spending under control and to resist calls for arms buildups, which the opposition had been demanding with its campaign slogans about the "missile gap."

Everyone agreed that the arms race had been a tragic mistake. But typically for 1987, all the men that evening were long on generalities and short on specifics—though I had no doubt they had some very strong personal opinions.

The conversation turned to the idea of retaliatory strikes, and suddenly we were playing a little game.

"If you were the President or the General Secretary and you were told that the other side had launched a full-scale attack against your country, would you retaliate?"

I answered first, and said that I could never press the button. It would assure the end of humankind, and I thought that the world did not deserve to be extinguished simply because of a long-standing bitter rivalry between only two of the world's nations.

Shishlin said he would probably not be able to push the button either, but he didn't give a reason. Kokoshin, who was a professional arms-control specialist, was slightly more evasive. To be honest, I'm not sure he ever really answered the question.

But when it was Roald's turn, he gave a clear and unequivocal response. Looking directly at me, he said, "I would not push the button if I knew you were on the other side."

Everyone laughed, but I was embarrassed by Sagdeev's impishness. What did these men think about his friendship with me, and would their assessments find their way to the Soviet intelligence community?

In Washington, summit fever was building and Gorbachev's arrival was imminent. But not everyone in the nation's capital was enthusiastic about the General Secretary's pending visit. The suggestion had been made that Gorbachev should speak to a joint session of Congress, but conservative members had mightily resisted. Said Senator Steve Symms, "To have a full-blown Communist dictator speaking in the hallowed halls of Congress is an absolute outrage."* Congressional Republicans threatened to boycott the session. Fearful of setting Gorbachev up for a humiliating reception on the Hill, the Reagan administration quickly moved to reduce the congressional gathering to a small breakfast meeting.

Skeptics, it appeared, were in the minority. It was hard not to be excited about the summit events. I had been sent at least two very interesting invitations. One was for "American intellectuals" to meet Gorbachev at the Soviet Embassy; the other was from Secretary of State George Shultz for a luncheon in honor of the Gorbachevs.

I was most interested in seeing the famous General Secretary and his wife close up. I had met them both at the Kremlin during the Nuclear-Free Forum, and I had been impressed by Gorbachev's demeanor, but that occasion had been too crowded, too staged, and his remarks had been too carefully prepared. Presumably the Embassy event would give the so-called American intellectual community a chance to ask questions and probe this man more deeply.

The Soviet Embassy gathering consisted of about sixty Americans and a slightly smaller number of Soviet Embassy personnel and summit advisers. As one of the latter, Sagdeev was in attendance. He greeted me warmly when he saw me and then insisted that we find Alexander Yakovlev. "It will be important for him to know who you are," he said. "That will help when he considers your letter."

In one of the large, ornate reception rooms, Roald found Yakovlev and introduced us. Short and bald, Yakovlev spoke very good English; he was quiet and low-key. I was not comfortable lobbying such a person at a public gathering, so we made pleasant forgettable small talk for several minutes. Despite his reputation as a powerhouse, I was impressed by how unpretentious Yakovlev seemed to be. His presence gave no hint that he was really the "progressive" mastermind behind the policy of *glasnost*. In fact, he seemed distinctly non-ideological, but then, during this short meeting he gave no hint of his viewpoint at all.

Gorbachev, it was clear, was the more flamboyant of the two. He mingled

* *Newsweek*, November 30, 1987, p. 36.

animatedly with the guests during the twenty-minute reception. Then, when we were called into the main room for his presentation, the crowd followed his trail like a pack of foxhounds that had been given a powerful scent.

We were assigned to seats at small tables scattered around the room. Gorbachev sat behind a French Empire–style desk and began his talk along the lines of *"Perestroika* and What It Means for the World." In all his lengthy remarks he made only a passing reference to SDI, hinting at its dangers to the global community and its potential to exacerbate a destabilizing arms race.

Then Gorbachev invited questions from the floor, and several people were ready. Most of the Americans who did speak prefaced their questions with statements like "Mr. General Secretary, all of us support and admire what you are doing to bring nuclear sanity to the world." Or: "Mr. Gorbachev, you are the only peacemaker on the world stage today." I noticed that Henry Kissinger and other former government officials sat in silence.

I had not intended to ask any questions, but now I was embarrassed by the ones the Americans were asking. Someone had to redress the balance, it seemed. With some nervousness I gathered my thoughts and scrawled a few notes on the back of my seating card. Several minutes later I raised my hand.

Gorbachev nodded his head, recognizing me the way a tennis player does when he's ready for the next serve. He sat poised, alert. Addressing him I said: "During World War II, the United States and the Soviet Union fought on the same side. Can you see any international situation in the future in which the United States and the Soviet Union might again become either diplomatic or military allies?"

Gorbachev gave me a penetrating look and began what seemed to be a rambling answer. In essence he said, "We should start now to build better relations. We don't want to be unprepared, as we were at the start of the Second World War." My impression was that he had not thought about such a question—not surprising, given the still tentative nature of the U.S.–Soviet rapprochement. But from what I knew about Soviet diplomatic activity at the time, I felt sure he would cite, for instance, the increasing importance of the United Nations. After all, the Soviet Union had, just weeks before, begun to pay their long backdated UN dues. Or, I thought, he might mention the Middle East, since the war between Iran and Iraq was still in devastating deadlock. But no mention was made of any of these matters.

Several minutes later, Gorbachev called for the last question. Stephen Cohen, a noted Sovietologist, was given the floor. In words to this effect, he said, "If everyone agrees that it is important to improve U.S.–Soviet relations and to increase our understanding of each other, why is it that American Sovietologists (and Soviet Americanologists) are looked down upon?"

Gorbachev listened, nodding his head in agreement. Then he said, with surprising acidity: "I don't know. Perhaps you should hold a symposium on the subject and see if you can find out." A slightly perceptible wave went through the room. I did not know Cohen personally at the time, but I was surprised that his simple question had elicited such a sharp and sarcastic answer. Interesting, I thought, that it had revealed something of Gorbachev the West had not seen before.

The next day I absentmindedly went off to the State Department luncheon for the Gorbachevs. The guest list was a veritable *Who's Who in America*: Armand Hammer, Donald Trump, Tom Brokaw, the leading members of the administration and members of Congress. The top echelons of the Soviet Embassy and the summit advisers were also in attendance.

Sagdeev and I said hello at the beginning and he introduced me to Alexander Bessmertnykh, then First Deputy Foreign Minister. Bessmertnykh, a slender man with an unreadable face, said, "Ah, you are the beautiful Miss Eisenhower I have heard so much about." We chatted for a few minutes, but my strong instincts told me that Roald and I should not remain at this gathering side by side. The way Bessmertnykh had talked unnerved me, and I wondered what he was getting at when he said he'd heard so much about me.

I excused myself and went to a table to pick up my seating card and opened it: Table 9. I put it in my pocket and got into the receiving line. Howard Baker, then Reagan's Chief of Staff, stepped into the line behind me. We spoke for a few minutes, then Baker opened his seating card and I noticed to my surprise that he was also seated at Table 9. I realized that protocol would probably put him at either the General Secretary's table or with Mrs. Gorbachev.

My guess was correct. When we finally found our seats, I discovered that I was at the head table with Baker, General Secretary Gorbachev, Mrs.

Shultz, Senator Sam Nunn, the *Washington Post*'s Meg Greenfield, Pepsico's Donald Kendall, and John Crystal.*

As far as I know, there has never been before or since a greater sense of excitement at any diplomatic gathering. It was potent and tangible, and impossible to reproduce. All of us in the room that day knew that we were present at a historic turning point. With the signing of the INF agreement, the future of the world would certainly change for the better. The United States and the Soviet Union had finally taken the first step in the history of the arms race to reduce and eliminate existing nuclear weapons. Euphoria was in the air. It was as if the whole room was on a high.

For some rather strange reason, the people at our table spent a great deal of time talking about Gorbachev's anti-alcohol campaign in the Soviet Union, which had not gone very well. Gorbachev displayed some humor on the subject, and as he spoke I watched him with real fascination. I had never seen a world leader in such a state of high energy, maybe even hyper-energy. He exuded something that dominated the table and the conversation, and it couldn't just be put down to power. When he looked at you, he looked *into* you. His dark penetrating eyes seemed to bore right down *into* your middle. Was the piercing quality a manifestation of self-confidence? Curiosity? Arrogance? Perhaps messianic zeal?

I said barely a word the whole meal. I had nothing to say. I was simply fascinated watching the others and the way they related to the Soviet leader. It was as if everyone at our table were engaged in a sophisticated minuet, with all the dancers looking to Gorbachev for their cues.

The protracted small talk about Gorbachev's anti-alcohol campaign did not stop him, or anyone else, from toasting the signing of the INF agreement. Gorbachev raised his champagne-filled glass and looked each one of us in the eye, and clinked each individual glass. To a new era in arms reductions! To a new era! To us!

What a day it had been. What a historic moment for me to have seen firsthand. What was I to do? When the Eisenhower Institute directors came to my office that afternoon and offered me an attractive pay raise, how could thoughts of returning to private business full-time have ever entered

---

* The next day, when the luncheon was reported in the *Post*, the reporter named everyone at our table but the two "unknowns": John Crystal and me. Crystal was an Iowa businessman who had known Gorbachev personally for some time and who was, interestingly, related to the Iowa farmer who hosted Nikita Khrushchev on his travels around the United States during the 1959 summit.

my mind? I was watching history before my very eyes. Didn't that compensate for all the other difficulties I had, even my personal conflict over the centennial? I wrote in my journal that the Gorbachev luncheon, and my directors' willingness to make a very good financial offer, was "a convergence that made my professional choice self-evident."

The summit ended the following day, with a lengthy press conference and rain-soaked goodbyes. The INF agreement had been signed, and many topics, from Afghanistan to human rights in the Soviet Union, had been discussed. The event had absorbed and consumed Washington like no other diplomatic event before. Special-interest organizations had descended on the city from all over the country. Demonstrators for Jewish emigration had staged rallies and nuclear activists held vigils. The press center had accommodated between three and five thousand journalists from all over the world. Washington, blasé by nature about foreign visits, had come to a stop for three days while siren-blaring police cars escorted the Soviet Union's first couple around town.

Even though an arms-control breakthrough had indeed occurred, most of all those three summit days may have marked a turning point in the American *public* consciousness. The indelible image of Gorbachev dashing out of his limousine at the corner of L and Connecticut to shake hands in the crowd, taking his security forces apparently by surprise, crystallized in the public mind the changes that were under way in the U.S.S.R. When an extremely knowledgeable Soviet émigré pooh-poohed the spontaneity of Gorbachev's plunge into the crowd with fairly convincing evidence that the General Secretary was nearly encircled by KGB men already placed on the streets,* our American friends accused him of ill-humored and misplaced skepticism. Americans *wanted* to believe that Gorbachev had emerged from his car without prior planning. After more than forty years of tension between our two countries, they were tired of the hostility and hoped for a change. People could be heard exclaiming that if Gorbachev were to run for President he would win!

But my friend Sagdeev, who'd already captured me with his honesty and directness, said before he left for Moscow: "Unfortunately, Susan, like most other goods and commodities of value in my country, *perestroika* and *glasnost* are for 'export only.' "

---

* The evidence was the clothing—the uniformity of the jackets and shoes—something that all Soviet citizens recognize as a classic KGB look.

6 : Resisting Compromise

Two days after the end of the summit, a member of Rostropovich's staff told the Institute that the maestro would no longer be available for a U.S.–Soviet concert. No explanation was given, but it was clear that it was not because of another commitment. The answer was just no.

I was puzzled by the sudden change of heart. Rostropovich's staff had been extremely encouraging from the beginning. And short of an outright apology to the man, which was extremely remote, Soviet approval for a performer to play with Rostropovich would have been tantamount to the regime's burying the hatchet.* It was also curious, because it had been reported that Rostropovich had flown in from Europe to attend the Reagans' state dinner for the Gorbachevs. I mentioned the whole inexplicable story to a colleague of mine who had been at the White House state dinner, and before I could finish my query he began nodding his head understandingly. He had been next to Rostropovich in the receiving line and had heard Gorbachev saying something to him in Russian, roughly translated as "I hear you are living well in America."

"Living well" may be the best revenge in America, but according to my colleague, it was regarded as treasonous in the Soviet Union. We speculated that Rostropovich had been offended by the remark. I predicted that now he would hold out for an official Soviet apology for his expulsion.

There was nothing more to be done. The next day I contacted the Soviet Embassy and we arranged to invite the Soviet classical pianist Stanislas

---

* Shishlin later said to me, "Too bad, Yakovlev was ready to agree."

Bunin to give a solo recital after the dinner at the State Department. I told the Soviet Embassy there would be no joint concert at the Kennedy Center.

During the summit I had been notified that an organizational meeting would be held in New York to discuss the formation of the new Western-style foundation that Mikhail Gorbachev had proposed at the Nuclear-Free Forum. Earlier that autumn I had been contacted and asked if I would consider being a founding board member. Although I was skeptical about much of its rhetoric, I thought the foundation had a great deal of potential as a kind of incubator for new cooperative efforts between Americans and Soviets. I expressed an interest in finding out more, and I said I'd decide about my participation after the first meeting.

Evgeny Velikhov, a Gorbachev adviser and the principal moving force behind this project, was in the United States for the summit and organizers wanted to take advantage of his presence here. Well known in scientific and political circles, Velikhov, a physicist and a longtime friend of Sagdeev's, was a large balding man, with sandy hair and a perpetual smile. He had a myriad of interests, and the foundation was his latest.

Quite separate from my recruitment on the American side, Velikhov, unbeknown to me, had asked Sagdeev to come to the same meeting to consider serving on the board as a Soviet director.

From the beginning, both Roald and I, for very similar reasons, had reservations about the foundation. We separately voiced questions about its independence, given that it was so closely tied to Gorbachev. While it was perfectly understandable why I might have been troubled about being "used" by the Soviet authorities, Roald's obvious concern about the same possibility was a different matter, and I was deeply impressed by it. As he said pointedly to a Soviet Foreign Ministry official at a reception we both attended, "The question is whether the foundation will appear to represent the 'heavy hand of the Kremlin.' " The official was not amused.

Aside from its associations, the foundation also had an image problem. It was persistently referred to as the "Survival Fund," in reference to its origins at the "Nuclear-Free Forum for the Survival of Mankind." I questioned this name when the meeting convened in New York and proposed that some other, more positive notion be stressed, such as "cooperation" —anything but "survival." This and many other issues revealed how much preparatory work was still left to do.

Nevertheless, Velikhov insisted that the new board of the Survival Fund meet with Gorbachev at the Kremlin on January 15, 1988—which was only weeks away. He was unmoved by the argument that we should have our own house in order before going to see the General Secretary about the new organization and its plans. I argued strenuously in favor of postponement. "If we are going to see Gorbachev, we should at least try to get on Reagan's schedule for a similar meeting," I said, advocating reciprocity. "If Reagan turns us down, at least we would have given him the option."* Velikhov remained resolute that the meeting with Gorbachev go forward on January 15. It wasn't until nearly the end of the meeting that I understood why that specific date was so important to him. Apparently the General Secretary wanted to meet with us then because it was the second anniversary of his speech on the nuclear threat to mankind—and his proposal for a "nuclear-free world." Another anniversary!

I was hesitant about participating, and I told Velikhov after the meeting that I was still undecided about joining the board.

Since I had begun my work in U.S.–Soviet relations, I knew it was important to have a philosophy to guide my approach to any given event or situation. There was something very seductive and exciting about being involved in these issues, with these people, during this period of history, but that was precisely what was so dangerous. It was easy to be compromised. I could see it happening with some of my colleagues, and sometimes I could even see it beginning to happen to me.

A few of my colleagues confessed that sometimes they found themselves afraid to speak out about Soviet policy for fear of losing access to the most powerful people on the Soviet side. For example, a very famous American Sovietologist, and a friend, later told me privately that he was afraid to write an anti-Gorbachev article because he didn't want to jeopardize his future chances to get an interview with the General Secretary or his aides. This was a phenomenon of the *perestroika* period because of the West's intense interest in this phase of Soviet history and because of the Soviet leadership's tantalizing accessibility.

I made myself promise that if I ever found myself at the stage where I couldn't walk away from a situation because I was too compromised to stand up for myself, I would get out of the U.S.–Soviet field first.

Roald seemed to understand these arguments perfectly. He told me about

---

* In the end, Reagan was never asked to receive our group, despite my arguments and those of a few other directors. But some of the American directors were curiously unwilling to meet with the American President.

how he hated, indeed refused, to make all the connections to the *nomenklatura* that would have assured him a larger apartment, say, or more and more promotions in the Soviet system. In the U.S.S.R. these came only in exchange for being what he called a "good little boy."

In this, as in so many other matters, we were on the same wavelength.

Sagdeev was also having his doubts about agreeing to be on the board of the Survival Fund, and he advised me against taking on this responsibility. After the dinner following the foundation meeting, he pulled me into a corner and said softly, "You are right to keep your options open. This probably isn't right for you." Later, when the guests had dispersed and we had the opportunity to do some walking around New York, he elaborated: "Susan, given the current and probable composition of the board, you are assured that you will always have to be the tough guy if you join it. Everyone else [on the American side] will be supporting more liberal things without too much regard to politics. Who wants *always* to be the tough guy?" Then he added gaily, "You are so much more wonderful when you are being yourself!"

Sagdeev was like a little kid those days in New York: full of energy, enthusiasm, and plenty of mischief. After arriving in the United States in early November, as Shevardnadze's representative at a UN session, he had spent his time *sans* bodyguard. Under the watchful eye and enveloping embrace of the U.S.S.R.'s UN Mission in New York, he had gone to Washington for what had supposedly been only a short stay. But in order to advise Gorbachev at the summit, he had been instructed to stay put, and this unexpected change in his itinerary had won him temporary freedom. As he waited for the summit to come and go, he did so without the usual KGB shadow that was routinely assigned to him and to other Soviet officials in important sensitive posts. He—and the assignment to escort him—had fallen through the pre-summit cracks.

"Evgeny Primakov has noticed that I have a special affection for you," Roald said as he settled into the plush leather settee at the Polo Lounge on Madison Avenue.

During the summit meeting, Roald told me, Primakov had pulled him aside and warned him that "this romance" had been noticed and it could be dangerous. It "would have to stop."

"What romance?" I protested.

So I had been right that Roald's behavior toward me had indeed attracted

t Camp David (named for my brother) in 1954: (left to right) my grandfather, with me on his lap; y mother, my sister, my father, and my brother sitting on my grandmother's knee (*U.S. Navy*)

My grandparents and me at the White House in 1957 (*National Park Service*)

The Eisenhowers entertain the King of Afghanistan at Gettysburg. He is standing behind me with his hands on my shoulders (*USIA*)

Roald and his father

Roald (at right) with his mother, brother, and aunt; Roald's paternal grandmother

Roald as a young student

Roald in 1986, being awarded the U.S.S.R.'s highest medal, "Hero of Socialist Labor." Boris Yeltsin, then newly arrived Party boss of Moscow and Politburo member, pins on the decoration

As a single parent: with my mother and Caroline, Amy, and Laura; a few years later after my return from the U.S.S.R., with my daughters and Delores, our housekeeper; and with Amy, in 1988

Sagdeev and I talk just after our first meeting. I look skeptical!

Sagdeev and I at a party given by Colleen Dewhurst (left) after the barbecue that first evening in Chautauqua

Sagdeev behind his cluttered desk at IKI, from which he proposed that we collaborate on a book, in October 1987

On the dais at the Space Conference. To my right, Roald's rival Guri Marchuk, president of the Academy of Sciences

the attention of the authorities. Primakov was an increasingly powerful man. His words carried weight, and I questioned whether or not he had been speaking only for himself. Sagdeev tried to reassure me that if there had been any high-level concern about him or us they would have "discovered" that they had forgotten to assign him a bodyguard and would have rectified their mistake. No, Roald was convinced that what he had heard from Primakov was conveyed as friendly but serious advice.

All the same, the futility of our friendship was never far from my mind. Roald was getting warnings from the Soviets and disturbing accusations from the Americans.

That evening, since we had managed to be alone, I finally asked Sagdeev directly about Charles McVey and any complicity he himself might have had in the IKI purchase of black-market American computers.

Sagdeev was silent for a moment. An awkwardness seemed to descend over him. He avoided meeting my eyes.

"I am glad you have asked me this," he said, still looking at his hands. "Do you know what my first reaction was when Marshall Rosenbluth* asked me about the news reports in the United States?"

I shook my head.

"I said to Marshall, 'I am worried about what Susan Eisenhower will think.' " He looked up at me as if he were waiting for the answer to his question.

"What should I think?" I replied evenly.

For the next half hour Sagdeev told me everything I wanted to know about the incident and answered my questions with a clear determination to erase any uneasiness I might have on the subject. He admitted that IKI had purchased black-market computers—an extremely common transaction in Moscow, he said. COCOM restrictions that regulated the sale of computers to Communist-bloc countries had created a flourishing black market. Beyond that, however, Roald was adamant in refuting the most damaging part of the newspaper allegations: that this black-market computer was being used for advanced research on a Soviet SDI system. "There is nothing top secret about what we are using this computer for," he said emphatically. "You saw that very computer with your own eyes. Remember when I took you to our computer center during your visit to IKI?"

To ensure that the West would understand he wasn't working on military

---

* A well-known American plasma physicist who had, over the course of years, collaborated with Sagdeev.

research, Roald had taken several distinguished American scientists who were visiting Moscow through IKI and had allowed them to videotape the sum total of its computer capability. Despite the considerable political risk he took in doing this, he said he had wanted to do everything he could to preserve the potential for international cooperation. "I told them to show the American authorities the tape if there were ever any question about my credibility or that of my institute," Sagdeev recounted. And then he added, with emphasis, "That is why I couldn't bear the thought that you might think I am someone I am not. I am a space scientist, and everything I have done I have done to promote the peaceful use of space and space exploration. As for my computers being used for a Soviet SDI program— hah! I have been one of its biggest opponents. You must believe me."

Our exchange had been so potent that night that we needed to walk. Roald put his arm through mine and squeezed it every so often, as if to verify that I was still beside him and still his "very dear friend." We circled the block around my hotel three or four times, like sweeping and swooping birds unwilling to land. The streets were nearly empty, but I was nervous and vaguely conscious of people in doorways, questionable loiterers sizing the two of us up. But still I was unable to break away. For some minutes we lingered at my hotel entrance, locked in a painful and protracted good night. Finally I insisted that I take my leave.

The next morning the sun shone with brilliant intensity. The air was crisp and cold. I hurried to pack for my return to Washington later in the morning. Roald, too, was leaving—returning home to Moscow later in the day. I had agreed to meet him for breakfast in his hotel lobby, only a block away. When I arrived, we set off down the street in search of a diner and an open drugstore where we could buy a Sunday newspaper. Roald had written an article on a joint U.S.–Soviet mission to Mars for the Sunday *Washington Post*.

We found a small shop on a side street and went in. As Sagdeev was about to purchase the newspaper, we were unexpectedly stopped by a man who began speaking Russian to him. Roald introduced us, but after a brief exchange of pleasantries, he ushered me out of the store. Once on the street again, Roald explained that the man's official position notwithstanding, he was known to work for the KGB.

This unexpected intrusion into our last moments together was a cold douse of reality. I worried aloud about it all the way back to the hotel. When we arrived, we collected my bags and then Roald asked me for the *Post*'s "Outlook Section," in which his article appeared. Without fanfare, he wrote something on the margin, folded the paper, and stuck it in the side pocket of my briefcase. On the plane to Washington, some hours later, I pulled the newspaper out. Under his article, entitled "Together to Mars: A Soviet Proposal," Roald had written: "Together on Earth, Love, Roald."

After I had returned to my home in Bethesda, and Roald, I assumed, was waiting to board his plane for Moscow, the telephone rang. He was calling from a phone booth at Kennedy airport. He had a collection of coins that he used, constantly, to feed the machine.

"I couldn't leave without saying goodbye again," Sagdeev told me. "Besides, I wanted you to know that Velikhov and I went to a Chinese restaurant and I think the fortune cookie I got could be very significant. It says, 'It is better to be respected than to be loved.' " Then he added brightly, "But I am looking for both!"

Several days after Roald left for Moscow, my friend who had asked me to help the undercover agent gave me a call. Over dinner I discovered that his absorption with the intelligence services remained. Now he was consumed by his interest in the high-technology electronic surveillance devices that are used to gain information about the Soviet Union at home and abroad. With great relish he spent the evening describing all the remarkable things they could now do to track people or bug their conversations.

I did not discourage his talk—not at all. I found myself listening with rapt attention. Everything my colleague told me only convinced me that Roald and I had been under surveillance.

For some time afterward I was paralyzed by the thought that someone might have "seen" Roald put his arm around my shoulders. Or perhaps our intense discussions, including the tentative ones about our feelings, had been picked up by microwave technology. Why not? Hadn't Sagdeev been in the United States to advise Gorbachev at the summit? Wasn't he also the Soviet Union's most effective anti-SDI spokesman? Even more significantly, wasn't he also under scrutiny for purchasing black-market computers, allegedly for Soviet SDI research?

It was a wet rainy afternoon, and I was sitting in a soft chair with my eyes tightly closed. The sound of the high-pitched dental drill bombarded my senses and a fine spray of water fell like dew on my face. It was "Moon River," I think, that echoed in my head—but I could only just hear it when the drill and the spray stopped. I felt a pinch somewhere in my lower jaw. A small pinch, just a little jab. But tears welled up in my eyes, tears from nowhere, unexpectedly flowing. My gums no longer hurt, but it seemed that a raw nerve had been exposed. The pain seemed almost unbearable. Not because of my teeth, but because of the loss. An overwhelming sense of past and future loss.

PART
TWO

1988

They could lay bare in the utmost detail everything that you had done or said or thought; but the inner heart, whose workings were mysterious even to yourself, remained impregnable.

—George Orwell, *1984*

7 : Assessing the Stakes

I had a great deal riding on the way I conducted myself not just with Roald but with his country.

I carried the Eisenhower name with deep pride and a sense of stewardship. My grandfather had been a strong and dominating force in my life, and after his death I desperately missed his presence and affection. My siblings and I often got a pat or a squeeze or a pinch, or maybe he would come up from behind us, bark something about West Point, and draw our shoulders back to "teach us how to stand up straight." I kept the memory of those little attentions like valuable treasures. When I could no longer close my eyes and conjure up his face, I mourned that I had lost him, but I really hadn't. His spirit stayed with me.

I was also proud of what his name represented in the Soviet Union. He was revered for his role as Allied Commander in Europe during World War II, and even the Cold War did not dim the Soviet people's respect for him. There were so many times, after I began traveling to the Soviet Union, that I would ask myself what he would have thought or how he would have reacted to a set of circumstances. I never forgot that my actions would never be judged independently. In the strongest sense, I carried Granddad with me, and I did not, under any circumstances, want to do anything that would darken his name.

As a single parent, I knew how much my earlier marital difficulties had hurt the children, and me. So I was wary about making another mistake in my personal life. Not only that, I had huge financial responsibilities for supporting my three children and our housekeeper. I earned virtually all the household income, and I was also responsible for putting my daughters through college. I had managed to overcome what seemed like overwhelming obstacles in getting my career launched, and I didn't want to do anything that would jeopardize my hard-earned professional reputation.

Such were the considerations of the head. Matters of the heart, I was beginning to see, were more complicated. Sagdeev and I fully understood the utterly taboo nature of our deepening friendship—which we observed on a strictly platonic basis—but a strong bond had already formed between us. We communicated with an emotional and intellectual shorthand that created an unavoidable intimacy. My dilemma was that my heart carried Sagdeev with me, but my head was demanding his immediate eviction.

I had a taste of what lay in store during the winter of 1988. Sometime in January I went to a cocktail buffet given by a former ambassador who had played a very important role in East-West relations. During the party, my host asked me about my trips to the Soviet Union. "The only explanation for your frequent trips to Moscow is that you have a man there," he said definitively.

"What a thought," I offered lightly. "Do you have any candidates?"

The ambassador responded without a smile. "Imagine if you did, what a scandal!" he said, his eyes widening. "What a scandal!"

I was sensitive about his offhand remarks for more than one reason. In addition to the Cold War impossibility of my growing friendship with Roald, he was still legally married. As his "very dear friend," I did not want to cause him any difficulty in his family life. When I had raised this matter with him, Roald would hear nothing of it. He told me flatly that he and his wife had been estranged for years, and he made it clear that he didn't want to talk about it.

What could I do? There was no way of making a judgment about Roald's situation. The usual benchmarks that we in America might use to determine a man's relationship with his wife—are they still living together? for example—did not work in the Soviet Union. Given the extreme housing shortages in Moscow, particularly of good apartments—and everyone's desire to live in the capital—it was common to find estranged couples still living together. In fact, it was not unusual for divorced couples to cohabit the same tiny flat long after their marriages had been dissolved, unwilling to make a settlement on it or unable to acquire another. I felt I had to respect Roald's own instincts on any questions he might face, either political, social, or moral.

Nevertheless, exchanges like the one I had with the ambassador were indelibly tattooed on my consciousness. And drawn to Roald as I was, it's not surprising that I felt utter futility about our deepening friendship. Good-byes had always been painful for me, and I feared I was setting myself up for an agonizing one in this case.

January 15 was nearing and the foundation meeting with Mikhail Gor-bachev was still scheduled. The time had come for me to make a decision about whether or not to join the board of the Survival Fund. I thought its potential as a vehicle for U.S.–Soviet cooperation outweighed its other problems, and certainly the momentum of bilateral progress had been established. In addition, the board of directors now boasted some very interesting and distinguished names from around the world, including that of Andrei Sakharov, father of the Soviet H-bomb and human-rights activist.

If I had residual concerns about the foundation's close association with Gorbachev, they were not widely held by the other directors or the public at large. The General Secretary was, indisputably, riding high in the in-ternational community. Just weeks before *Time* magazine had named him "Man of the Year," and his book, *Perestroika*, had become a worldwide bestseller.

Two days after our arrival in the Soviet capital, we were bused to the Kremlin and, without any security checks, ushered into an anteroom to wait for Gorbachev. I was flattered, of course, by his warm recognition of me: "Susan, we meet this time in Moscow!" But I was absorbed and distracted by the historic happenstance taking place before my eyes. When Gorbachev shook hands with Andrei Sakharov, it was the first time they'd ever met. Their greeting was cordial, if rather cool.

Gorbachev opened the meeting with a lengthy summary of the state of his country and the world; then each of the board members was asked to say something. When my turn came, I openly expressed my concerns to Gorbachev that this foundation's credibility could be at stake unless it maintained its independence.* Others used their time to make statements about the challenges facing the global community and the General Sec-retary's leadership in finding solutions to them.

Tension mounted when Sakharov started to speak. He took a list from his pocket and demanded the release of two hundred "prisoners of con-

---

* At the end of the meeting he said to me: "I admired your remarks and the spirit in which you delivered them."

science" still incarcerated in Soviet prisons. Slowly he started to read the names, before giving the list to Gorbachev's aide.

Despite the much-touted telephone call that had released Sakharov from his internal exile in Gorky, it was clear that the General Secretary was not particularly an admirer. I could see the General Secretary's ready temper was threatening to flare.

I was surprised by Gorbachev's demeanor that day. His body language and mannerisms were strikingly different from what I had observed during the Washington summit week. Unlike the understandable high of Washington, in Moscow he seemed to be under much more strain.

Soviet society had become a wellspring of the unexpected. The unthinkable was a daily occurrence. Several days before our arrival, for instance, Boris Pasternak's long-banned *Doctor Zhivago* had appeared in *Novy Mir*, a popular weekly magazine. The Supreme Court was also considering the rehabilitation of the old Bolsheviks Nicolai Bukharin and Alexi Rykov, victims of Stalin's purges. Although one might have imagined that Gorbachev was proud of such developments, I sensed that something about the process he had unleashed worried him deeply. He spoke about the "politics of realism" and about a time to "sober up" from the "inebriation" that the U.S.S.R. had been experiencing with *glasnost*, the liberalization of expression.

At the end of the meeting, I was standing next to Sakharov when Gorbachev left the room. Utilizing even the last moment to squeeze in another favored topic, Sakharov said, "Mikhail Sergeiivich,* I have an idea to bury nuclear power plants underground to enhance safety. I would like to come and talk to you about this idea sometime."

Gorbachev looked directly at Sakharov and then said, "Why don't you do that, Andrei Dmitriivich. Come see me before you hold another press conference for the Western press."

The following day we had an even keener insight into how Sakharov was regarded by the General Secretary and his Communist Party colleagues. When news reports came out about the meeting of the Survival Fund, a number of Moscow newspapers ran a front-page photograph of all of us at a large conference table, with Gorbachev in the center. The photo had been taken from such an angle that Sakharov's face could not be seen. In some versions, including the one in *Sovietskaya Rossiya* and even more

---

* These are Gorbachev's first and middle names. The second, his patronymic, means "son of Sergei." This is the proper Russian form of formally addressing a person. The same form is used for women; the suffix *ovna* means "daughter of."

mainstream papers like *Pravda*, the back of Sakharov's white head of hair had been airbrushed black! Unless one read the article with extreme care, one could miss the fact that Sakharov had been at the meeting. I was astonished when I saw it. Such things were common in Stalin's and Brezhnev's times. In fact, the airbrush was to the Soviet leadership what the ray gun was to science-fiction villains—an excellent way to vaporize an enemy. But what a shock to see such an old Soviet trick used in this "new age" of Gorbachev.

How could I have guessed when I left Moscow for home that I would be back in the Soviet Union less than a month later?

Not long after the Eisenhower Institute's successful State Department dinner and four-day conference and exhibition, the American side of the Survival Fund met in Boston. What I heard at the meeting prompted me to wire Velikhov to ask for immediate visa support to come to the U.S.S.R. to discuss urgent business. I was troubled that the fund had already taken some ill-advised steps.

As part of the foundation's start-up documents, its Soviet staff had developed an unprecedentedly radical document for approval by the Soviet Council of Ministers. It proposed that the foundation be given special status, which included preferential currency exchange, exclusion from customs regulations, and a long list of other "privileges." If approved, the request would essentially give the foundation extraterritoriality, liberating it from many of the Soviet Union's laws. This first-of-its-kind application was bold and risky. To submit it to the authorities required the signature of the foundation's Soviet board members. But I doubted that Sakharov, Sagdeev, and Velikhov had actually given the document full consideration. They were not in Boston with us, and I worried that the Soviet staff would return to Moscow to say that the American board had insisted on these terms.

Knowing that some employees in the Soviet Union were "organizational plants," put there to spy on others and provoke them into making fatal political mistakes, I did not trust one particular employee who had been charged with drafting the document. When I questioned him at the Boston meeting, he swore that the Soviet board members had read the draft and approved it. I just didn't believe him.

I came away from the meeting convinced that I must talk with Sagdeev about this. I needed to look him straight in the eye and ask him if he was really willing to risk his precarious political position on such a radical document. To me, it looked like a certain way to commit political suicide.

The ramifications of this question went far beyond the simple political safety of the Soviet board members. During the Washington summit, Roald had told me that Gorbachev had not been as accessible to his advisers as he had been during the Geneva summit in 1985. According to Sagdeev, just after Gorbachev came to power, he was still finding his way and seeking counsel from a broad spectrum of people. But by 1987 Gorbachev had moved from a free-flowing reliance on many advisers to a predictable dependence on his staff. A man named Valery Boldin, a Central Committee apparatchik, who was to become his chief of staff, was already on the scene.* At the same time, advisers like Sagdeev, Velikhov, Georgi Arbatov, and others were finding it more and more difficult to gain access to the General Secretary with their ideas and their concerns.

I feared that conservatives around Gorbachev could point to the foundation's request, spearheaded by Velikhov, Sakharov, and Sagdeev, as "provocative" and "adventuristic"—and use it to drive a bigger wedge between these important liberals and the General Secretary.

The night before leaving for Moscow I wrote in my journal:

It is the night before I go to the Soviet Union and I cannot sleep . . . Despite the fact that I should stay home and try to lead a more normal, personally satisfying life, I cannot stop. I felt the utter necessity to go to the Soviet Union after our Fund meeting in Boston last weekend. The Council of Ministers document is so radical that it would be thrown out of our Congress for being impossibly foolish. At best it makes the Soviet legislative initiative asymmetrical,† at worst politically crazy . . . The Americans insist that it is quite appropriate that our Soviet colleagues should push the limits as far as they can. But I think, rather, it is in our best interests to produce a reasonable document that will assure that the foundation can do business. We should avoid anything that would play into the hands of those who would like to have an excuse to further isolate the General Secretary.

As my plane neared Sheremetyvo Airport, I was in a state of high anticipation, anxious to discuss all this with Sagdeev. He had promised to meet me at the airport and he did not let me down. When I arrived, he

---

* Boldin was later arrested as one of the conspirators in the August 1991 putsch.
† Our American members of the board would never have tried to have special legislation passed granting the American branch of the foundation similar rights.

was standing at the end of the jetway, awkwardly clasping a large bouquet of flowers.

While we waited for my luggage to appear, we discussed the reasons for my trip. As it turned out, Sagdeev had not seen the most recent complete draft of the fund's document, and neither Velikhov nor Sakharov had either. The large dose of manipulation that had been liberally administered to these three busy men, and their discovery of it, generated a full-blown debate that went on for nearly a week.

Sakharov was also disgruntled about other early steps that the foundation had taken. In a memo to the board he had distributed a few days before my arrival, he had demanded that board elections be conducted all over again and that the foundation start from scratch. With the help of Roald's staff—and the use of his computer and printer—I wrote a counter-proposal, designed as a compromise for the board's consideration. These were delicate issues which were not easy for the Soviets and Americans to work out. It was all such a new process, in fact, that the board had hired a Swede to serve as the foundation's director—a friendly intermediary in a relationship that was still fragile and somewhat volatile.

These and other issues were discussed at a small gathering of the Soviet board held one evening at the Sakharovs' apartment. I had not fully formed my impression of Sakharov from the brief exposure I had had to him in January, but this get-together at his home gave me that chance. In his own setting Sakharov projected quiet introspection, a purposeful peacefulness. It was his wife, Elena Bonner, who seemed to be the family's engine of activism. She would regularly, and passionately, interject thoughts on the matters being discussed.

That evening Sakharov expressed his worries (as I did) about how the foundation would be perceived.* On reading my memo, he said quietly that he thought we had "some common ground for discussion." We went through my memo and his, point by point, and slowly some consensus began painfully to emerge.

In an odd sort of way, I think I had a tremendous advantage over the Soviet board members when it came to Sakharov. To them he was more than a scientific colleague and a hero of the human-rights movement; he was an icon. Whatever their relationship with him, there was a general reluctance to stand up to him with any different viewpoint. Perhaps it was

---

* Ironically, the name the Foundation for the Survival and Development of Humanity was one that Sakharov had insisted on.

easier for me to disagree with Andrei because I had grown up with powerful personalities in my family and I knew how badly famous men need and respect honesty. I was also from another culture, and Sakharov had not been among my childhood or professional role models. But whatever the reason, I enjoyed many lively disagreements with Sakharov and I know that he appreciated nearly all of them.

After a lengthy debate on foundation issues, thoughts turned to the recent crisis over Nagorno-Karabakh, where ethnic violence between Armenians and Azerbaijanis had erupted over the disputed enclave. The Sumgait massacre had been followed by an official national news blackout, orchestrated at the highest Soviet levels.

Elena Bonner, who was partially of Armenian ancestry, spoke heatedly about the situation in Nagorno-Karabakh. She and Andrei also expressed their deep concern about the fate of Soviet "new thinking" and the re-emergence of the conservative viewpoint. What else could explain the Soviet leadership's suppression of the news story?

The openness of the evening was exhilarating. However, I noticed that one board member at the gathering rarely spoke but watched and seemed to keep track of everything that was said. I made note of it that evening in my diary. Then I put it out of my mind, perhaps because I doubted that our fellow board member Metropolitan Pitirim, one of the Russian Orthodox Church's leading officials, could be reporting to the Soviet intelligence authorities about what we were doing. But my instincts had been sounder than my reasoning. The KGB archives, opened after the abortive coup attempt in August 1991, showed that the KGB had assigned Pitirim to file reports about the foreigners with whom he came into contact.*

After a long and stimulating evening, the group dispersed, and Roald and I also left the warmth of the Sakharovs' cozy kitchen. Ivan had been waiting for us at the curb near the apartment. As soon as we got into the

---

* In *The Washington Post*, February 11, 1992, Michael Dobbs reported:
A few weeks ago his holiness Metropolitan Pitirim was publicly exposed as agent Abbott of the KGB security police. But this has not prevented him from his normal business as one of the leaders of the Russian Orthodox Church—conducting divine service, receiving Ambassadors and performing various charitable activities. Pitirim, who heads the publishing department of the Orthodox Church, was "unmasked" due to the publication of the KGB archives . . . and credited them with exerting politically favorable influence on foreigners at various public events.
Pitirim has acknowledged submitting reports on his contacts with foreigners, but denies that he sent them directly to the KGB (external affairs department instead). However legislators who reviewed the documents doubt his denials.

car, Sagdeev said with some finality, "So you see, I am identified with the Sakharovs."

"Do you mean politically, or do you mean that you identify with them?" I asked him.

"Both," he said simply.

For nearly ten days Roald organized and orchestrated every nuance of my trip. To ensure that I had what I needed, on more than one occasion he sacrificed his own car and driver for my benefit. On one such occasion— before taking the subway to the Kremlin, where he was to chair the INF ratification hearings—he wrote a note that he had Ivan deliver to me:

Susan,
I would feel better if you are taken care of. So Ivan is in your disposition. Probably you will be in IKI before me. Don't hesitate to ask for typing. See you soon.

　　　　　　　　　　　　　　　　　　　　　　　　　　　Roald

I folded the paper and put it in a safe place, where I would not lose it or it would not be taken from me. I was profoundly moved by that little note. In the Soviet Union, a society motivated by the pursuit of position and privilege, the very idea that a deputy of the Supreme Soviet would take the metro to the Kremlin was unimaginable. Yet Sagdeev did it genuinely and without false modesty.

I don't know if he could have possibly guessed that no man I had ever been close to had said that he would feel better if I were "taken care of." All my previous experience had told me that men knew how to exploit my strength with little or no regard to the age-old notion of "taking care." His obvious desire to win my heart was also in stark contrast to the ambitious but afraid-to-commit men of Washington.

I was captivated by all the little things he did to be thoughtful. But his ardor caused in me a strange sense of imbalance—almost vertigo. As my diary described one sleepless night, I lay awake "searching my mind for a workable scenario [for our relationship], even evoking help from the Almighty."

For instance, one evening Sagdeev and Georgi Managadze arranged for us to go to the Taganka Theater Restaurant with a number of other friends.

Managadze had filled his briefcase full of Georgian wine and Russian vodka.* With all the beauty of rich Russian folksongs, minstrels serenaded us while we ate our generous four-course meal.

During one of their breaks Managadze got up and disappeared. I had failed to notice his prolonged absence when suddenly a guitar-playing minstrel and several other singers emerged from behind a large potted plant— only ten feet from my seat. Although sometimes haltingly executed, the trio sang a Russian-language rendition of "Oh Susannah." I could tell from Sagdeev's expression of suppressed satisfaction that Managadze had arranged this serenade for me on his instructions.

When Managadze returned to the table after the trio's performance, he apologized for his absence. "I am sorry I was gone so long. I had to teach them the song in the kitchen."

I could tell how much Roald had come to mean to me when he apologetically told me that he would have to leave Moscow on my last day in the city—his father had gone into the hospital in Kazan, and Roald's brother had asked him to come quickly. I tried hard to squelch the thickness that formed in my throat as we said goodbye. How could I know when I would see him again? International phone lines were nearly impossible to secure and, anyway, out-of-bounds for any personal exchange.

Characteristically, Roald wanted to be sure I was "taken care of," so he arranged that his friends Managadze and Alexander Zakharov, another scientist, take me to dinner at the Zakharovs' house that evening. He also assured me that they would drive me back to my hotel and deliver me to the airport the next morning. Content that those details were fixed, we said goodbye. It was one of the most difficult partings I can remember.

That evening Alexander (Sasha) and Georgi and their wives treated me to a splendid spread of caviar, chicken, and cakes. Managadze had again brought his favorite red Georgian wine.

"The first toast is for Roald, the man whose spirit is here with us tonight,"

---

* During these last days of prohibition the only way to get a drink in a restaurant was to bring your own bottle, even though, only a month before, the government had conceded that the anti-alcohol campaign had been a disaster and that the regulations would be relaxed. That was small comfort for the countless Georgian vineyards that had been destroyed as part of the government's implementation of its earlier decree.

said Georgi. I lifted my glass, comforted that Sagdeev's closest friends understood that it was here he wanted to be. The next toast was to me: "To our Susan, our very dear friend."

I hadn't noticed that Sasha had slipped out some time after that toast, but when I looked up some minutes later, I was floored to see Roald standing next to him in the doorway of the kitchen. The candlelight from the table just barely lit his features, but I could see that his eyes were twinkling with that special gaiety that had drawn me to him initially. Lifting a brown and orange object up for me to see, he said, "I couldn't let you leave Moscow without giving you a *chaplashka*, a traditional hat from my native Tatarstan. I thought I should deliver it myself."

We left the Zakharovs', but despite the late hour Roald insisted that we go for a walk on Lenin Hills. As we had done on so many occasions before, we left Ivan with the car and walked up to the railing that overlooked the whole of the city of Moscow.

The air was clear, and the full moon, directly above our heads, bathed the looming Stalinist structure of Moscow State University in its eerie light. As we leaned against the railing, I asked Sagdeev what had happened in Kazan, and how it was that he had come back so unexpectedly.

After Roald had visited his father at the hospital, he had decided to go to the airport to see if there was any chance of returning by air the same night—instead of taking the night sleeper as he had planned. "It was meant to be," he said. "There was only one remaining seat."

We both agreed that it was the perfect ending to a remarkable ten days. I had been taken into people's hearts and homes, and I had gained some real experience of Soviet life for the first time—from the dirty barren grocery stores I had gone to with Roald to the crumbling interior of a dilapidated apartment he had managed to acquire for his daughter, Anna. We had dined with the Sakharovs twice at their apartment; we had had lunch with Deputy Foreign Minister Vladimir Petrovsky; and I had had a meeting with Anatoly Dobrynin, former ambassador to the United States and head of the International Department of the Central Committee. I had also seen Velikhov on more than five separate occasions. Roald was amazed, he said, that I had so successfully managed to get Evgeny to focus on the issues facing the foundation.

There was a lot to distract people like Roald and Evgeny in those days —for one thing, the constant escalation of infighting among different rival groups. Perhaps it had been that way in earlier times, but then there had been clearer lines of authority—and little outward opposition to the "big bosses" or those with special influence with the regime.

That night Roald told me about a fight at the Academy of Sciences that had gone on during my week in Moscow. He and a few of his colleagues had blocked the election of what he termed one of the Academy's "bad guys." He didn't go into much detail, but I gathered that they had managed to defeat a scientist who had falsified some of his scientific results but whom conservative forces nevertheless wanted to elect to the Academy's Presidium. *

Perestroika had not come to the Academy at all, Roald said grimly. He told me that after my departure, with the exception of a few days in Paris, he would have to stay in the Soviet Union indefinitely. He needed to concentrate on writing some articles for publication and on using *glasnost* to bring to light a number of serious issues that needed to be aired. He warned me that these efforts might jeopardize his ability to get an exit visa and to travel. The KGB and the Central Committee still had full control over that "privilege."

"It also depends," he said, "on what the authorities think is going on between us."

I did not have good news to offer in that respect. Earlier in the week I had been to see Valentina Tereshkova, who had been at Chautauqua when we met. Even though it had been six months since then, she teased me about Sagdeev's great affection for me. Her comments had made me feel confused, embarrassed, and downright worried.

Roald and I both sensed that there were any number of wild cards in the deck. "The political situation is very fluid," he said. "Who knows how things will develop?"

Then he said quietly and without any warning, "I want you to consider being my visiting wife."

In his estimation, he said, a "visiting wife" status was the only workable scenario for the two of us if we were to be together. "I will wait faithfully for you to come when you can," he said.

There was silence between us for some minutes. Leaning over the railing,

---

* I later found out that the scientist whom Sagdeev had "taken on" had been the one who convinced Gorbachev that he had discovered a new technology for verification of warheads on submarines, a technology which Gorbachev had announced at the Washington summit. Sagdeev and others, however, understood that Gorbachev had been misled about the feasibility of such technology and proved, mathematically, that it was an impossible claim. Although they had communicated their findings directly to the Kremlin, Gorbachev stood by the idea that such a verification "miracle" was possible.

both of us stared at the city lights below us. I felt Roald deserved a response, but I was at a loss to know what to say or how to say it.

I was touched by Roald's hopes for our future, but I saw mostly the impossibility of it all. I thought that Roald underestimated the difficulties of conducting a marriage on a "visiting" basis. There would be the strain of long absences from each other, and it might make my job as mother all the more difficult. As it was, I made a concerted effort to spend every possible moment with my three girls when I was at home. But how would I resolve an even more complicated and emotionally fragmenting situation?

Not only that, there were some financial realities that also had to be considered. I told him I had to think about my career, since I provided virtually all the financial support for my daughters. With Roald in Moscow and with me in the United States—as a discredited American—I would most certainly have to change my work. If things were bad enough, I might even have to move to Europe. If I was married to Sagdeev, I would find that many open doors would most likely be closed. I wasn't sure I was ready to do that. I explained to him that I had been raised to think I might have something to contribute in public service. "Perhaps this is where I should be concentrating my efforts. I might someday want to negotiate one of those agreements between our two countries—and I don't want to do any-thing foolish that would prohibit me."

For some minutes we stood quietly and looked at the lights of the city. This was a desperately important topic, but it was getting very late and I asked him to take me back to my hotel. He showed some resistance, but I insisted.

When we finally reached the Rossiya, Roald wouldn't let me go. I reluctantly agreed to walk once around Red Square, but then I finally broke away and went up to my room. The ultimate futility of it all preyed on my mind. What was the point of getting close to Roald when every barrier in the world stood in our way?

The next morning, at the appointed hour, Sagdeev phoned my room as a wake-up call. Shortly after 7:00 a.m. he arrived to take me to the airport.

Halfway there, Ivan screeched on the brakes again—and in keeping with Roald's little tradition, he emerged from the public market with a bouquet of carnations.

Just before putting me on the plane, he emphasized again his feelings for me.

"His care and thought are things I will miss a great deal," I wrote the next day in my diary. "We are so very cut off from each other when I am at home. Maybe that makes the struggle/dilemma easier to handle. Or does it?"

I had left Moscow with a heavy heart. I was frightened by the way the regime could manipulate people into obedience, with the threat of denying them basic human rights and the freedom to travel. Although I was concerned for Roald, I was moved by his instinctive bravery. He was even more of a miracle, given that this quality ran counter to Soviet history and cultural indoctrination.

As I prepared for the long, lonely months ahead, I thought about what must be going on in Sagdeev's mind. The words he had shared with me at the Rossiya Hotel one evening kept echoing in my head.

"The concept of an exit visa is rather like prison bars," he whispered to me with a note of sadness. "You are raised to play by the rules and you follow them. It's not until the game is put into another context that it all seems so stupid, so unjust."

8 : Paris Spring

That same winter, not long after my return to the United States, Soviet watchers were stunned by the publication of a letter written by a Leningrad schoolteacher, Nina Andreyeva, in *Sovietskaya Rossiya*, a conservative national daily newspaper. In a long, rambling article entitled "I Cannot Deny My Principles," Andreyeva attacked Gorbachev's *perestroika* and *glasnost* for bringing shame on the great Soviet nation. She also defended Stalin and Stalinists for having made the Soviet Union a superpower, and she damned the pernicious influence of the West and of Soviet émigrés, whom she accused of betrayal.

What underscored the importance of this letter was the timing of its appearance just when Gorbachev was departing for Yugoslavia and Gorbachev's closest ally, Alexander Yakovlev, was leaving for Mongolia. The Soviet intelligentsia understood immediately that it had been printed as an effort to discredit Gorbachev and his reforms and that Gorbachev's most serious rival, conservative Yegor Ligachev, was behind it. In fact, some sources even suggested that Ligachev himself had had a hand in writing parts of it.*

The Andreyeva letter was reminiscent of the tactics the authorities had used during the Stalinist era, when they would lay out an example of wrongdoing in order to set the stage for subsequent campaigns of retribution. These had led to the loss of jobs, imprisonment, and worse.

A swift rebuttal by Gorbachev or Yakovlev would have been reassuring

---

* See Robert Kaiser, *Why Gorbachev Happened* (New York, 1989), p. 208.

to those in the Soviet Union who were already outspokenly in favor of the reforms initiated in those first Gorbachev years. However, a bewildering twenty-three days passed before Yakovlev finally responded. Meanwhile, the Moscow rumor mills claimed that Gorbachev was in panic. Although the General Secretary and his allies finally prevailed, the whole incident deeply shocked the intellectual community, which began to ask how stable Gorbachev's position could be if Ligachev had managed to find enough support to issue a statement so successfully challenging official policy.

The Andreyeva incident was on my mind a lot, too. I'd often lie awake at night, thinking about these disturbing political developments, trying to imagine what Roald's assessment might be. I wondered about his intention to write his exposé of the Academy. And I wondered about us.

Soon I learned that the Initiating Committee of the Space Future Forum would be meeting for a conference in Paris, followed by a dinner honoring Sagdeev and Roger Bonnet, chief scientist of the European Space Agency, for their contributions to international science. To my surprise I was invited to attend. I could see Roald's hand in this planning and I guessed that he had carved out a seat for me at the meeting because he wanted to see me again. The telex I got said as much, through a little code we had begun to use.

> To: Susan Eisenhower
> From: R. Sagdeev, IKI Moscow
> I had a long phone conversation with Roger Bonnet on the agenda of informal discussions at ESA. It seems we could have a few people left after the Initiative Group of October Space Forum to discuss the broad issues of future space policies. Exploration vs. national programmes, International Space Year. On top of it I have suggested to talk on approach to the future Mars programme. I believe all invitees would have special messages from ESA. On bilateral side I hope to have further discussion of our project.
>
> > Sincerely yours,
> > R. Sagdeev

"International Space Year" might have been thrown in there because of me, as a member of the advisory board of the year-long events. "Bilateral" in our lingo usually meant Roald and me and "our project" was our future together. Moreover, I knew that Paris was his last foreign trip before his self-imposed exile.

I greeted this invitation with both excitement and dread. I knew that a showdown regarding our relationship was inevitable. As the date neared, my deep ambivalence dominated everything. I could think of nothing else but the quandary of whether or not to go. I was in such a state of confusion about what I wanted to do that I made numerous reservations on several airlines for various times and return dates. Each one represented a different state of mind.

Two days before my departure, I went to a small luncheon at the French Embassy. There I discovered, from a couple who had recently returned from Paris, that France was now requiring visas. An odd sense of relief swept over me. When I got home, I called Roger Bonnet and told him that I was terribly sorry, I was unable to come to the conference: with the weekend in front of us, it would be impossible for me to get a visa in time.

Bonnet, deeply distressed to hear of this problem, assured me that he could arrange to have a visa issued over the weekend. Then, before I could protest, he put Roald, who had just arrived in Paris, on the line.

"Getting a visa to France has got to be easier than invading Normandy," Roald quipped. "I suggest you take Bonnet up on his offer."

Several hours later the science and technology attaché from the French Embassy called to say that he would have a visa for me in time for my departure.*

The hand of fate had been felt. Now I knew that there could be no backing away. If I was going to put a stop to all this, Paris would be the time to do it—before any irrevocable mistakes were made.

My days in the French capital were perhaps the most taxing few days I can ever remember spending. During the breaks in the meeting, I walked up and down the tree-lined streets, intensively weighing my options.

It might seem surprising that such serious discussions of marriage were going on, in the 1980s, between two people who had a constantly chaperoned platonic relationship. More than once I mused that this was how it had been a century before, in an era when greater priority had been placed on knowing the person and the circumstances before jumping in with both feet.

---

* The requirement of a visa for American citizens lasted only a short time.

But the truth is, our relationship had already progressed quite far, and the deep affinity I felt for Roald had blossomed in the last months into a trust and confidence that I had never experienced before. The quandary we both faced had to do with politics and feasibility. If that could not be satisfactorily settled, I thought, then we should take no more risks with each other on any level. Too much was at stake.

At the end of the first day's session, Sagdeev joined me for a short walk. We talked about what was happening in the Soviet Union and the nervousness that he and many of his intellectual colleagues felt about the Nina Andreyeva affair. He confirmed that they had been very shaken by the incident, but he seemed philosophical, not out of optimism about the overall picture, but because he had come to expect less and less from the Gorbachev regime.

He acknowledged that a power struggle was under way in Moscow and that it was not clear how it would be resolved. In thinking about "us" in this political context, his mind, too, scanned the list of problems. Relations between our two countries were improving, but he warned me that even though he ran the only nonclassified institute in the Soviet space program, it was, nevertheless, part of the omnipotent military-industrial complex. Improved relations between our countries would have little bearing on the chances of us being together "full time." Many refuseniks, with considerably less knowledge about the "complex" than Roald had, were denied permission to leave the Soviet Union altogether. *

Nevertheless, there were a number of options. Roald could defect to the West—a choice we both discarded from the outset. I could be his "visiting wife," as he had proposed. Or we could try to persuade the Soviet authorities to give Roald permission to work in Paris or some city in a neutral country. That, actually, was my naïve idea. I say naïve because Roald assured me that the authorities would never let him live, even for a short while, in a third country.

It is interesting, in retrospect, that neither of us even discussed the option of living in one another's country full time. Defection in either direction —as it would have been considered—was the most unacceptable of all options, including that of ending our relationship.

After the awards ceremony that evening, Roald refused to let me retire for the evening. He had made plans for us, he told me. With a bundle of

---

* Roald had been given permission to travel largely as part of his job—and the mark of reliability that comes from being a member of the Party.

hard currency he had been saving, he hailed a taxi and took me to the Left Bank, where he had chosen a restaurant in one of the cave cellars. Both of us were giddy with the notion that we had escaped the Soviet delegation. We reveled in this, one of our few rare moments alone.

We went down a long flight of stairs to a crowded, dimly lit room, where we finally found a small table. We drank champagne and listened to a French guitarist with a deep raspy voice. We were so absorbed in each other that we barely noticed when the room began to empty. At 3:00 in the morning, the only customers left, we made our way back to the modest hotel where both of us were staying.

The doorbell of the *pension* roused the sleepy concierge, who let us in. Crossing the lobby we summoned the tiny elevator from the floors above. The outer doors clattered open and we pulled back the metal elevator grid. Roald pushed the button for the fifth floor and I extended my hand to press the button for 3. We awkwardly said good night.

As on many other occasions, the combination of the late night and jet lag made it virtually impossible for me to wake up the next morning. I was fortunate that I had already made my presentation the day before, so I was free to relax and to take in Paris. Arising late, I dressed and went to the corner café, where I drank strong black coffee and consumed piles of crusty French bread, cheese, and ham. After that I rode the métro to visit my old stomping grounds from the days when I had been a college student in Paris.

The city felt oddly familiar and yet strange at the same time. The touchstones of times past naturally jogged my memory. In my wandering mind, I revisited my early years, the happy days of my childhood when security and love were inextricably intertwined with my own optimism for the future. Then I saw myself at college in Paris, before the women's liberation movement was widespread in America, when sights were set primarily on marrying and having children. I saw my years as a young mother in London and then the painful ones in Rochester. I thought of those challenging times as a single parent, taking risks with no margin for failure. I also thought about the promise the future held, and the expectations that people had for me. "You'll be a senator someday," people often said, "or an ambassador." I didn't know if that's what I wanted, but I was certain that if Roald and I ever crossed the line, that option would be gone. But if I saw myself in public service, was elective or appointed office the only way to make a difference?

My mind drifted. I felt again the acuteness of loss, the end of my marriages, the futile investment I had made in other people. And then there were the untimely deaths of several friends, particularly Bill Sharpless, a close friend who had died at the age of forty, only months before. Two of my cousins had also died in early middle age. And, of course, I thought about Roald—his gentleness, his intelligence, his kindness, but most of all our mutual trust.

If life can be unpredictably short, isn't the loss implied in not doing something—not risking oneself—the thing one regrets? I couldn't possibly predict the future political situation, but even if nothing really improved, wouldn't I perhaps gain more than I might lose if I took the chance that something might work out for us? What if I were cruelly rejected by my countrymen? Hadn't I, in my own frame of reference, hit the bottom and survived?

Some vague thought, some scene from long ago, suddenly crossed my mind.

I am sick in bed with a monstrous cold. The dull light of Sunday afternoon pierces the thin curtains of my room. I stare at the television set, unable to change the channel or fathom what blares from the screen. The movie's name is *The Girl from Petrovka*, I think. There's a scene where the American newspaperman, in love with a young Soviet girl, poignantly says goodbye to her for the last time. Accused of trumped-up offenses—of parasitism*—she is finally arrested as punishment for the illicit love affair she has been having with the American. Her fate is prison.

Even in my stupor of congestion and fever, her final words penetrate my consciousness. They aren't words of defiance: she'd known there was always the danger that the authorities would intervene. Her words are words of passionate regret that she and her American lover hesitated so long; that they lost the chance to make memories together that would have always sustained her, memories so imbedded in her being that they would be, perhaps, the one thing not even an authoritarian government could take away from her. I too knew that memories live inside you and feed your inner life, and fill the empty moments that crowd our days.

That night, after the parties were over, Sagdeev and I went out for a walk in the chilly spring night. We were undeterred by the lightly falling rain. We raised the umbrella I had brought along. One side of it was bent, so we huddled close together to stay dry. Exhausted by discussions of our dilemma, we spoke about mundane subjects. There did not seem to be

---

* Parasitism was an accusation made frequently during the Brezhnev years. As the name implies, it suggests that the person accused is sponging off the state. People who found themselves between jobs or out of work were frequently accused of this.

any more reason for talking. Roald showed no signs of backing off, and though I said nothing to him, my own personal breakthrough had come while walking miles and miles of Paris sidewalk that afternoon.

Around one o'clock in the morning, Roald and I came in from our stroll. Except for the bleary-eyed concierge, the hotel was quiet, and all our colleagues had already retired. As we had the night before, we got into the tiny elevator together. Roald closed the metal grid and the outer doors clacked shut. He silently pushed the button for the fifth floor. But this time I made no move to press 3.

The smell of damp earth filled our nostrils. Paris seemed alive with spring. The drizzle had stopped, giving us the chance to take one last walk before leaving. We chose one of the boulevards that led to an embankment along the Seine. When we reached the river, with the Eiffel Tower in the background, I took a few photographs of Roald—as a memento of our days together in Paris.

He seemed distant, and I was confused by this. Had he also visited his past and future life? Was he struggling with the implications of our days in Paris, especially now when things had come so intensely into focus? There was a wall between us that morning that I could not seem to penetrate. Weeks later, when the photographs came back from the developer, I was struck by how pensive Roald looked, how uncomfortable, or maybe sad. I didn't know.

So I went back to America ready to set about rebuilding my life. Roald's aloofness, and the political realities, left me with few illusions. Nevertheless, I was at peace.

I made no diary entry for several weeks. It was impossible to write. I couldn't put anything on paper, perhaps for fear of permanently trivializing what had happened. Only a few cryptic lines summed it up: "I have many memories that are deep and lasting—but in between there is very little."

Given the sensitivity of the phone lines and the absence of mail, I had no contact with Roald at all, except for an occasional telex—usually constructed in formal colleaguese. The only thing I really knew about his activities I gleaned from reading the Soviet newspapers and an occasional reference in the Western press.

To take my mind off things, I thought I should start making some plans to see old friends, to reconnect. The previous months had been a period of such intense ambivalence and confusion that I had gone out of my way to avoid seeing people. I thought that by getting together with old friends now I could start to put my life back on track.

By coincidence, not long after my return from Paris, Paul Michel, a close friend of mine, called and asked me to have dinner with him. I was delighted at the prospect of seeing him again. We hadn't seen one another for quite some time, but Paul and I had been confidants many years before, and I regarded him as one of the most thoughtful and responsible people I knew. If misery and distress love company, as I soon discovered, we were ideal dinner companions. He was deeply involved with a well-known plastic surgeon, Elizabeth Morgan, who had become famous for a controversial child-visitation dispute she was having with her ex-husband. At that very moment she was serving time in jail for contempt of court, since she had refused to reveal the whereabouts of her child. She'd hoped to deny the father access to their daughter because she was convinced that her ex-husband had been molesting the child, so she had persuaded her own parents to take the child into hiding.

That evening Paul and I found a quiet booth at the back of the restaurant and began to catch up. He had been seeing Elizabeth seriously for some months, but now he had to content himself with visits to her prison cell and telephone calls. I was impressed by his absolute devotion to her, which he expressed with remarkable stoicism.

As Paul recounted all the most recent developments in Elizabeth's case—many details of which he was sharing with me in confidence—it occurred to me that I could, similarly, confide in Paul. He of all people would be responsible enough to keep my counsel, yet sympathetic enough to such emotions and hardships not to be judgmental.

In addition, Paul understood Washington. He had served on the staff of the Senate Intelligence Committee, had been administrative assistant to Senator Arlen Specter, and he was currently a federal judge. Since he was no longer associated with intelligence work, Paul would have no obligation to share my story with anyone. At the same time, however, he would have some insight into how serious my situation might be.

Without telling him Sagdeev's name, I briefly described Roald's position in the Soviet Union and our dilemma. Paul listened carefully but impassively, but when he spoke, I was surprisingly unprepared for his advice.

Leaning forward, Paul took my hand. "Susan," he said gravely, "although I am happy for you that you have finally come to feel this way about someone, you should know that you are playing with real fire. You must start with the obvious certainty that the Soviet regime will never let your friend go. *Never.* Now the question is: are you directly jeopardizing his safety?"

He paused and then said thoughtfully, "I think the answer to that is that you could be. I don't have to tell you, it is a ruthless regime and he has a high-ranking position in its most sensitive sector."

I covered my face with my hands, struggling to maintain my composure. Tears began to fall involuntarily.

"If you decide to continue to see him," he cautioned, "make sure everything is out in the open. *Never* do anything that appears to be at all secretive. If you do, the KGB could misconstrue what you're doing and assume there's something more serious than love going on. They have accused people of being spies for a whole lot less."

He reiterated the point: "The KGB just might be able to understand a love affair, but certainly not clandestine meetings."

In fact, this was virtually the same opinion Roald held. Both men felt that openness was the only tactic we could use. This was harder for me, since my natural inclination was to avoid drawing attention to our relationship. Yet the thought that my attachment to Roald might jeopardize his safety was too painful to contemplate.

Paul understood this quandary, but he reminded me that it was no ordinary situation. And in this context, any kind of secrecy—even what you might call ordinary discretion—was extremely dangerous.

A wave of rebellion washed over me. *This goddamned Cold War could destroy this gentle wonderful man—and maybe even me. And for what? So our governments can score points about the righteousness of our respective systems—and tell our people that massive overkill capacity is necessary to secure the peace? It seemed so ironic that love could be shattered in the name of peace.*

My anger lasted for days. But at least it ensured that I was no longer trying to deny reality. Paul Michel had firmly outlined something I had not wanted to face, and he had convinced me that the intelligence community was now a very big factor in my life.

9 : Authorities on Alert

That month I heard rumblings from a mutual friend about an article Roald had written in *Izvestia*, the Soviet government newspaper. Despite the Nina Andreyeva business—and the strength it showed the conservatives had—he had apparently decided to launch his attack against the old men of the Academy. I had the odd experience of hearing the Eisenhower Institute's chairman, General Andrew Goodpaster, tell the other directors that a Soviet scientist, Roald Sagdeev, had written a "remarkable piece" called "Science and *Perestroika*."

In it, Sagdeev was sharply critical of the way the Academy of Sciences was managed:

> To a great extent, science is a product of the social conditions in which it develops. During the last past half century, Soviet science has suffered deep, and still bleeding, wounds from ill-conceived government policies. Today, although the Soviet Union has one of the world's largest scientific work forces, it has only a modest record of achievements and is contributing too little to the world's scientific knowledge.

In the article Sagdeev launched a direct salvo aimed at the Academy leadership, its relationship to military industry, and its aversion to change. As he knew full well, the Academy's president, Guri Marchuk, was close to Yegor Ligachev. His article, the first publicly to challenge the Academy in this way, required real bravery. I was tremendously proud of him, but

I fretted because I could vividly imagine the number of enemies he was making.

Nearly two months later I got word that Sagdeev was coming to America. I was virtually trembling when his plane arrived at National Airport. Rain was steadily falling as Roald alighted, followed closely by his bodyguard, a new KGB shadow named Valery. Roald gave me a collegial kiss on the cheek and I drove them both to their hotel on Pennsylvania Avenue. While they checked in, I parked the car a block away. Valery was still at the registration desk when I rejoined them; taking advantage of this, Roald suggested to me that we get away a bit later and have a drink at a quiet bar, somewhere nearby.

A half hour after Valery and—supposedly—Sagdeev had retired for the night, Roald came back downstairs with a raincoat over his arm. Headed down the street toward the Watergate Hotel, we found a tiny jazz club midway whose entrance could barely be seen from the street. We tentatively opened the door and asked a heavy-set bartender if the place was still open. He nodded. Given the late hour, the saxophonist had gone home, but music came intermittently from the jukebox at the back of the long, smoky room.

Roald and I ordered drinks and found a table. As soon as we sat down, he took my hand and everything came pouring out: news about the Soviet withdrawal from Afghanistan and stories about the selection process under way for the Nineteenth Party Conference to be held later in the summer. This was to be the first Party conference of its type in decades, and Gorbachev was going to use it to call the Party together and press for wider reforms. As we went on talking about all of this Soviet political news, Roald slowly wrote something in Russian on a bar napkin. *

Suddenly he stopped talking about politics and looked at me squarely. "I have something important to tell you," he said seriously. "I can no longer resolve my love for you and the role I have to play at the Space Research Institute and in my other official positions. So I have submitted my resignation as director of IKI. I won't know for a few months whether they will accept it or not. But anyway I have done it."

---

* I folded the napkin up and took it home. However, it was some time before I found out what all of it said. It was written in Russian and I didn't dare ask anyone to help read the whole thing. He had written:

> Suzannah,
> I love you like crazy.
> R.S.
> 27/IV/88

I was stunned. Sagdeev resign? He had run IKI for the last fifteen years. He had built it from a poor stepchild of the Soviet space community to its most prestigious asset. He had been the U.S.S.R.'s first real pioneer in international cooperation, with his Vega mission to Halley's Comet. IKI was preparing to launch a probe to Mars that summer. It seemed impossible to imagine that he had done such a thing.

"If we're going to have any future together, I have to reject my official positions," he said, "and begin to distance myself from the authorities." The first in the long series of steps, he explained, had already been accomplished with the publication of "Science and *Perestroika*," with its appeal for fresh blood in the Academy and its argument for the rotation of institute directors.

"Roald," I said, "I have some news for you, too. Since I saw you in Paris I've also given everything a lot of thought. And a few weeks ago I also handed in my resignation as president of the Eisenhower Institute."

The impact of what Paul had said, and the concern that my relationship with Roald might be scandalous for the Institute had prompted me finally to make the break: I certainly did not want to bring shame or controversy to the centennial or to the Institute, both of which were to honor Granddad's memory.

Then I asked Roald if he had had second thoughts after Paris. I wondered, I told him, given how detached he had seemed that last morning.

"I knew in Paris," he said, "that my love for you would be incompatible with my positions. It wasn't distance you felt but my mind already working on how we could resolve this."

The hour was late and we walked back to my car. He opened the door for me and then paused. "I need to know if you think we will be together, if you are willing to marry me. I need to know before I leave for Moscow."

"I understand," I said.

He squeezed my hand and I got into the car.

Full of thoughts of what it would be like to be a "visiting wife," I drove toward home, down the long, dark, glistening streets of Washington.

Several nights later we managed again, somehow, to shake Valery. That evening we dined by candlelight at my dining-room table. As had become our habit, we had a brainstorming session on the political situation in the Soviet Union.

"You must not be surprised if you discover that I can no longer get an exit visa," Roald said solemnly. "That is typical of the way they issue warnings. Now that I have submitted my resignation, I can expect it at any moment."

"If that happened," I blurted out, "I would come immediately to Moscow and marry you. I would *make* them set you free."

In a flash I had the answer to Sagdeev's question about marriage that he had posed to me the first night: If I love him and I'm prepared to stand by him in the worst of times, then my choice for the best-case scenario is also clear. My reasoning seemed natural and obvious. I had faith that ultimately our plans would be successful, even if I had to be only a "visiting wife" for a while. At the back of my mind I knew I would do whatever had to be done to fight for his freedom. I couldn't imagine it otherwise. And I told him so.

It is difficult to explain why I made such a tremendously important decision—to throw my lot in with him—when there were so many negatives in place, so many reasons to think it wouldn't work. The explanation goes to the heart of what Roald and I had come to mean to one another. We were very much alike in our approaches, in our interests, in our outlooks, and even in our foibles—qualities that would surely make such a marriage work. If a wedding weren't possible, and the authorities intervened, then *not* to come to his defense—*not* to fight for him would be like giving up on myself. I had had plenty of opportunity to do that in the past, starting a life in Washington with more expenses to cover than job experience. But I stuck with it, even when I was frightened, exhausted, and humbled. I sensed, deep in my gut, that I had every reason to invest the same tenacity and long-term faith in him, and in us, as I had in myself.

Suddenly our conversation was full of plans, scenarios, political problems, and logistics. We were like two military generals about to make an assault on a well-fortified camp; our recent resignations now gave us a new opportunity and presented new challenges.

Though resigning from our jobs might have been the right moral course, the consequences of the decisions—financial and otherwise—were daunting. Any new work that either of us would find had to be impervious to potential scandal. This was more of a problem for me. I was working directly in Soviet-American relations and if the Soviet authorities were to punish Roald, I would surely become *persona non grata*, which would have a dramatic bearing, at least in the short run, on my ability to earn a living. Roald, as a scientist, would not have the same difficulties with his foreign scientific colleagues, many of whom had championed human-rights causes, but their support would be useless if the Soviet authorities prohibited him from leaving the Soviet Union.

One encouraging prospect was an offer Roald had received to write his memoirs. We both saw that such a project would give us some financial independence, and I agreed to help him put together an outline for the book. He was excited about doing the book, because in a way it was the realization of his dream that we would collaborate—the suggestion he had made during the Space Forum. Working on it would also give us a useful pretext to be together.

Later that night, after Roald had gone, my daughter Caroline and I sat on stools in the kitchen and drank cups of hot steaming tea. I felt very close to my daughters, an intimacy forged by our shared experiences. And when they spent their customary two-month summer vacation in Rochester, I always felt that a part of me had also gone. Being the oldest, and a junior in high school, Caroline was accustomed to more than her load of responsibility, but whatever burdens she carried, she did so with uncanny perception.

I started to say "Sagdeev" and she interrupted me: "—wants to marry you. He does, doesn't he, Mom?"

"How did you know?" I asked.

"It's so obvious he's crazy about you. But, Mom, you are pretty obvious, too." Then she added, "I know I can't tell anybody. I know it might get you into trouble. But I hope you don't mind if I say that unfortunately I don't think this country is ready to accept you and Roald."

And then she paused and said with a hint of apology, "Do you think you could wait until I finish high school?"

Just before Roald's departure, another U.S.–Soviet summit meeting was announced for the end of May. Scheduled for Moscow, it was to be Reagan's fourth and last summit with Gorbachev.

Although U.S.–Soviet relations were improving rapidly, the Communist bloc was seething with potential serious unrest. Strikes were breaking out in Poland, and the Western news media expressed deep misgivings about what these developments could portend. The popular uprisings of 1980–81 had led to the imposition of martial law in 1981, and the recent round of strikes and the way police and armed forces were used to break them up felt frighteningly reminiscent. Zbigniew Brzezinski, the Polish-born former National Security Adviser, made a dire prediction about the escalation of

Solidarity's resistance to the Polish government. "If there is a revolution, there will be suppression. If suppression fails, there will be Soviet intervention. If there is Soviet intervention, that is the end of *perestroika*."*

There were disturbing signals coming from Moscow, too. Two dissidents, an Armenian nationalist named Paruir Arikyan and Sergei Grigoryants, publisher of a newspaper ironically called *Glasnost*, were arrested. I was especially alarmed by Grigoryants's detention, for "resisting authority" and for allowing opposition groups to meet at his dacha outside Moscow. Gorbachev was unrelenting about Grigoryants's offenses, which he articulated in a pre-summit interview with *The Washington Post* and *Newsweek*:

> "People know that Grigoryants's 'organization' is tied not only organizationally but also financially to the West, that his constant visitors and guests are Western correspondents. Therefore people think of him as some kind of alien phenomenon in our society, sponging on the positive aspects of *perestroika*. This happens—it happens in nature, too. There are such parasites living off healthy organisms and attempting to harm them. But we are sure that our country is strong enough to overcome such a thing."†

Later in the interview he stated that the Soviet people were "firmly in favor of renewal . . . only within the boundaries of socialism and on the basis of socialist values."

Such insights into Gorbachev's mentality fueled the concern Roald and I both felt about the direction the Soviet Union was taking, and I wondered to myself how honest scientists like Roald could restrict their "human values" only to the areas that coincided with Gorbachev's "socialist values."

Once "values" became a concept of importance, wouldn't it be impossible for a nation of questing souls to draw artificial boundaries around their intellectual search?

That June, Ronald Reagan went to Moscow to meet Gorbachev—the first American President to visit the Soviet Union since 1974. After twelve years, the Soviets were placing great importance on it. The authorities were even using the occasion to doll up the city with fresh coats of badly needed paint. Roald was asked, again, to serve as a summit adviser to the General Sec-

---

* *Newsweek*, May 9, 1988.
† Cited by Kaiser in *Why Gorbachev Happened*, p. 220.

retary. And I myself was surprised to be invited by Valentina Tereschkova to participate in the events.

Valentina told me she had been asked by the government to invite a few of her counterparts to meet with Gorbachev during that week. I accepted the invitation, but promised myself that I would use the opportunity of being in Moscow to assess the commercial potential in the Soviet Union. Although my resignation from the Eisenhower Institute was not yet effective, I was already thinking about what I would be doing after that.

As interesting as Valentina's invitation was, it came without much information. I asked the Soviet Embassy if it would be a small or a large group meeting with Gorbachev, and I tried to get the names of some of the other participants. When none of that was forthcoming I decided to rely on my old rule of thumb: "If you don't like the situation you find yourself in, you can always walk out and go home."

The day before I boarded the plane for Moscow, a messenger brought me a first-class ticket on an American carrier, paid for by the Soviets in hard currency. I was surprised at the lavish treatment but was determined that it not affect my judgment.

At Sheremetyvo Airport Elena Loschenkova met me. She was Roald's assistant at the Committee of Soviet Scientists, a non-official group he chaired that made "independent" assessments on arms-control questions and other global issues. Elena, an amiable and efficient woman, had an office not far from Roald's at IKI. She protected him and looked after his interests like a jealous mother hen. In my case, she spread her wings wide, bringing me into the fold of IKI and life with "the Boss."

While Elena and I drank coffee and waited for my luggage, she filled me in on everything she knew about the forthcoming meeting with Gorbachev. She said that a rather controversial group of people would be attending. She confided that Roald had also been asked by the Gorbachev people to invite some of the committee's American counterparts and that he had declined to do so. The meeting with Gorbachev, she told me, was going to be used as a counter-gathering to the one President Reagan was holding for Soviet dissidents at the United States Embassy. I was troubled by all that I heard.

Sagdeev was at the Kremlin for negotiations, but Elena said he would leave at lunchtime and meet us at a Georgian restaurant. After I had retrieved my documents and luggage, we went directly to the restaurant.

This newly opened cooperative Georgian bistro had a stark, unpretentious private room where a long table had been already laid for the main midday meal. We waited there until Roald finally blew in, harried and distracted but full of summit stories.

Before long, the conversation turned to my problem. The meeting with Gorbachev, to which I had been invited, was precisely the kind of propaganda situation I had always wanted to avoid—an occasion at which my own presence could be used against my country. At the same time, I didn't really blame Gorbachev: he wasn't doing anything that the Americans had not done, even if the United States might have thought it had a higher moral right to gather political dissidents and internal opponents of the Soviet regime. Whatever the case, I simply didn't want to be a part of it.

"I'm concerned about this meeting," I said. "In fact, I simply can't go."

"And you shouldn't!" Sagdeev immediately replied.

I told him I was going to see Valentina Tereschkova later that afternoon and I'd have to say something to her. Valentina was a formidable woman who had proven herself to be an able infighter. I was impressed by her professional demeanor and appreciative of her friendliness, but I was rather intimidated by her. I wasn't looking forward to telling her of my decision. Roald, who of course knew her much better than I did, suggested that he call her before my appointment and ask her not to put pressure on me to go to the meeting. Although I was grateful for his offer, I rejected the idea. I didn't want Valentina to think I was too timid to deliver my own message. I thanked him but insisted I tell her myself.

At the end of lunch Sagdeev refused to listen to my protests and insisted that he forgo his afternoon plans and come with me. So together we arrived at Valentina's ornate office, prominently located in one of the pre-revolutionary palaces on Kalinin Prospekt. She greeted us warmly and led us to a long conference table, where she invited us to have tea and cookies.

As we were sitting down, Roald said something to her in rapid-fire Russian and I was conscious of the stiffness with which she took her seat. But before she could answer him, I started to talk, thanking her for bringing me to Moscow and expressing my pleasure at seeing her again. Then I said that since I had arrived in the city I had learned more about the Gorbachev meeting and that I would be unable to attend.

When I finished, she shifted slightly and said with some strain, "Well then, it's settled. We will say that you have come to Moscow on business and to pursue our future cooperation."

I was grateful to Valentina for letting me off the hook. I could tell that she had her own concerns, but she was gracious nonetheless. With that out of the way, we had a very pleasant visit, and later, without a trace of animosity, she made sure that I had tickets to the final event of the summit—a performance at the Bolshoi Ballet. More than that, she gave me a ticket for one of the best seats in the house, in the center in front of Reagan and Gorbachev. It was from that vantage point that I watched the most riveting performance of *Romeo and Juliet* I had ever seen. Nobody could have guessed how unnerved I was to see this drama—which I now so closely identified with—in the heart of the Soviet empire.

In the days that followed, I met with commercial and policy people, and in the evenings Roald always seemed to have something planned. On one occasion he arranged for us to meet some friends at the Taganka Restaurant, attached to the famous theater. Nicolai Shishlin came, as well as Yuri Osipyan, a slender graying Armenian whom I had met before in Moscow at the Space Forum. Yuri was an increasingly powerful man, but he had a gentleness and warmth that drew me to him. I was always touched on these occasions that these busy men, with important and pressing work, took time from their official schedules to see me. More and more I thought of them as real friends.

On my last full day in the city, we had plans to see another friend, Georgi Managadze. It was swelteringly hot and humid, so before our luncheon Roald suggested that we go for a walk in a cool forest near Lenin Hills. He had acquired a video camera while he was in the United States and wanted to test it.

We parked the car not far from the university and walked down the hill, Roald slowly filming as we went. Then he put the camera back in its case, and we walked for more than an hour in the refreshing forest, leading down from the crest of the hill.

Roald filled my head with gossip from the Academy and what he had heard about the Kremlin struggles. He was not alone in expressing growing anxiety about Ligachev's apparent comeback and Gorbachev's perceived instability. But perhaps Roald's most troubling story involved "us." During the state dinner that the Soviets had held in the Kremlin the day before my arrival, Roald had been seated at the same table with Valentina Tereschkova and Vladimir Kryuchkhov, then deputy chairman of the KGB and soon to be chairman.*

---

* Kryuchkhov eventually played a role in the attempted coup of August 1991.

"Sagdeev is in love with Susan Eisenhower," Valentina had announced to Kryuchkhov.

Kryuchkhov had mumbled something inaudible.

Valentina said more loudly, and with greater emphasis, "No, I mean, *serious* love."

Turning to Kryuchkhov, Roald said, "You would be, too, if you knew her."

Roald's clever comeback may have diffused an awkward situation; it may have even avoided any real suspicion. All the same, our relationship had been brought directly to the KGB deputy chairman's attention. When Roald told me that this incident had taken place *before* he had gone with me to see Valentina at her office, I understood that the risks he had taken on my behalf were even greater.

We completed a broad circular path through the woods and Roald checked his watch to see how much time we had. He suggested that we head back to the car. Climbing up the steep path, we reached the top of the hill, and finally our car. Roald unlocked the vehicle and we got in. He turned the key to start the engine, but the car was utterly dead. Again and again he tried, in vain.

Roald gave up in frustration, and we walked silently in the penetrating heat until we found a taxi stand.

We arrived at Managadze's house late and distracted. After a typical Georgian lunch, with massive quantities of food and wine, Georgi took us back to Roald's disabled car, still parked on Lenin Hills. To our astonishment, the car now started without difficulty.

"Roald," I asked, "do you think that the car was tampered with?" The question was clearly on his mind, too.

"I don't know."

One could never rule out the possibility that the KGB had meddled with it as a form of harassment or warning. One knew of other such incidents.

I kept replaying the day in my mind, looking for some clue that would make some kind of sense. We knew the KGB bosses were alerted—we had Valentina to thank for that—but it was logical to think that the lower levels had known about "us" for some time.

10 : A Sanctuary from Prying Eyes

I found myself in the Soviet Union again only weeks later. The Survival Fund, now known as the International Foundation, had scheduled a board meeting in Leningrad. The American members flew to Moscow and then took the night sleeper to Leningrad. Work started as soon as we arrived.

The board had agreed that grants would be made at this meeting, and Andrei Sakharov, well prepared, had very specific projects he wanted the organization to support. It was impossible, however, to get across to him that the foundation's directors themselves could not receive this money for their own use. Rather, it was their responsibility to provide grants to worthwhile projects that came in from outside the board apparatus. Sakharov was resolute. Determined that the foundation support two of his projects —one on "the right of emigration" and the other a comparative study of Soviet and Western prisons—he conducted a virtual filibuster, until a positive decision was made in his favor. The board was in a quandary. We realized the worthiness of his topics and his unique position to address them, but explaining conflict of interest to this Russian was next to impossible. In fact, not only were we unsuccessful, but Andrei's insistence ended up changing forever the nature of the foundation, which effectively moved from being a grant-giving institution to being an operating foundation. As in so many other matters that required tenacity, Sakharov had demonstrated his mettle.

Sakharov is perhaps remembered as having been one of the U.S.S.R.'s most important democrats, but I often look back on that meeting as evidence that he was an activist, by the nature of his personality and his political direction. In a broad sense, he used the power of his determination not to bring about consensus in society, which is what democracy requires, but to redress the imbalance that existed between the regime and the Soviet people—which probably had to be accomplished before the next stage of democracy could even be attempted.

Few people wanted to admit this was so. By virtue of his stature as an icon, Sakharov was expected to be the man for all seasons, infinitely wise and all but infallible. But failing to see Sakharov objectively was to rob him of his humanness. He was a richly complicated man of many contradictions. For all his commitment to human rights, for instance, I was frankly amazed that, even privately, he never expressed regret or remorse for delivering the deadliest of all nuclear weapons into the hands of Stalin, a ruthless dictator who was one of the greatest mass murderers of all time.

This man of soaring spirit used his own stature to influence many critical issues. But I had an insight into his anguish over his years in exile in Gorky. Once, when I was in Moscow, I was invited to see the Peter Kapitsa House and museum, the onetime home of the late former director of the Institute of Physical Problems. Kapitsa, a Nobel Laureate and one of Roald's mentors, was one of the most outstanding Soviet scientists of his generation. And through a long, tangled history, he had developed a unique line of forthright communication with the Soviet leadership, from Stalin to Brezhnev.

At the Kapitsa House, where I was asked to sign the guest book, I noticed that Sakharov had been there the day before me. A Kapitsa family member told me that Andrei had been to the archives there, to search Kapitsa's correspondence for anything that would show if Kapitsa had ever written the Soviet leadership in protest over Sakharov's internal exile in Gorky. Andrei had been suspicious, perhaps because Kapitsa had never signed any open collective letters of protest. To his unexpected relief, there was ample evidence that Kapitsa had taken a very strong line with Brezhnev on behalf of his exiled colleague. Kapitsa had preferred to work behind the scenes.

I was fascinated by this story, because it demonstrated that even the most towering figures in human history find it difficult to rise above suspicions of collegial treachery. Whatever trust Sakharov had in his friendship with Kapitsa did not stop him from checking to see whether Kapitsa had stood with him. Allegiances and betrayals were the connective tissue of Soviet society, where the negative outcome of any important event could be categorized in the darkest terms.

However, Sakharov, the same man who worried about the steadfastness of his friends, was not incapable of lighter moments. I saw an example of that in Leningrad. At the end of our meetings, we all had dinner at the city's first private nightclub. Known as the Troika, it was what would be called in the West "dinner theater." It was a gaudy kind of a place, with red plush carpet and thick flocked wallpaper. Tables scattered around the dark cavernous hall were piled high with caviar and smoked sturgeon and other Russian specialties. And each table was replete with bottles of vodka, cognac, mineral water, and Pepsi.

Roald and I sat with Andrei and Elena at a small table for four. Andrei seemed to be in high spirits. Fresh from his victory at the foundation meeting, he looked around the room with great anticipation, waiting for the performance. The nightclub act, in fact, was similar to the one I had seen at the Hunters' Restaurant, the cabaret outside Moscow that Roald had taken me to just after the Space Forum—an interesting combination of Russian and European traditional dancing and burlesque.

When the performance began, Elena leaned over to Roald, shouting above the noise of the accompanying band: "Andrei is very upset. He has forgotten his long-distance glasses. He is complaining that he can't see the dancing girls. I told him, 'Go sit in the front row. Nobody will mind. Go down to the front row!' "

Roald and I looked over at Andrei with great amusement. I don't know whether or not he heard Elena telling stories on him. His eyes were fixed on the row of women doing a Paris cancan.

Andrei was so intent on the sight, in fact, that some of our colleagues began to notice, and this caused a commotion at one of the other tables. Loudly a few of the men shouted over in jest, "So, Andrei, this is the freedom you were fighting for!"

Andrei did not divert his gaze, and no one could tell whether he had heard the remark. But we all liked knowing that not all of Andrei was consumed "in the fight." His appreciation for beautiful women proved that the man was made of flesh and blood, not just pressure-treated human timber.

Before the act was over, Roald and I were told that if we were to catch the night sleeper we'd have to leave. We were a bit surprised to find that of all the board members, we were the only ones leaving Leningrad that evening. We collected our coats and briefcases and bid our colleagues goodbye.

It was nearly 11:00 p.m. and still light outside. We were only weeks from Leningrad's "white nights," when the sun never really sets. The city looked especially beautiful that summer night, as amber light cast a honey glow on Peter's imperial city. Roald and I rode silently in the car, wondering each to ourselves how the tickets had been booked and what it would possibly mean for the trip back to Moscow.

A young man with neatly combed hair and impeccable English took our bags from the back of the car and led us in the direction of the waiting train. When we had reached our car, he showed the conductress our tickets. Then he led the way down the narrow companionway and found our spot. "Here we are," our escort said, "5 A and B."

Roald and I realized that we had been placed in the same sleeping compartment. Without exchanging so much as a look, Roald thanked the young man and politely dismissed him.

After it was clear that our escort was out of earshot, Roald roared, "Can you believe that! The KGB has put us in the same compartment. *Very interesting!*"

"What?"

"He is KGB all right. You can tell," Roald said.

It was true. Characteristically KGB agents spoke excellent English (special schools), had very good deportment, and wore well-cut suits. This one had also given Roald his business card, which said, "Foreign Relations, Leningrad Division of the Academy of Sciences." The KGB often filled such posts in the "Foreign Relations" departments of institutes and enterprises.

"Nobody can accuse us of trying to sneak into the same compartment," Roald exclaimed. "They put us here themselves!"

This thought instantly made me feel uncomfortable. Had they given us this compartment because it was bugged? That was, after all, the standard in allocating hotel rooms. I slept badly all night, conscious that perhaps Big Brother was imbedded in the metal walls of our carriage.

Stiff and tired, we arrived in Moscow in the morning, with a full slate of meetings ahead and very little rest.

That Saturday, Roald picked me up at the Rossiya Hotel without Ivan. He was driving his own car, a bright orange Lada.

"We are going to go to the store, and then I am going to take you on a picnic," he said cheerfully.

Roald drove like a maniac through the half-empty streets of Moscow. In less than ten minutes we had arrived at an all-purpose store, a barren little shop somewhere on the ring road. Fortunately all we needed to buy was bread and tea, since he had brought sausage with him. It did not take long to find those modest items.

"We'll make one more stop," he said, "to see if we can get some cheese."

This time the store was larger and, unlike the other state store, much more crowded. There were two lines, one to pay, which they expected you to do first, and another to pick up your goods.

"What happens if they run out of the products you paid for before you get through the second line?" I asked him.

Roald gave me a look of resignation. "Then you get to stand in line again to have your money refunded!"

Despite the unpleasant ordeal of standing your ground in a line of impatient people, twice, we finally secured a block of cheese. I was beginning to feel like a real Muscovite: full of a sense of victory after such a feat.

"Why don't they make the line more efficient?" I asked on the way out of the store.

"Simple," he replied. "If they had only one line, with the food products and the cash register together, it would take no time to sell out everything in the store. They'd have to close by 9:30 a.m."

The big food store was just around the corner from a huge Stalinist structure, the Foreign Ministry—nearly identical in appearance to Moscow State University. A block away, we pulled into an inner courtyard, bordered on one side by the Belgrade Hotel and on the other by an aging brick building that overlooked the Moscow River. At the back was a row of entrances to apartments and small shops.

"Where are we going?" I asked.

"Sh-sh . . ." Roald admonished. "Don't talk anywhere around here, or in the elevator." He seemed very serious, so I instantly obeyed. But it was curious. We had been to many Moscow apartments before to see friends and he had never issued such a warning.

We entered a gateway connecting two nondescript buildings and walked along a roadway, passing three *babushkas* sitting on a rickety bench nearby. Several entrances closer to the river, Roald stopped. Taking out a piece of paper and checking something, he tapped some numbers into the console on the wall and the door clicked open. The smell of dust and urine hit me in the face. Floor tiles lay everywhere unwashed and broken.

In the hallway a tall slender man passed us and Roald looked at me blankly as a signal to stay quiet. We summoned the elevator and Roald pushed the button for the seventh floor. When we got out, he approached two padded brown doors on the left. Then, pulling out some keys, he quickly opened it. A dog in the neighboring apartment started to bark.

After the door was closed securely behind us, Roald seemed to relax. So did I as I began to assess my surroundings. A cramped little hallway led to a room on the left, which appeared to be a combination sitting room, dining room, and bedroom. Straight ahead were the bathroom and WC. The kitchen was at the end to the left, overlooking the leafy inner courtyard.

As he put his white grocery bag down on the kitchen table, Roald explained to me that this was a new apartment he had somehow managed to secure on the unofficial rental market. He told me that his landlady was nursing her mother somewhere in the city, and he was able to rent it from her for 100 rubles a month. We decided right there and then to call the little flat "Belgrade," after the seedy hotel just down the street.

The apartment's furnishings gave some hint of the landlady's taste for nice things. An Oriental rug decorated the wall in the main room and a collection of crystal was displayed on the living-room shelves. There seemed to be an ample supply of dishes and cookware in the kitchen, so we put a pot of water on the gas stove to boil and laid out the sausage and cheese on plates. After a search of a minute or so, Roald found a knife to cut the bread.

There was poignancy in this intimate moment. A similar small repast at someone's apartment in the States would leave no impression of any kind, except perhaps for its modesty. But this meal seemed full of meaning. As our life had developed, it was a rare and forbidden moment—in circumstances that were all too fleeting and uncertain.

I was leaving for Washington the following day, back to the life I had built for myself, back to my children—but six thousand miles from Roald. "I think when I go home," I said, "I will start writing to you instead of writing to myself in my journal. That way when I see you next I can bring a whole sheaf of papers and you can really begin to share with me the things I can't tell you about on the telephone."

I looked out the window of the little apartment and felt a rush of emotion. Despite the restrictions and the constant worries, there was a closeness and warmth in this country that I would miss dreadfully. Those who constituted a circle here could count on the support, love, and constant concern of the rest of their group. Their mutual involvement was in stark contrast to the way American society seemed to be evolving. In Washington, anyway, there was a disconnectedness because everyone was so busy. Even among the oldest of friends you seldom had time to be in touch, to stay engaged.

Without explaining why, I walked over to Roald and gave him the full force of a hug that had been pent up inside me from the moment I had stepped off the plane.

My last evening in Moscow, several of us went to a cooperative restaurant together. Yuri Osipyan and Roald had just returned from registering at the Kremlin for the forthcoming Party conference, which was to begin in a few days. As we dined, both of them recounted how the conferees had been told to line up and pass by Lenin's tomb, a ritual that had been institutionalized for big official gatherings ever since Stalin's day. They humorously described the incident as if it were a silly ritual from a more primitive and pagan past.

Osipyan had to leave early that evening because he was going back to his institute in Chernogolovka, on the outskirts of Moscow, and soon Roald and I went, too. When we got into his black Volga, Roald gathered a few items from the back ledge of the car. "Here," he said, "you should have these as souvenirs. Your grandchildren may appreciate them." He handed me a pen-and-pencil set and an official notebook with *Nineteenth Party Conference* embossed on them. I was touched by the gift, but I was also struck by the gesture, given to me, as they were, as if I would be enjoying my grandchildren alone, without him.

As it was my last evening in Moscow, we went for a walk around Red Square before I retired for the night. The sky was azure and the air pleasantly cool but still. Roald and I agreed that we would have to be more careful. We did not know the extent to which we were being observed, but we had to assume that the KGB was now trying to assess the nature of our friendship. So we decided that Roald would send me an invitation to come to the launch of his Phobos mission to Mars, and I would wire him back and regret. We thought that might, perhaps, put the authorities off balance. At least for a while.

Roald confided in me that he had been told he was to go with Gorbachev to Poland in July. With those dates firmly fixed on the calendar, it appeared that we would not see each other until a conference the International Foundation was hosting in Stockholm in August.

Each separation was personally painful and politically nerve-racking. August seemed like years away.

11 : Displeasure from the Top

All eyes, that hot summer of 1988, were trained on Moscow. The Communist Party of the U.S.S.R. held its Nineteenth Party Conference in July. As distinct from Party congresses, conducted every five years by the Central Committee, Party conferences were held only when fundamental policy questions needed to be approved. They were much more than rare: the last one had been held in 1941.

Gorbachev promised to use this conference to codify a number of reforms that would assure the future of *perestroika*: the introduction of a presidential system, the establishment of two presidential five-year term limits, the formation of a new parliamentary body (the Congress of People's Deputies), the separation between Party and state officials all the way down to the grassroots level, and the initiation of secret ballots, to replace the old "show of hands" method. Perhaps the most revolutionary proposal put forward by Gorbachev in the conference "theses" was the establishment of "a socialist state based on the rule of law."*

These far-reaching goals notwithstanding, the late spring elections to the 5,000-person conference had gotten off to a shaky start. Gorbachev had instructed local Party bosses to nominate only dedicated followers of *perestroika*, but his instructions had gone unheeded in many areas. Roald had regaled me with stories of how local Party bosses were appointing conservative apparatchiks as delegates. And, indeed, this is how he got drawn into the fray.

---

* See Kaiser, *Why Gorbachev Happened*, p. 226.

When Roald returned to Moscow from his visit to the United States in May, he was met at the airport by some of his colleagues from IKI, who told him that during his absence they had discovered the corrupt way in which their district Party bosses had been selecting delegates. At a big meeting at IKI, they adopted and sent a collective letter of protest to the district Party committee, demanding a more democratic approach. In addition, they had contacted *Izvestia* and *Pravda* with the story.

"The bosses were fearful of the negative publicity," Roald later told me. "They decided to compromise with IKI's dissenting factions." Out of six seats allocated for the district, it was agreed that two would be filled by popular election. Roald's colleagues had placed his name in nomination for one of them while he had been in the United States.

Roald had resisted the nomination and tried to pass on the "opportunity" to another like-minded person, but his colleagues had pleaded with him. "Please don't let us down," they said. "We fought like lions to push the system this far. You are the only person we can be sure will win in an open ballot."

Reluctantly Roald allowed his name to be submitted along with six or seven others.

Accepting such a candidacy meant campaigning at organizations all over the district. Roald often enjoyed the shock value he could create. He gleefully recounted to me his first campaign speech. He told the audience that if Soviet history was anything to go by, the candidates had to be very brave to put themselves forward for such an assignment. Of all the Politburo members in the post-Lenin period, he had told them, only Stalin had survived. "All the rest were shot—except, of course, for Comrade Tomsky, who had the privilege of shooting himself before he was arrested."

"My speech created a furor," he told me. "But I was elected anyway by a very large margin."

Roald's election, as it turned out, was counter-trend. There were some surprising defeats among the liberal intellectual community, among them, fellow foundation board member Tatyana Zaslavskaya, a pollster/sociologist who had been one of the most outspoken advocates of reform during *perestroika*. Their defeats were a testament to the power of the conservative undertow.

When reports from the Nineteenth Party Conference began to filter in, newspapers recounted, with astonishment, that a genuine debate appeared to be under way among the 4,991 delegates meeting at the Great Hall of Congresses in the Kremlin. In fact, it could have been described as a free-for-all compared to what the country had been used to. In stark contrast to earlier Party gatherings, deputies for the first time actually described the dreadful condition that much of the country was in. One after another they went to the podium to detail everything from poor health conditions (infant mortality on a par with those of Mauritius and Barbados) to the crisis in education (half the schools in the U.S.S.R. had no central heating, running water, or sewage systems). What was happening in Moscow was nothing short of a public confession that the Communist system had failed the Soviet people miserably. Seventy-plus years of propaganda on the "accomplishments of socialism" were debunked for all time as sheer mythology.*

The most dramatic moment was the appearance of Boris Yeltsin, who had been elected a delegate from his native Sverdlovsk. Yeltsin denounced the ruling Politburo as being made up of men who had voted for what Brezhnev wanted "every time." He also accused the ruling elite of squandering huge amounts of money on dachas, sanatoriums, and other perks.

At the end of the four-day conference, Gorbachev got his new presidential system, the elections he wanted for a new Congress of People's Deputies, and the institution of secret ballots. But he unexpectedly abandoned his proposal to separate the chairmanship of the local soviets (legislative councils) from the post of local Party Secretary.

I scanned the newspapers every day to see if I could find some reference to Sagdeev, but I found none. It was not until I saw Dmitri Simes, a friend and colleague, that I understood what had happened. "Your friend Sagdeev was the hero of the conference," he said in passing. (I inwardly blushed, wondering if he had heard any rumors or had any idea of how much of a friend Sagdeev really was.) During the ballot vote on the powers of the soviets, Gorbachev had proposed that the Party chairmen would automatically become chairmen of the local soviets. Simes told me that Sagdeev had counterproposed instead that the Party chairmen be compelled to run in competitive elections for the soviet chairmanships.

"His amendment was absolutely to the point," Simes said.

I anxiously waited for Stockholm, where, I was sure, Sagdeev would tell me all that had happened in his usual colorful manner.

Hearing such stories about Roald made me feel his absence all the more acutely. One moment we were vividly engaged with one another in every

---

* See Kaiser, *Why Gorbachev Happened*, p. 233.

way, the next moment we were separated with virtually no contact. The only verification I had for the reality of what had happened between us was the trust we had, and my memories.

Writing to him kept him alive for me, however. I did not address the letters, in case they were ever read by a third party, but this was a useless precaution. Anyone reading these letters would have immediately guessed for whom they had been intended.

July 3, 1988

Dear

I just plunked myself on a hard straight-backed bench amid the grimy rows of passenger seats in the railway waiting room. From lugging my heavy bag with me, I can feel twinges in my back and I am wondering why it takes half a day to travel from Kennebunkport, Maine, to New London, Conn., when they *sound* so close.

To be honest, I have been somewhat anxious and distracted during this day's trip. I have spent the last two days with Vice President Bush and his wife, Barbara, in Kennebunkport, the Maine village in which they have their summer home. This morning before I left for the airport, the Vice President gravely reported that it appeared the United States had (accidentally) shot down an Iranian passenger liner over the Gulf. Apparently 300 people were on board. Before we left he confirmed the news.

I wondered immediately how the news would be received in Moscow and whether your commentators would ridicule us: shades of KAL 007.

Sitting on the hard plastic chair, my back continues to twinge, despite the fact that I feel very well rested. The children have finally arrived in Rochester and I just finished two idyllic days with the Bushes. I slept in; read (Vasily Aksyonov's *In Search of Melancholy Baby*) and went fishing. I was childishly delighted at catching five mackerel (three more than the Vice President).

I was also warmly and graciously welcomed into the Bush family fold for those days. They are generous with their warmth and inclusive in their humor. In fact, I was delighted by the Vice President's breezy repartee. It is a fashion of humor that I understand; lighthearted factiousness. The two of us managed to go at some pace.

I must say, though, I couldn't help feeling that I was witnessing the dying rituals of a family life that exist for almost no one anymore: where the still-married grandparents play host to the still-married children, who have come to stay with the beautiful healthy grandchildren, well-behaved and knowledgeable of their place. I was struck by envy both for their luck and for this lifestyle, so reminiscent of my own upbringing (including the Secret Service men!).

. . . I will never forget seeing the Vice President sitting on the living-room couch with his granddaughter Ellie nestled under his arm. The sun flooding in from the window highlighted her baby-fine hair. The VEEP said to her with great seriousness: "The dog mustn't eat the pieces from the Peggity board, they are very valuable pegs," referring to one of the family board games.

Just as final thoughts, I was most impressed with Bush for, among other things, his great ability to relax and for his easygoing thoughtful ways. In those two days, he, by example, absolutely challenged us to forget what we'd left behind. And except for a few thoughts that would creep in, the challenge was pretty much met.

Memories of Moscow and themes from the Aksyonov book are most thought-provoking. It draws me back to the previous weekend when I was in Moscow.

I am feeling twinges now—but not from my back. Another kind. I am thinking about you and the smile you would bring to my face if you were here.

Take care of yourself.
Susan

The week after the Party conference ended, I got a message via a friend that Sagdeev wanted me to know he would be in London later in the month. I was curious about this; weren't these the dates when he was scheduled to be in Poland with Gorbachev? Through a series of obscure telexes we sent each other—and one telephone call—I managed to piece together his plans. He was intending to participate in a conference in Oxford and could possibly be in London for a few days. He wanted to know if there was any prospect that I might be in England at the same time.

I did have good reason to go to London. I had potential business clients to meet, and I had promised to go to Scotland and Paris in connection with the Eisenhower Centennial, before leaving my position. With the kids on vacation, I decided I might as well make the trip that month.

It is still a mystery to me how Roald and I managed to coordinate all our logistics to arrive in London at the same place at the same time. But once Sagdeev reached Oxford and was consequently near an unbugged phone, he was able to confirm at least some of the details with me before I left America. A few days later we were in London together. We couldn't believe he had managed to slip away without his bodyguard.

Roald arrived at the Grosvenor Hotel with a beautiful navy blue briefcase. He explained that he had purchased it in Oxford. As soon as he had seen it, he said, "I thought it looked like you." We both got tremendous fun out of programming the numbered lock on it to coordinate with my room number at the hotel.

After we settled into our separate rooms, we met downstairs for supper. Sagdeev was predictably full of stories about the Party Conference and his own role in it.

"The good news is that two hundred ten delegates voted in favor of my resolution. The bad news is that 4,789 voted against," he said with a smile.

Roald speculated that his amendment had annoyed the General Secretary. He told me that he had felt it at the time but had clear confirmation of it later.

"I got a telephone call from the Central Committee," Roald said. "They told me that my name had been taken off the list of people to go with Gorbachev to Poland. Apparently Academician Dmitri Likhachev was also removed from the list. Poor guy," he added, "they cut him out so that the reasons for my removal wouldn't be so obvious."

"Why would they care if anyone knew why you had been cut from the list?" I asked.

"I think Gorbachev's aides were a little frightened of me," he speculated. "The Polish intelligentsia had made it very clear that they were interested in having me come on this trip. I have many friends there from the Halley's Comet mission."

Perhaps I, more than Roald, was nervous about what his alienation from the top brass would mean. Roald himself seemed quite cheerful about it. He thought that this distancing from the regime enhanced the chances of having his resignation as director of IKI accepted. But in truth, neither of us really knew what the final outcome of this estrangement would be.

We decided that we would not think about it. We did not want to spoil the short time we had together by worrying about such developments, and anyway, courtesy of the General Secretary, we managed to have these unexpected days together in London. We planned and prepared a picnic to take to one of the parks and later in the afternoon we went to see some old friends of mine from my days in London more than a decade before.

We parted the afternoon of the following day. Before reconnecting with his KGB bodyguard, Roald hailed me a cab. Overwhelmed with presents for my children that he had insisted on buying, I got into the cab as he whispered, "I will not forget these few days. But the problem is, I need you *every day.*"

July 28, 1988

Dear

I am enjoying a few minutes of unexpected quiet. I am home waiting for a delivery and I have several delicious hours to drink in the quiet of a childless house.

I was expecting it—and I wasn't. In the course of reading the newspapers this morning, I opened *Moscow News* and there you were! I was interested in the "letter" you wrote calling for the restoration of Sakharov's awards. I thought your piece was really well done. I was moved by your analogy of the universe and the individual: "Physicists know how bold one must be to deal with such deep . . . 'closed zones' in the contemporary models of the universe . . . but isn't every human being on earth a universe unto him or herself, full of feelings, concerns, and alarms? And is it possible to speak about the establishment . . . of relative order in a stormy nuclear age without social justice for all?"

When I read this I wondered what *you* are feeling: what concerns you, and what alarms do you experience now—after these two weeks since I have seen you? Have things changed for you? Is your sense of optimism still with you? . . .

The "restructuring" of my career at the moment gives me an insight into the vast personal instability that *perestroika* must be causing in your country. While they are hardly analogous situations, I am increasingly aware of the toll that uncertainty takes. My situation is complicated by an intense desire to keep my long-term options flexible enough to accommodate any future plans I (we) might have . . .

As for Washington, the city is abuzz with discussions about the presidential campaigns. Michael Dukakis has been dominating the press for some time and the Bush supporters seem to be getting restless and frustrated. Many Republicans have expressed concern that unless Bush gets out there more assertively, the campaign is lost.

I maintain an interest in all of this, though I confess that my own professional and personal situation weighs more heavily on my mind.

Last night I had some people over for dinner. During dessert, I got a phone call from someone who called to ask me to verify a rumor that was floating around. Apparently someone had just returned from Moscow and said that you had been relieved of your position at IKI before your retirement date. "Fired" was the word he used. I went back to the table and tried to concentrate on the discussion under way, but at the back of my mind I was turning this rumor over and over in my mind.

I expect to be calling you in the next few days. While I don't think for a moment that any conversation we might have will reveal any insight into what is happening in your life, your voice will be reassuring.

You have touched the lives of a great many people here. That was implicit in the phone call last night.

I am no exception. As I sit in the stillness of my empty home, I wonder and long to know what you are feeling right now, what concerns you have, and whether you face them with alarm.

Take care of yourself.
Susan

A little more than a week later I was delighted to have Yuri Osipyan for dinner. He was traveling in America with a number of influential Soviets. For me, the main reason for giving the dinner was to have an excuse to monopolize some of his time. While the guests that evening mingled and moved between the living room and the garden, Yuri and I sat in the corner and talked about the political situation in Moscow, and about Roald. I didn't lead the conversation to him. I guess Yuri just had an instinct that I wanted to know as much as possible about what people were saying about Sagdeev these days. Since Yuri didn't know that I had been with him in London, I was careful to avoid any impression that I had already heard most of the stories he was telling me.

That night, in one of my "letters" to Roald, I took note of some troubling references Yuri had made to Roald's position.

Dear
Osipyan told me that you went to his dacha recently and that the two of you were discussing your next moves within the Academy of Sciences. It occurred to me that you must share the same conflict I do, at times. It can be hard to know how to proceed, leaving as many doors open as possible.

During our discussion he did confirm my worry that you are increasingly regarded as very outspoken and that that is becoming a problem in certain quarters. I worry about it, you know. Although I recognize that it is none of my business, I can't help having it on my mind. I have a great impulse to stay out of your most personal decisions, offering neither advice nor encouragement, because I have no way of gauging your best interests. But that should be some indication of how I feel about you. I have no urge to control you or prompt you into anything that doesn't come naturally. Your well-being and happiness means a great deal to me . . .

In closing, I was going to say "take care of yourself" and then I remembered that little anecdote about Yuri. I will never forget the time I saw him in Boston. After a very long and penetrating discussion about you, he said at the end, "Be careful."

I fretted about that for months. When I told you, you were amused, assuring me that there was nothing ominous about what he had meant. "It's really his poor English," you said. "He meant to say, 'Take care of yourself.'"

So much for verbal communication.

> Stay well and I will see you soon.
> Susan

The International Foundation's arms-control workshop was nearing. I stopped in Moscow for a few days beforehand to work with Roald on the book outline, which was due in New York on my return. For three days Roald and I worked intensively at IKI. He opened up the offices on Saturday and Sunday, and we spread out our papers on the director's conference table and used a small kitchen not far away for tea and light snacks. I worked at the computer while we discussed the book's contents, a process we continued in Stockholm in between the scheduled workshops.

In Stockholm there was no logical place to work on the text except in my room, in between the meetings. One afternoon we discovered that Roald's KGB escort had been put in the room next door—he was coming out of his room as Roald and I were leaving mine. It was interesting, we both thought, that he, too, had been in his room in the middle of the afternoon while everyone else was touring Stockholm or in meetings. Had he been listening in?

During conferences like this, Roald and I were all business, exuding a friendly but collegial face. Sometimes this was stressful, but he would liven things up by passing notes down the table to me: "I never had anything like this, even in my imagination," or, "I am already missing you. 83 hours and 43 minutes before your departure." These notes were my good-luck charms. I would fold them up and put them away to take home, where I'd lock them in my file cabinet. In times of deepest longing and loneliness, I would get them out and read them over, to reassure myself that our relationship, so intense and fulfilling when we were together, still existed when our absence made it seem to evaporate.

In between working sessions on Roald's book and the conference meetings, Roald and I walked the streets of Stockholm, brainstorming the implications of Roald's alienation from Gorbachev's circle. Although Roald understood he was on a tightrope, neither of us could guess that his growing distance from the Gorbachev camp would position him prominently as one of the new progressive leaders—looked to by the Soviet intelligentsia to keep *perestroika* on track. His stature and his courage would create a new set of complications for "our project," of comparable proportions to those posed by the Soviet regime itself.

12 : Taking on the Complex

Stateside, my time was absorbed in making the final transition from the Eisenhower Institute back to the company I had started in 1985, the Eisenhower Group. Although I had finally made my break with the Institute, I had an informal agreement that I would conduct occasional projects in the Soviet Union under its auspices. Apart from that, all my energy was now focused on building my own company, this time with a special interest in representing companies who wanted to do business in the Soviet Union.

Underlying these changes, though, was a deep anxiety about what my relationship with Roald would mean for the future. I could well imagine the problems we would have with the Soviet regime, but I was not at all convinced that things would be much easier for us in the United States. Implicit in returning to my company was a recognition of the flexibility it afforded me. It would be possible to open a new office in Europe if I felt the girls and I needed to move—into a kind of self-imposed exile. I started negotiations with a major New York company with branches all over the world, about the potential for an overseas affiliation.

The president of that company asked me to attend their annual meeting in Brussels, and when Roald heard the news he begged me to stop in Geneva, where he was giving a series of lectures on space. As it was on the way to the Soviet Union, where I would attend the 1988 Chautauqua Conference and a meeting of the International Foundation, I agreed.

Within hours of my arrival in Brussels, Roald telephoned me. The spacecraft Phobos, which IKI had just launched, had been lost, he told me somberly. It had developed a communications error: with one false prompt by a land-based computer, it had been instructed to close up its orientation thruster caps and, in doing so, had lost its equilibrium and its energy source. After the glittering success of the Vega mission to Halley's Comet, this was indeed bitter news. All hopes were now focused on the second identical backup spacecraft, still on course to Mars.

I was expecting Roald to be depressed when he met my airplane in Geneva, but we were so glad to see each other that all thoughts of Phobos' problems vanished, at least for a while. After I checked into a hotel not far from where Roald and his colleagues were staying, we went for a stroll along the walkway next to Lake Geneva. It was already dark and the colors of the city lights of this peaceful Swiss city shimmered on the water.

Roald was so happy to see me, he didn't seem to hesitate in putting his arm through mine. As we walked he squeezed it intermittently, recalling his first visit to Geneva—indeed his first trip abroad. Ironic or fateful, perhaps, he had been given his first opportunity to join the international community of scientists because of my grandfather's Atoms for Peace initiative. "It was here in Geneva that the Atoms for Peace conference took place in 1958," he said. If it had not been for Eisenhower's speech, he told me, Khrushchev would have had no incentive to declassify the Soviet Union's controlled-fusion program.

Not long after, Igor Kurchatov, the head of his institute, had asked Roald to serve on a committee that would welcome Eisenhower to the Institute of Nuclear Energy during the summit scheduled for Moscow. I told Roald that had it not been for the U-2 incident and my parents' refusal to bring us along, I might have come to Moscow on that very trip.

What a fortuitous path had brought him to the world of international science. But it was precisely those valued international links that now concerned him. Roald was obviously worried that the loss of Phobos would jeopardize international cooperation with his country.

"There is a big fight going on in Moscow right now over the loss of Phobos," he said.

"Should you be gone at such a delicate moment?" I asked.

We walked for a moment or two in silence.

"I needed to get away and gain some perspective on the whole mess. Everyone will still be fighting when I get back."

It had been determined that the technical failure had been traced to a prime contractor from one of the "mailboxes" in the space industry. "They found that their own computer programmer had made the error, and they were going to fire him. But I stopped them. It is no time to change personnel in the middle of the project. But the man is on notice. I said to his boss, as Lavrenti Beria used to say, 'Make them work, we can always shoot them later.' "

I laughed, and he smiled at his own black humor.

"Seriously," he said, "the important thing is not to lose the backup spacecraft. Nearly every experiment had been duplicated, so it's still possible to have a successful mission. But things will have to be watched very carefully."

A chilly wind began to pick up along the lakeshore. Neither of us was wearing a warm coat, so we decided to stop in a café and have a cup of hot tea.

"I visited Alexander Prokhorov about my resignation," Roald said, rubbing his hands together to warm them up. "He is the chairman of the Physics Division in the Academy. He agreed to support my request to resign from my position at IKI. In fact, I should know their decision by tomorrow."

I asked him if he had any feelings of regret or any second thoughts. He seemed surprised by the very idea.

"I did not sleep well last night, in anticipation of your arrival. I want you to know that I want to go through with this no matter what. You are the most important thing in the world to me."

The next morning was clear and crisp. I got up early and joined the scientists for breakfast at their hotel down the street. When Sagdeev came into the dining room, his eyes were gleaming mischievously.

"Let's go for a short walk after breakfast," he said as if he could hardly contain himself.

As soon as we were out of the shadow of his hotel, he told me that he had spoken with Moscow that morning and that his resignation as director of IKI had been accepted. He was excited about the prospect of being free to do creative science again, and he was sure that this would help with the implementation of "our project."

Indeed, leaving the IKI directorship must have brought some relief. It is perhaps impossible for a Westerner fully to fathom what it must have been like all those years to make space science projects actually happen— from building the spacecraft to navigating the gigantic Soviet bureaucratic establishment. But Roald was excited and eager to start this new chapter of his career.

With only two days left to complete his book outline for New York, we were at least filled with optimism that tactically, at least, "our project" was on target.

Although I had initially declined to participate in the Chautauqua conference that year, Greg Guroff, director of U.S.–Soviet Initiatives at USIA, had finally persuaded me to go, so I joined the delegation straight from Geneva. The conference was being held in Tbilisi, the capital of Georgia. Located in a natural bowl formed by the Caucasus Mountains, it was a beautiful city of cathedrals, museums, and Mediterranean-style architecture. Miraculously, its flavor had survived Russification and Sovietization. Although Georgia had lost her briefly held independence in 1921, she had never really forgotten it. A new awakening was under way, prompted by *glasnost*. One sensed that Georgian national pride, so amply evident, would eventually be further fueled by the increasing power of a free press. In fact, within a few days of our arrival, we heard about a few small demonstrations that had taken place at various points in the city. Nationalism was still defined in Soviet political terms, however, not as a separate, ultimately decisive force of its own.

The subject of Georgia and its unique role in the Soviet Union—homeland of Stalin, a Christian nation bordered by Islam—was not covered at all in our Chautauqua meeting. As in years past, the conference agenda was still set in Cold War terms: one panel on regional conflicts, one on arms control, one on human rights, and so on. It seemed surprisingly outdated against the backdrop of this dynamic Georgian location, particularly when word came that the police had broken up an even larger demonstration outside our hotel and had made numerous arrests. Still, the cordiality between the Soviets and the Americans was much as it had been at Chautauqua.

On the first evening, at a large gathering in the town hall, I saw many people whom I already knew well, among them Valentina Tereschkova and General Nicolai Chervov. When I approached the head table to say hello to my hosts, General Chervov gave me an affectionate kiss on my cheek. The poor man was being teased unmercifully about all the women he had kissed that evening. When I joked to Valentina that she and I would just have to share the general with the other ladies, Valentina said, without missing a beat, "How can you say such a thing? *You* can't share your heart with anyone: Sagdeev has all of it!"

"Oh, I forgot," I quipped.

Repartee or no, Valentina's tease put me on notice that she had no intention of stopping her campaign to alert the world to my friendship with Roald.

More important for me to gauge, however, was the mood of Evgeny Primakov. Primakov's power had grown significantly since the previous year, when he had issued Roald a few warnings about our relationship. Here in Tbilisi, the half-Georgian Primakov seemed to be in his element. Although we had often dined with him and other mutual friends in Moscow, I had never seen him like this. Georgia seemed to do something to Primakov's soul. He was more outgoing and spontaneous. I'd even say downright fun.

That evening Primakov had a table in the middle of the room, where he was inviting people to join him. After dessert he plucked me away from another group and insisted that I sit beside him. "She may be a President's granddaughter, but she has really made a name for herself in her own right," Primakov announced to the others at the table. Then he suggested that we raise a toast to me.* When he discovered that I didn't have a glass, he found a clean one and picked up a bottle of Borgomi, one of Georgia's unique sulfur-spring waters. I had never liked the thick salty taste of it, so I raised my hand in polite refusal. But Primakov poured ahead. "You can't have an empty glass for a toast," he scolded, filling the glass with the clear liquid.

I courteously took a sip and nearly choked. It was not Borgomi water at all but vodka that Primakov had had someone put into the dark-green bottle.† He leaned over to me and, in his wonderful half-Georgian way, put his hand on my arm and said, "Syousan, we lavvve you. We *accept* you as one of us."

Later that night, when I wrote in my diary my impressions of what had happened, I remarked on the way I had been so warmly and inclusively treated. The final line of the entry, however, spelled out the ever-present worry: "When Roald and I follow through with our plans, I wonder if they will be friends (Tereschkova, Chervov, Primakov, et al.) or if they will turn on us, quickly and ruthlessly?"

Despite a number of delightful social events and a moderately interesting conference, I decided to leave Tbilisi before the end of the week. The International Foundation was about to have a meeting of the board's

* In Russia, even the person being toasted is expected to drink.
† Although regulations about the purchase of alcohol had been liberalized, remnants of Gorbachev's anti-alcohol campaign could still be found.

human-rights subcommittee and I decided to go to Moscow a day early. I went to the conference service room to see about changing my plane tickets. There, an American woman was loudly complaining to the coordinator that her handbag had been taken. They speculated that it was probably a KGB warning: she was known to be involved in helping dissident causes.

This woman's plight was on my mind when I finally got Sagdeev on the telephone at IKI. I asked him about the foundation schedule for the two-day meeting, and Roald said he would check on it. Then, to my surprise, he went through a elaborate little speech about how he had just gotten back from Geneva, where, he said, he had gone to a conference on joint cooperation on space. It was perfectly obvious that he was saying all this for the benefit of probable wiretappers. But I had made no secret about being in Geneva with him, and the KGB knew perfectly well I had been there. Roald and I had even gone to the Soviet mission together! Had Roald outsmarted himself on the telephone? I stewed that the authorities would have this odd phone conversation in their file—with the first confirmation that we were playing games and had, perhaps, something to hide.

The next day when we landed in the Soviet capital, Roald was waiting for me at the bottom of the airplane stairs with an armful of flowers. He and Ivan dropped me at my hotel, before returning to his meeting at IKI. Later he came back to take me to lunch at a Soviet version of a fast-food restaurant, a dreary place with dirty floors and unwashed tables.

Roald and I ordered a greasy version of beef stroganoff, while he recounted to me the dramas of his face-to-face meetings with the aerospace industrialists. He had come back from Geneva earlier than he had planned because of the internal investigation of the Phobos spacecraft loss. He didn't say too much about the details, but I could tell that he was deeply disturbed.

Even to me Sagdeev was extremely negative about the bosses who ran the Soviet space industry. Not only was he in conflict with them over Phobos, but, he said, they were people whom Gorbachev was listening to more and more. "These are the kind of men that Gorbachev is surrounded by now. Westerners are entirely too taken in by Gorbachev's charm," he said grimly.

By the tone of his voice I could sense how complicated and dangerous the situation had become. He didn't confide in me, but I could tell he was under tremendous strain. I guessed that something had gone very badly at the meetings. I thought back to our walk on Lenin Hills, just after the Space Forum, and all that Roald had said about the complex's penchant for secrecy. With Roald's insistence that the foreign partners of Phobos also attend the meetings, one could be certain that the long knives were now out for him.

Before he went back to more meetings that afternoon, he pulled two long boxes out of his pocket. He told me that they were two watches he had bought in Geneva for me.

"Just like Phobos," he said, "you must have two. One can serve as a backup in case the other one no longer works."

On the last evening in Moscow, Roald and I went for a brief walk around the Ukraina Hotel. He seemed ever more troubled by the political situation and what it could mean for us. In addition to the intense difficulties he was having with the industrial suppliers for Phobos, the unresolved power struggle at the Kremlin disturbed him deeply.

As we walked, I was surprised to hear him talk so pessimistically. "Are you afraid of a potential coup d'état?" I asked, referring to rumors that had been carried in the international press.

"Of course, who knows what will happen? Perhaps the military might finally take over. But in such a case Gorbachev would be at the head of the coup," he speculated. "He's too smart to be otherwise."

13 : The Man Who Knows How to Say Nyet

Roald's prediction that the political struggle in Moscow was coming to a head was right. Not long after my return to the United States, Yegor Ligachev was demoted from chief ideologist of the Party and was given the thankless responsibility for agriculture, although he was retained as a full Politburo member. Alexander Yakovlev, seemingly perfect for the ideological post during these times of change, was given a rather secondary position, dealing with international Communist Party organizations. The old Party stalwart Andrei Gromyko was not so fortunate. He was forced into "retirement," and Viktor Chebrikov, a Ligachev ally, was removed as KGB head—replaced by Vladimir Kryuchkhov. In the shuffle Gorbachev acquired the title President in addition to his role as General Secretary of the Party.

It is ironic that while the West was celebrating Gorbachev's consolidation of power, Moscow intellectuals were disquieted by it. Their concern was fueled by their analysis of the recently issued draft laws to establish new legislative structures. The laws stacked the selection process for candidates in favor of the Communist Party, and the new system would also allow Gorbachev to serve as chairman or president of the legislature *and* retain his position as General Secretary of the Party.

Sakharov, for one, was deeply disturbed by what this could mean for reform. He feared that combining the two positions would give Gorbachev almost "boundless powers," which in Sakharov's judgment was "just insanity." "Today it is Gorbachev," he said, "but tomorrow it could be somebody else. There are no guarantees that some Stalinist will not succeed him. Once more, everything boils down to one person, and that is extremely dangerous for *perestroika* as a whole and for Gorbachev personally. This is an extremely important question, one on which the fate of the country depends."*

Concern about Gorbachev's acquisition of power was underscored with the publication of a piece of draft legislation that would restrict public meetings and demonstrations. During my Moscow visit, when the International Foundation's human-rights subcommittee had met, Andrei Sakharov and Tatyana Zaslavskaya had brought this draft law to our attention. Apparently it had already been adopted by the Presidium, under Gorbachev's chairmanship, sometime during August. If the draft was confirmed by the full Supreme Soviet,† they told us, it would severely restrict free expression. For instance, any demonstrations held without appropriate permission could be subject to "dispersal" by special paramilitary troops that were to be created. (These troops were similar to the future troops used in the crackdown in the Baltics.) Roald, the only member of the Supreme Soviet among us, had asked both Andrei and Tatyana to collect as much information and legal advice as they could before the late October session of the Supreme Soviet, when a vote on the law would take place.

The importance of this issue came into sharper focus when Estonia declared its "sovereignty" and, thus, the precedence of its own laws over Soviet ones. Gorbachev condemned the move as "totally unacceptable." But unacceptable or not, Estonia's move and the growing ethnic and national awareness all over the U.S.S.R. were not going away. The nationalities question was now in the newly empowered hands of Mikhail Gorbachev, the only Soviet premier since Lenin who had never lived outside the Russian Federation proper. And it would be his actions that would decide the fate of the Soviet Union.

In late October, Bill Miller,‡ who had been acting director of the American branch of the International Foundation, called my office with news. He had just heard that Sagdeev's demand that Sakharov have his medals returned to him, by decree of the Politburo, had been successful. Sakharov

---

* See Kaiser, *Why Gorbachev Happened*, p. 245.
† This was the old Supreme Soviet, which existed before the Nineteenth Party Conference authorized the formation of a new one. The draft laws would be rubber-stamped by the old Soviet body.
‡ Currently U.S. ambassador to Ukraine.

would have all his scientific decorations and prizes reinstated.* He also said it looked probable now that Sakharov would get an exit visa to come to the United States for a promotional tour for the foundation. It was a breakthrough. For all his international fame, Sakharov had never visited the West before.

This all sounded quite positive; then Bill said something curious. "Sagdeev was nominated for the presidium of the Academy of Sciences."

I was not expecting such news. I could feel the blood drain from my face. "He was?"

"It created quite a sensation," Bill went on. "He yielded his nomination to Sakharov and embarrassed his colleagues into electing Andrei to the post."

I was taken utterly by surprise. I had not even had a hint that such a thing was looming. But I was scheduled to leave for Moscow on business the next day, and I knew I would hear the authentic story from Roald.

No sooner had my plane landed than Sagdeev began to tell me everything. After his nomination, the president of the Academy, Guri Marchuk, had persuaded one of his colleagues to attack Sagdeev publicly, a maneuver he hoped would assure Roald's defeat. Every imaginable accusation was made, though fortunately none about his relationship with me. Despite the attacks, many of Roald's colleagues in physics firmly defended him, and his nomination was maintained. Then Sagdeev dramatically raised his hand and asked for the floor. When he was recognized, he took the podium and relinquished his nomination to Andrei Sakharov. There was complete disbelief in the hall.

Roald told me that he and Sakharov had planned this maneuver for almost a week. "But even Andrei doesn't know my deepest motivation," he whispered.

News of Roald's brilliant move spread like wildfire around the city. Everywhere we went, people stopped and congratulated him. His office was inundated with flowers, cards, and telegrams. He had created a sensation. †

Sagdeev also confirmed that the article he had written about Sakharov's

---

* Sakharov had quite a collection of decorations. The most important of them were three "Hero of the Soviet Union's," the highest number after Brezhnev's five.
† It is interesting that many prominent Western newspapers and magazines gave Gorbachev credit for this development. Nothing could have been further from the truth.

medals had prompted the Politburo to restore them. Andrei, as we discovered, rejected the gesture on the basis that he couldn't accept them until all prisoners of conscience from the Brezhnev era had been rehabilitated. Doing this was certainly Andrei's right, but I worried that Roald had used up valuable political capital to no real avail.

That night, as I tried to fall asleep, my mind kept turning over the significance of all these political developments, wondering what they would do to Roald's standing with the authorities. "He has turned down his leadership position at IKI," I wrote in my journal, "yielded his nomination to Sakharov, and now this. How long can it go on before the government begins to react against him?"

During the previous month I had seen a political window open that I thought could probably be very important for "our project." The political situation had reached a turning point, in fact, and we needed to decide how to respond. So on the Sunday after my arrival, Roald and I went for a walk around the lake at the Novodevichy convent, a monastic sanctuary in the heart of Moscow. The wind was sharp and the temperature had dropped; we buttoned up our coats and turned our collars up.

Moving quickly, I outlined for Roald the various scenarios I had put together in the middle of the night. I was anxious because so many factors were converging that might call our hand.

To start with, in the Soviet Union, Gorbachev had just consolidated power in a Kremlin shakeup, and elections to the Congress of People's Deputies were forthcoming. It was important for our future that Roald not get swept up in that. Our relationship would be sure to drag him into serious trouble. If he were to take on a position of trust in the Congress, it could discredit him and the reform movement, and our relationship might even give the authorities an excuse to accuse him of some breach of duty.

In the United States, I figured George Bush would probably be elected President and he would presumably build on Reagan's opening to the U.S.S.R. More important, he knew me, and I felt he would stand up for me in case of difficulties.

For all these reasons I felt very strongly that we should not delay our marriage. I also did not want to get it mixed up with the Eisenhower Centennial. I had to assume that in America there would be a rash of criticism of me, and I didn't want it to coincide in any way with the national effort to honor Granddad's memory. If we moved now, we would take a "hit," but we would be respected for it, especially by the people who were counting on us.

Roald agreed. "Are you feeling brave?" he said to me seriously.

"I'm working on it," I replied lightly. "But you have more practice than I do. I was leaving this decision up to you."

"It is decided, then," Roald said. "This is an important day."

I was surprised that he seemed to be so ready to take decisive action, just like that. But it did seem to both of us that there had been a political turning point. The time seemed right.

Roald made one amendment. We should not adopt a rigid game plan, he said. "In chess you make your move and you don't make the next one until you know how they will respond to your initial play."

Unable to sleep that night, I lay awake for several hours, occasionally getting up to write things down in my journal. Around 3:30 in the morning I began to write a draft of a public statement that I thought we could make to explain what we were doing.

The next day Roald and I went to "Belgrade." There we were able to discuss the matter without concern about being bugged. We went over the draft I had finished at 4:30 in the morning. It read:

> In the last year and a half, in the course of our working relationship, we have experienced a deepening sense of trust, respect and love for one another.
>
> The relationship that has developed between us has become so compelling and central to our lives that we have finally recognized the need to unite our futures.
>
> For that reason, we have decided to take the necessary responsibility and the personal risk associated with being together. In addition, we feel that under the circumstances full disclosure of our personal commitment to one another is the only moral course. Against the backdrop of changing political times and improving relations between our two countries, we fervently hope that our decision will be accepted with understanding and support from our friends, and in a spirit of goodwill and best wishes by our respective countrymen.

Roald read it and approved it, but he was vague about how and when we should issue it. In retrospect, I think he was buying time, even if he didn't know it himself. Perhaps intuition told him that perhaps the time was not yet right. Maybe he knew that his fight with the complex would pose greater dangers to him now, he didn't say. But when I asked him a few days later if he had any doubts about me, or about getting married, he seemed surprised.

"No, not at all," he said. "But I do worry a great deal about the obstacles that could be put in our way."

Over those next days, in snatches of privacy that were only infrequently available to us, we would discuss the whole business. I felt rising frustration that we couldn't find the time or place to have a proper talk, and I was beginning to feel resentful and bitter about all the distractions. The stress and powerlessness we both felt was beginning to make even the smallest things intolerable.

One night I nearly had a temper tantrum when Roald told me that we were going to a concert. With so many friends, we had managed to be out every evening. Even though these gatherings had been pleasant enough, all I could sense was time ticking away before my departure and no resolution to our difficulties. The tension between us was palpable. That cold windy evening I wasn't wearing a hat. One of the women in our party admonished me for not having one. After several efforts to get me to borrow hers I finally exploded: *"I don't want a hat!"*

Embarrassed that I had lost my composure with such a well-meaning friend, I said to Roald at the end of the evening, "I have to talk to you."

"You don't think I have to talk to you!?" he snapped.

Ivan drove like a madman through the streets of Moscow, while Roald and I sat in the back seat without uttering a word. When we got to my hotel, Roald walked me to the door. Taking my hand, he said suddenly very tenderly, "I know we haven't had much time alone. The lack of privacy is a function of our 'situation.' Our problem would be solved if you didn't sleep in a hotel. Apartment living would be one of the benefits of getting married."

A moment or so later he looked me straight in the eye and said, "You know, I can live without most things, but I can't live without your smile."

I wasn't so sure it was that simple. I wondered about the feasibility of living as man and wife on a "visiting basis." His pessimism about the hostile powers in the Soviet military-industrial complex led me to believe that he was serious when he said that a visiting basis was the only feasible way.

That evening I wrote in my journal:

I am probably unduly pessimistic, however. Many people panic not long after discovering the full scale of the commitment they have made. I am no exception. Sometimes I am nagged by feelings that I may be doing something wrong, perhaps even unpatriotic, or that Sagdeev will blame me for being underutilized and passing up important positions. He will have the book, and then if he can travel, he can have other things. But what if he can't?

As much as anything, my bad mood had roots in my deep dislike for ambiguity. I was eager to either get on with life or face the music. The anxiety of being an interested but helpless bystander was wearing on me, and the maddening lack of resolution yawned without end before me.

A few days before I left, the old Supreme Soviet, as one of its final acts, was about to convene to take up the draft laws on meetings and demonstrations and the establishment of special paramilitary troops. Roald told me that he had talked to Anatoly Lukyanov, then deputy chairman of the Presidium of the Supreme Soviet.* He had used the opportunity to register his opposition to the pending law. Lukyanov told Roald that he, too, had had reservations about the bill but that deputies from the "working class" had been eloquent during the Presidium meeting in support of the draft. That's why there would be no chance to soften the wording of the bill.

Roald had replied that he wanted the podium during the forthcoming debate in the Supreme Soviet, but Lukyanov resisted: to avoid confusion, it had been decided there would be no verbal debate and instead the Presidium leadership would cite different written views during a general presentation. "If you wish to be quoted," he told Roald, "hurry and send me your written statement."

Roald quickly wrote out his principal arguments on why the draft law was anti-democratic, and on October 28 sent them to the Grand Kremlin Hall.

Roald and I had lunch together in the cold and drafty director's dining room at IKI, on the day the bill came up for a vote—October 31. He told me that a number of his colleagues had warned him against sticking his neck out. "After your performance at the Academy over Sakharov's election

---

* Lukyanov was speaker of the Congress and a longtime friend and adviser to Gorbachev. They had been classmates at Moscow State University. Lukyanov was later jailed for his role as a coup conspirator in August 1991.

to the Presidium," they told him, "you can't take a similar action a second time, especially since only a few days have elapsed in between."

I couldn't tell what Roald was going to do, but I guessed he would abstain when the vote was taken.

That evening, when he picked me up at my hotel, he was still flushed with excitement from the day's events. Despite some effort to get Gorbachev to postpone the hearing, the drafts had been read unchanged, and the Secretary of the Presidium only briefly mentioned that there were other opposing views. No effort was made to read or quote from any of them.

"I felt cheated," Roald told me without apology, "so I voted against the law." Both chambers of the Supreme Soviet had considered the measure. In the House of Nationalities, five or six Estonian delegates voted against it; in Roald's chamber he was alone.

There was nothing really startling about the Estonian votes. Estonia had already declared its sovereignty and the Baltic nations had even boycotted the Congress. But a "no" vote from a member of the Soviet establishment, a lone dissenter in the Council of Unions, was utterly unexpected.

"When I raised my hand, there was noise and excitement all around the hall and journalists ran over to me and took pictures," Roald told me. "I don't think they were prepared for any opposition. No one seemed to know how to count a no vote. I had to keep my hand up for fifteen or twenty minutes!"

The same afternoon came the vote on the establishment of paramilitary troops. Roald again voted against the proposed law, but this time five more deputies joined him. "Perhaps they were encouraged," he said ironically, "when they saw I had not been taken away."

Those two no votes of Roald's in the old Supreme Soviet created a sensation. Within days, articles all over the U.S.S.R. cropped up heralding Sagdeev as "The Man Who Knows How to Say *Nyet.*" Even *National Geographic* featured a picture of him sitting in his seat, his arm assertively raised. This image signified the country's first parliamentary resistance to the rubber-stamp mentality of the Soviet Union's legislative process.

Sagdeev was now decisively outside the ruling circle, permanently alienated from the General Secretary himself. Six months later such bold moves would be more commonplace, a year hence a part of the new system. But Sagdeev was an unapologetic pioneer, and there could be no doubt that he was now dangerously vulnerable.

I left Moscow the following day. It had been a troubling trip—and there seemed little prospect that anything between us could be resolved quickly. I was overcome with sadness and confusion.

On the return flight, I discovered that an old friend, Stephen Rhinesmith, was also on the plane. I was so consumed with sadness and concern about Roald's and my situation that in the course of a few hours I confided my dilemma to Steve, swearing him to absolute secrecy. He assured me that he understood the need for confidentiality. And he listened very carefully. But as soon as he spoke I could tell he was deeply skeptical about the feasibility of our plans. In his judgment, my relationship with Roald would be possible only under two conditions: if Roald and I were not to marry, or if I moved to Europe. He did not believe that my marrying him would be accepted in the United States. "But, Susan," he said gently, "do you really want to persist with this? I mean, we're all older, we've had experience in life. You know it's possible to fall in love with more than one person. Do you *really* want to be in the middle of all this?"

I listened to him without response, unable to give him any rational explanation.

The next day Bill Miller called me at the office and told me that President Reagan had agreed to meet with Andrei Sakharov on his forthcoming visit, but *not* with either of his traveling companions: Evgeny Velikhov and Roald Sagdeev. I asked him if the President understood that it was Sagdeev who had secured Andrei's place on the Academy Presidium and that it was he who had prodded the Politburo into returning Andrei's medals; more important, that Sagdeev had stood up against the regime for the first time in the seventy-year history of the Supreme Soviet. Bill acknowledged that all these things were true, but he surmised that Reagan was refusing to see Sagdeev because of his anti-SDI position.

Bill's words underscored for me what Rhinesmith had said. Americans were probably not ready for my marriage to Roald either. The U.S. government, it seemed, was still incapable, beyond convenient photo opportunities, of making meaningful distinctions among the new players on the revolutionary Soviet scene.

PART
THREE

It was possible, no doubt, to imagine a society in which wealth, in the sense of personal possessions and luxuries, should be evenly distributed, while power remained *in the hands of a small privileged caste. But in practice such a society could not long remain stable. For if leisure and security were enjoyed by all alike, the great mass of human beings who are normally stupefied by poverty would become literate and would begin to learn to think for themselves; and when once they had done this, they would sooner or later realize that the privileged minority had no function and they would sweep it away.*

—GEORGE ORWELL, *1984*

14 : "It's for My Own Protection"

In early November 1988, the International Foundation discovered that
Andrei Sakharov's first trip to the United States was in jeopardy. But the
planning for his visit had been troubled from the start. His first application
for a visa had been turned down by the Politburo, based on the secrets he
knew from working on the bomb project roughly thirty years before. But
Velikhov persuaded Gorbachev to convene a special commission to consider
the trip. Finally they agreed to let Sakharov participate in the foundation-
sponsored promotional tour. When I was in Moscow, some of the board
members had met with Andrei to discuss his itinerary, which had already
been prepared and circulated. We had not been together ten minutes when
Sakharov pulled out a piece of paper and announced: "This is my program
for the United States." He read out his own typewritten plan, citing a
number of places and events that were completely unrelated to his scheduled
appearances. Evgeny Velikhov protested, saying that the itinerary was already a final one and that people in the United States had already been
invited. Sakharov refused to combine his new plans with the old ones.
It would be too taxing, he said. Then with characteristic resolve he told
Velikhov, "My wife said she didn't stick it out with me in Gorky to have
me die in America."

Fellow board members had grumbled plenty about Andrei's position, but
now some weeks later they were virtually speechless when Sakharov delivered a new ultimatum. He had already received his exit visa to leave the
U.S.S.R. when, the day before his departure, he went into the foundation's
headquarters and said he wouldn't make the trip unless several of his dis-

sident colleagues, who had spent time in jail as political prisoners, could go with him. This required a twenty-four-hour turnaround request to the Politburo. It was sheer blackmail, but it worked. The next day, in time to make the flight, the exit visas for Andrei's associates were ready—though they had been granted, apparently, with some cynicism. Later we learned that a few Politburo members had wagered a case of Scotch on the likelihood that Sakharov and his colleagues would defect.

Sakharov's most recent demand had created a major crisis for the foundation. According to Roald, Velikhov, who had gone out on a limb getting Sakharov's exit visa in the first place, now felt angry and used. I must say, I had some sympathy for him. Although these high jinks may have been a boon to Sakharov and maybe even to human-rights groups in the Soviet Union, they had exacted a toll on our board members. While his crusades were valuable—perhaps indispensable—he dragged everyone into his fight with or without their consent. As one American said, in frustration, "We should demand human rights for foundation board members."

As we anticipated, Sakharov, accompanied by Roald and the other Soviet board members, arrived in the United States to a media firestorm. But unexpectedly, from the moment Andrei stepped off the plane, he spared the International Foundation nothing. He used nearly every press opportunity to denigrate its work, notwithstanding the fact that he and his dissident colleagues were in the United States entirely due to its efforts. Though his complaints about the foundation might have been shared privately by others on the board, it was hard to imagine that the organization deserved the public beating it got at the hands of one of its founding members.

Roald, who knew Sakharov much better than I, tried to explain how it was that even though the foundation had given Andrei and his dissident colleagues a chance to come to the West for the first time, Andrei publicly expressed animosity toward it. "Sakharov probably feels used, put on exhibition like a dancing bear," he remarked.

"That may well be so," I said, "but he wasn't exactly a loser here. He gained a great deal in the bargain, as did his associates." Some appreciation was called for, I thought.

Jerome Wiesner, co-chairman of the International Foundation board, was deeply saddened by the whole affair. He shrugged and said wistfully that in fact it had been Sakharov who had asked to join the foundation board in the first place. But he had another theory about why Sakharov was handling himself this way. The Soviet board members were unused to the prominence given them by the barrage of Western media attention during *perestroika*; many progressive Soviets had been catapulted overnight onto the international scene. That had been the case even with Sakharov, who until this time had dealt primarily with the press corps in Moscow, a smaller and more manageable body than the full crush of the American Fourth Estate.

I thought that had a lot to do with it. But there was another trend of even greater importance. Given the deep pessimism shared by many Soviet citizens, it was not untypical for people to try to get as much as they could, *now*, before the gains of *perestroika* were inevitably, as they imagined, rolled back. This kind of attitude might have been driving Sakharov, too.

Ever since *perestroika* had started, the progressive elite of the U.S.S.R. had been under enormous strain. I was surprised by the number of positions of responsibility any one person might be filling. Velikhov, for example, was holding perhaps four different full-time jobs; Yuri Osipyan had almost as many. While this layering of titles, honors, and positions of power—a form of empire-building—might have been typical during the Brezhnev era, it continued and increased throughout *perestroika*, and little effort was made to change it. Perhaps because the elite was so clearly divided between liberal "good" guys and conservative "bad" ones, no one was willing to relinquish a position to the other.

In order to discharge manifold responsibilities, it was vital to delegate considerable authority. This had been possible during the Brezhnev era, when subordinates knew the rules and tended to be even more cautious than their bosses. But during *perestroika* there were no rules anymore, and the bosses spent a lot of time putting out near-fires started by their subordinates—if they were lucky enough to smell the smoke in time. This was the most probable explanation for the earlier Council of Ministers fiasco, when the foundation's Soviet staff had pushed so hard for approval of such radical by-laws. *Perestroika* required *genuine* management and oversight, but no one knew how to do it. Not surprisingly, chaos ensued and tempers were constantly being tested.

After an exhausting week-long series of events, and the upset created by Andrei's performance, I suggested to Roald that he and his assistant, Elena, who was traveling with him, stay through the Thanksgiving holiday. We were all invited to spend the weekend with Dielle Fleischmann, a friend of mine who lived in Planes, Virginia. The weekend would give everyone a chance to rest.

The day after Thanksgiving, Roald and I went out for a long walk in the Virginia countryside. It was brisk that morning and frost sparkled on the meadows and on the trees that lined the roadway. It was good to get outside, far from the others. We had had very little time since his arrival for our usual political brainstormings and assessments about "our project."

News from the Soviet Union was not good. More than 500,000 people, it was reported, had just demonstrated in Baku, the capital of Azerbaijan. The Baltic republics were also showing signs of unrest. One could imagine these developments escalating into bloody confrontations—especially now that the Soviet government had the laws in place to use force to break up demonstrations legally.

As we walked, Roald suddenly said, "And now I want to ask you something very sensitive." He hesitated. "What do you think I should do about leaving the Party?"

I could tell by the way he said it that he had been wrestling with the question for some time. I thought for a moment.

"A bold move right now might certainly alarm the authorities," I answered carefully.

Roald and I walked in silence.

I was resigned to the idea that major changes in his life and in our relationship would occur only gradually. That seemed to be the approach that had evolved. While I wasn't sure his caution would bring him greater political safety, the political situation was so unstable that I did not want to push him beyond his own natural instincts. Nevertheless, the agonizing uncertainty of everything continued to create some tension between us.

Since his arrival in America with Sakharov, Roald had seemed very conscious of his political vulnerabilities. Both of us understood that the book Roald had contracted to write, and I had agreed to edit, would be critical in ultimately providing political protection. While writing it might bring some danger, the finished text would give him a visibility that could be used to mobilize the Western press, if he was singled out by the Soviet authorities. We had agreed that he would start by making audio tapes, with me, of his story. The cassettes would be transcribed and assembled into a text by me, in Washington. It would take longer to produce a manuscript this way, but it would ensure that the book would be written in the United States, and ready to go, in case the worst happened.

"You're probably right. Better to have the book almost done before making any more big waves," he said.

. . .

Later that day, when I drove Roald and Elena to the airport and we waited at the Pan Am gate, Roald peeled off a Post-It note I had given him earlier and stuck it on the magazine I had on my lap: "Someday when we are rich and famous we'll look back on this and laugh."

Shuffling through his papers, he found another note I had written him and put with his things, knowing he would see it later. He opened it casually and then read to himself: "You will never know what you mean to me. Love, S."

Roald looked up and caught my eye in one of the deepest, most enveloping looks I have ever seen. Moments later, he gave me a long, hard hug, and I waved him and Elena through the boarding gate.

I arrived in London in early December. Roald was there to meet me at the airport. He put his arm through mine and held it tight. We sat at the back of the bus from Heathrow, laughing and whispering, barely able to stop smiling.

Both of us were feeling much better. With some distance from Sakharov's visit to the United States, I could see that Roald had been under immense pressure then. Now, on the surface at least, Roald showed none of those signs of strain.

Although we had set aside two days for working on Roald's book, he was not exactly a free man. He could arrange to see me only when he could sneak away from a conference he was attending. With limited time, we concentrated on taping politically sensitive parts of the book that we did not want to tackle in the U.S.S.R. or in the United States. Time was short, but we managed to have the equivalent of two highly productive days of work during which we finished a critical mass of material. For me, the tapings made many parts of Roald's life come together in a cohesive way —giving me a better idea, too, of the problems we were facing now.

Roald told me that at the end of his studies at Moscow State University he was chosen to do his diploma work at a top-secret nuclear installation, code-named Arazamas-16. There he met Sakharov, who was, at the time, working on the hydrogen-bomb project. Sagdeev's nine-month experience at the weapons laboratory convinced him he never wanted to do military work. Despite his resolve, the entire group of graduating physicists at the university in 1954 were assigned to the U.S.S.R.'s newest nuclear installation, Chelyabinsk-70 (the counterpart to the Lawrence Livermore laboratories). Through his highest-level contacts, he pleaded with his mentor, the Nobel laureate Lev Landau, to find a way out for him. The result was an assignment to Igor Kurchatov's Institute of Nuclear Energy, the central brain trust for the Soviet nuclear-weapons program. However, rather than working in the heavily guarded weapons program, he was put in the controlled-nuclear-fusion program.

"From the time I was young," Roald told me, "I valued my freedom. Joining the weapons program was a pact one made with the devil. In exchange for better living and material conditions, you gave up what scientific and physical freedom there was."

From the beginning, he told me, he had hated compulsory things. While still in high school during the Stalin regime, he had been chosen to lead his school chapter of Komsomol, the Communist youth organization. He had declined. His parents were supportive of him, he said, but his refusal had been unprecedented if not downright dangerous. He thought that his rejection of the post was a precursor of his ultimate desire to avoid being ensnared in Soviet politics.

Now, after all these years, he was more than ready to admit the compromises he had made in his life, specifically his deep regret that he had given into pressure to join the Communist Party. But I noted a frustration in his voice—the sound of regret, as if it was too late to rectify even the smaller mistakes he had made, choices that now hampered his ability to act freely in pursuit of our future.

On our last evening in London, Roald warned me that he would have to get back to his hotel by 10:00 p.m. Elena, he said, would be looking for him. During a break in our work, we talked about more personal matters for the first time. I hadn't realized that events were moving quite so ominously in Moscow. Roald admitted that he was under fresh attacks because of his recent radical positions, especially his vote in the Supreme Soviet. He said that they were coming from people who did not want Sakharov in his present positions. "Sakharov is a sacred cow in the U.S.S.R., just as he is in the West. But since they can't go after Andrei, they focus on the people around him. There will be others like me who are targeted instead of Andrei."

There were other worrying signs. I had been riveted by a recent newspaper article about a U.S.–Soviet marriage—between the Soviet Union's leading female chess champion, Yelena Akhmilovskaya, and the American Olympic chess captain, John Donaldson. "It's a real love match—a marriage, not a defection," one of Donaldson's American teammates was quoted as saying in *The New York Times*. But I had interpreted the story differently. The couple married while they were out of the U.S.S.R., and according to the report, Akhmilovskaya "hoped that [her] daughter would eventually be allowed to join them in the United States. The seven-year-old girl is staying with her grandmother in the Soviet Union."* It was clear to me that despite *perestroika*, the Soviet chess star did not think she would be allowed to marry her American counterpart, and so she had taken matters into her own hands. If she had thought otherwise, she would have taken her daughter with her.

If a chess champion had been so pessimistic about her chances of getting permission to marry an American and decided to defect, what would the prospects be for a man with strong ties to the Soviet military-industrial complex?

I produced the newspaper clipping about the chess champions from my bag. Roald read the article, his brow furrowed. "Imagine," he said gravely, "even a chess champion didn't think she would get permission."

Dark predictions overtook the joy of our day's collaboration. Abruptly, Roald looked at his watch and said that he had to go. I wasn't stopping him, but he pleaded, "Please, Susan, it's for my own protection." Suddenly he jumped up, grabbed a few reports I had collected during my business meetings, and started for the door. If asked what he had been doing, he said, he could say he had been discussing business with someone in London. He didn't want anyone to know that I was in the city.

This was an excruciating moment for us both. There was still so much that needed to be said. I could sense Sagdeev's panic—but I was at a loss about what I could do to help him.

I walked Roald down to the lobby and out to the portico. It was raining hard as the doorman hailed him a cab. He kissed me briskly on the cheek and jumped in. Through sheets of water, I watched him wave to me until the taxi was out of sight.

That was the last I saw of him before he caught an airplane for Moscow and home.

I had been scheduled to stay in London a few more days to do business when my office called to say that I had an invitation to attend a reception for Mikhail Gorbachev at the Soviet UN mission. He was in New York to

* *The New York Times*, November 27, 1988, p. 22.

speak at the United Nations and to meet with outgoing President Reagan and incoming President Bush. I was relieved to know they were willing to include me.

Then, very soon after, the news broke that there had been an earthquake in Armenia. When I heard that on television, I knew that I would not be seeing Gorbachev, but I thought there might be a chance the reception would be held anyway, with someone like Foreign Minister Shevardnadze hosting it. But when I arrived in New York I learned that the entire event had been canceled. Beyond my disappointment, I was surprised that Gorbachev had gone back to the U.S.S.R. and not left anyone behind. Symbolically it would have gone a long way toward dispelling the notion that the reform movement in the Soviet Union was only one person deep. Later, when I asked a Soviet official why the entire leadership, including the Foreign Minister, had returned to the Soviet Union, he replied that it would have been unthinkable not to be on the plane with Gorbachev. The culture of the omnipotent tsar still existed.

I had arranged to stay with my sister Anne the night of the reception that never took place, so we had a free evening together. During one of our long discussions about family matters, I decided to confide in her about Roald. Anne, who had met him as "my collaborator," was surprised. But she listened with sympathy to my woes, underscoring something I had felt all along: if you are serious about this, she warned, disclosure assures you the greatest safety. She advised us to move quickly, given the favorable political climate and because, she said, clandestine affairs are always risky.

She was telling me something I knew all too well. But things were not quite so easy. Roald had been living as a separated man, but he still had to get an official divorce before we could marry. Under the circumstances, I did not trust the Soviet officials at all.

From the work Roald and I had been doing on his book, I had learned why he was so pessimistic about being allowed to live freely, whether in the Soviet Union or in the West. He had not merely been part of the military-industrial complex; he had made major decisions about the U.S.S.R.'s valued space program. This was an area of intense competition between our countries, of course, and the rocketry end of it had a direct tie-in with nuclear weapons. Despite Roald's insistence that he had always kept IKI "open and clean" of military contracts, it was part of the military-industrial establishment's pyramid, whose rule paralleled that of the Mafia: "Once in, no way out."

I figured that when the regime realized that the only thing standing between us and marriage was Roald's divorce, they would tie up the paperwork on it to block our effort to be together. In that case, if there was a crackdown and Roald needed my help in order to leave the Soviet Union, I would be all but useless: Western governments would not be able to declare us a "separated family," a human-rights category used by some refuseniks and others in this kind of plight.

Unfortunately, there was no assurance that being Roald's wife would even make a definitive difference, though international attention would help. As I knew, an American wife did not always suffice. Sergei Petrov, a friend of mine, was married to an American, but he spent a decade in the U.S.S.R., separated from her, before he was released. A great deal of international pressure had been brought to bear on his behalf; the matter had even been raised during U.S.–Soviet summits. Petrov had held a junior position within the military-industrial complex and Soviet law prohibited people who had access to secrets from emigrating to another country for at least ten years after they'd left their posts.

After London, I sensed that Roald and I were now entering an increasingly dangerous and difficult phase. This feeling was further exacerbated when several people in Washington warned me that rumors were circulating in Moscow about us. My friends could not have known how terrifying this news was. If the Soviet authorities decided to take the rumors seriously and regard our relationship as a threat, the worst-case scenario, Roald told me, was that he would find himself in a car crash, a collision that would be made to look like an authentic accident. Somewhere between that scenario and a happy ending, was the third possibility—that they would deny Roald an exit visa and me an entry visa.

I was so desperate thinking about all this that on some nights I could barely sleep. I racked my brains to think of a way to confuse the authorities and lead them to believe that the rumors floating around were just that, only rumors.

One Sunday afternoon, as I was trying to take a nap, I had what I considered a brilliant idea. I thought, why not ask one of my male friends to stage an "engagement" with me? That would, at least, serve as a cover until Roald and I could straighten out the increasingly complicated situation we had put ourselves in.

Just before Christmas, I got a call from Sergei Ivanov at the Soviet Embassy. Although I liked him personally, I was more and more convinced that his

Embassy job was a cover for his work as a KGB agent. Suspecting that going in, I rarely hesitated to get together with him socially, since it was always an opportunity to gauge the "thinking" of the day.

On December 16, Sergei asked me to meet him at the Hay-Adams Hotel. Over lunch we discussed recent events, including the Armenian earthquake. Sergei told me that the disaster had had an unexpected benefit. He spoke solemnly, his ashen face lined with fatigue. "It has really put things into perspective," he said. "All the gossip, all the trivialities, all the rumors about who is doing what to whom just pales next to this tragedy. People are working together much better at the Embassy and there is a real sense of purpose.

"We're putting in sixteen-hour days," he added, "and still there is more to do."

Then Sergei asked me some friendly and seemingly benign questions about my health and my family. I had a sense that he had been instructed to feel me out, so I decided to encourage him a bit, knowing full well that everything I said would, most likely, join the other volumes about me in my file. During this small talk, I found the opportunity to tell him that I had the reputation in my family of being very stubborn and determined.

Sergei said without irony, "I can imagine. You have a beautiful smile, but I bet you can be pretty tough."

I nodded with mock seriousness. We both laughed.

Then, looking at me attentively, he said, "You have a successful career and you have made a name for yourself. Does a woman like you ever think of getting married again?"

"Sometimes I think about it, but it's highly unlikely," I told him. "I work such long hours and travel so much that when I'm home—outside of office hours—I'm with my daughters. There really hasn't been much time to settle down and date anyone. Maybe that's just another way of saying I value my freedom."

We talked a good deal about marriage, and I told him a little of my background. Sergei returned our discussion to the topic of freedom again. I was surprised by the passion with which he spoke about what it meant to him. "You have no idea what it is like to have to take instructions for everything—to have no real right to do what you want. I value every little bit of freedom I get—from my bosses, from my wife—freedom is precious," he said with great emphasis, "*precious.*"

He smiled. And I returned it broadly.

Sergei suddenly became pensive, full of observations about life. "But you certainly find time for reading and learning a lot about issues. It is impressive that Dr. Sagdeev, for instance, one of our most brilliant scientists, values your views the way he does."

It was indeed flattering, I told Sergei. "Sagdeev has a great mind, and we have many similar interests—including those related to space. It makes for many lively discussions."

Perhaps the most interesting part of our conversation centered around Sergei's next observation, which I had been waiting for him to make. "Sagdeev is a dissident of sorts, you know," he said.

"Really? Would you call him that?" I asked. "It strikes me that he is both constructive and affirmative. Isn't that what *perestroika* is trying to encourage?"

Sergei passed over that comment and moved to the heart of the matter. "But such a talented man as Dr. Sagdeev is being underutilized at the moment. Now that he is no longer director of IKI, surely he will want to run for the presidency of the Academy—or maybe he is interested in another job."

"What job do *you* think Sagdeev would be best suited for?" I queried.

"I think he should put himself forward as head of the Science and Technology Division of the Central Committee. That would be my advice."

I did not respond, but inwardly I was laughing. Wait until Roald hears that! It was a powerful position, but only apparatchiks need apply!

"Sagdeev tells me that he wants to do science again," I offered. "Maybe that job would be too administrative."

"Maybe so," Sergei said, "but if he wants to concentrate on science, it doesn't explain why he yielded his nomination to the Presidium of the Academy to Sakharov. It just doesn't add up. There must be more to it than that."

Now I could see what Sergei was driving at. My relationship with Roald was under intense scrutiny—and now Sergei was probing to see how much I had had to do with Roald's decisions.

"I understand that creative science takes a great deal of concentration. Perhaps that was his reason," I ventured vaguely.

We finished lunch on a very friendly note, and I volunteered to assist with Armenian earthquake-relief efforts. I told Sergei I would think carefully about what I might persuade the Eisenhower Institute to do on that topic.*

---

* Eventually Roald and I brought a delegation of Soviet earthquake specialists to the United States to exchange information with their American counterparts about the Armenian and San Francisco quakes, the latter taking place almost exactly a year after the former.

Roald's mood, the political situation, and now my lunch with Sergei were all crowding in on me. But the worst part of it was our separation. I desperately missed being with Roald, and I worried about his safety all the time. I wrote in my diary sometime that month:

There is no way to gain any insight into this situation from such a distance. We are again cut off from one another with no communication. It feels like a death—the total and complete severance from a loved one. It is going to take great courage and strength to pull this off—no matter what happens.

15 : Rowing in Rough Waters

Moscow was in pandemonium when I arrived in the middle of January 1989. Nominations for the Congress of People's Deputies were under way. A third of the candidates would be elected through "social organizations," and the others would be directly elected from regional constituencies around the country. From that body of 2,250 members, which would probably meet only once or twice a year, a smaller Supreme Soviet of 542 deputies would be selected to run the country's daily affairs. The Congress would serve as a kind of constitutional convention, though the real work would be carried out by the Supreme Soviet, whose members were to be elected from one-fifth of the Congress.

Since the process had begun, Sagdeev had been told by institutes and organizations all over the country that he had been nominated as their candidate. Because of the different nomination venues, his name was also being put forward in other regional channels, all of which would meet at different times to narrow their list of final candidates. However, most of the organizations that named him were tied in some way to the Academy of Sciences, which had been given twenty-five slots to fill. In addition, the local Party bosses in Moscow, remembering all the troubles they had had only months before with Roald's election to the Nineteenth Party Conference, decided to preempt the potential pressure from their constituency and nominate Roald for the popular vote in their district.

I was staying at the Cosmos Hotel on this trip, a teak-and-plastic attempt at a modern Western commercial hotel. Somewhere near the tacky shops of second-rate souvenirs, Roald found a restaurant where we could have a light supper.

It had been six difficult weeks since I had last seen him. There was so much news to catch up on. After we placed our orders, Roald told me an extraordinary tale about a recent visit he had made to the Kremlin. Gorbachev had asked a hundred members of the intelligentsia to meet with him at the Central Committee building. Apparently so exasperated with the burgeoning power of the press and the outspoken position of the intelligentsia, he had decided to take them to task, to plead with them to unite in the cause of *perestroika*. He begged them to end what he thought were critical and unconstructive attitudes which in his estimation threatened their socialist society.

Lowering his voice, Roald described for me the details of this extraordinary gathering. It had started in the morning and lasted well into the evening. The entire Politburo sat behind Gorbachev, yet no one but Mikhail Sergeiivich spoke.

"What do you mean no one but Gorbachev spoke?"

"For seven hours, Gorbachev carried the meeting," Roald said. "He took questions from the audience, but imagine what the Politburo members must have felt like, sitting there literally all day listening to Gorbachev go on."

"Did it take seven hours for him to get his point across?" I asked.

"To tell you the truth, I am not sure what his point was," he said, lowering his voice still further. "It was like being a schoolboy again and being lectured by a teacher for misbehaving. At one point, he even lost his temper and said, 'If you think you can do better, here, come try this job.' "

We were all too aware of how much of *perestroika*'s success depended on the calm and the wisdom of one man, and Gorbachev's general attitude and behavior would also be decisive for "our project."

Although I was uneasy about Roald's report on Gorbachev's mood, I was even more troubled by his own apparent plans. He was actively considering running in the elections. Roald's ambivalence about his nomination for the Congress concerned me greatly, but I was not surprised by it. Given the historic changes under way in his country and his growing influence within the progressive camp, I could see that his political activity might be a form of that repentance about which he had spoken on the very first walk I had taken with him at Chautauqua two years before.

As admirable as that was, I was desperate to get some clear signal about what he'd do with respect to the elections. I knew he was under tremendous pressure to run, but he had often told me that given our relationship, it was critical not to accept an official position. What would our future be now?

Roald reiterated how much he missed me and how much he wanted to proceed with all we had discussed. He was no longer concerned, he said, that his nomination and eventual election to the Congress of People's Deputies would have a negative effect on "our project." Indeed, he thought it would give him a "play ball" status, and then we could get on with our plans.

"It is fine if you really want to do this," I said, "but I remember the days when you told me you wanted nothing more than to do science. There are no options closed right now. Why don't you take some time and think as broadly as you can about what you want to do with your life at this stage—from science to politics? It all gets down to what *you* want. It is *your* life," I added.

Roald and I ate in silence for some minutes.

"What I really want more than anything else," he said confidently, "is to do my work as an international scientist and be a citizen of the world. I have never been a politician."

I didn't say anything more. I left his words as they were: a clear and unencumbered statement.

That night, burdened with jet lag and relentless worries, I woke up in the early hours of the morning in tears. I was surprised at my state—I could not remember what I had been dreaming, and I did not know, at first, why I was crying.

That afternoon Roald and I went to "Belgrade" to do more book taping. When we settled into the sanctuary of the little flat, I decided to tell him what had happened. Over a modest supper of sausage and bread, I described how I had woken in the middle of the night in tears, convinced he was being reckless. On the one hand, I very much wanted him to make his decisions freely, based on his genuine desires, but there were problems enough associated with his being connected to the military-industrial complex; if he were to become a member of the Congress, our relationship would be absolutely untenable. My position was based on a simple formula: if I were a U.S. senator, on the Armed Services or Foreign Relations Committee, say, there would be no way politically that I could be married to either General Zhukov's or Nikita Khrushchev's son or grandson. Roald, I figured, would find himself in even more pronounced circumstances.

Roald protested, saying that the Congress of People's Deputies would be little more than honorific, meeting only once a year to set broad policy.

I told him I thought he was naïve.

"Naïve?" he said curiously.

"Naïve," I repeated. "Do you really think if you get in that you will escape being tapped for the Supreme Soviet? That would be an offer you couldn't refuse, especially since you have declined all the other positions."

I told him about Sergei's observations that he was underutilized. Others in the U.S.S.R. might have accused Roald of "parasitism."

"Furthermore," I said passionately, "a full-time position in the Supreme Soviet is completely inconsistent with being an international scientist. How can you be a serious scientist and fight the revolution at the same time? Politics alone take so much time there'd be nothing left for science."

I told him that his happiness was the most important thing of all to me. I promised that I would support him whatever direction he chose—even if it excluded me—but only as long as I was convinced that his decision was genuinely his and not the result of outside pressure.

Roald was already with me. "You're right," he said, "I must act now. We had always said that official positions must be avoided. The only thing I can say is that I was swept up in the tide of the moment. I was busy being the hero of my own book!"

He stood up and began to pace around the kitchen floor. "Tomorrow," he said, "I will write an urgent letter to the Party boss of Moscow and tell him I have to decline his proposal to be their candidate. I will say I am going through a divorce and my personal life precludes it."

The very next day, I arrived at Roald's office just as he was giving his letter to the Party representative in IKI—for urgent delivery to the district Party headquarters.

"It is done," he said cheerfully when we were alone in his office.

Despite his brightness, it was a sobering move. The die had been cast. There could be no more speculation. The authorities, at least the local ones, had now been alerted by Sagdeev himself that his personal life was in transition.

Our talk, he told me, had been "going round and round" in his head. He could think of nothing else. "If I am going to do as you say," he said half jokingly, "that means we will no longer feed the monsters." In a bugged room he could say no more, but I knew he meant the monsters of the Soviet system: the monsters of coercion and control.

As we had decided not to go to "Belgrade" that evening, Roald suggested that we walk on Lenin Hills instead. Ivan patiently dropped us at the corner and waited while we had our ritual walk, up the long promenade toward the university and then back toward an ancient Russian Orthodox church.

"From now on," Roald said emphatically, "we should be talking and thinking about the best-case scenario."

He started to outline how our life would be. Given the age of my children, we would have to base ourselves in the United States while they were in school: "We will travel together, write a book every two years, buy a country house, and have the children coming and going—and later their children. And we will come to the Soviet Union for the summers. I will find a position at a university and give public lectures. And you will be my lover, my agent, my collaborator, my friend, and my wife."

What about his status as a Soviet citizen? He said he could see himself as a goodwill ambassador explaining his country's policy, "except," he said, "when it conflicts with my conscience."

Although I contemplated the coming months with some trepidation, our objectives were clear. Roald would make an effort to find a position with an American university, and we would try to secure permission to come and go. Then if, for some reason, the state wouldn't give him permission to travel, I would stay with him in Moscow. But I emphasized to him again that I would never agree to live in Moscow unless the choice was freely made.

The next day we asked Ivan to drop us at the Belgrade Hotel and Roald told him that we were going in for a bite to eat. We asked him to return at 7:00 p.m. As soon as Ivan had disappeared, we walked down the alleyway into the courtyard of Roald's apartment building, past the *babushkas*, and silently up in the elevator. Roald fumbled for his key, and the dogs in the adjacent apartment started to bark. The pounding in my throat did not subside until we were safely behind the closed door of his flat.

Roald put the kettle on for a cup of tea and we both began to relax. It felt different to be here: the first major step had been taken in our drive to be together. We were both excited but wary about what the coming months would bring.

"I am glad I sent that letter," Roald said confidently. "If I had taken those nominations, later they would have felt cheated—like I had misled them and used them as a cover for our relationship. Directness is the best course."

Unfortunately it was not so simple. It had occurred to me, in the intervening day, that Roald had sent only one letter to the Party organization. "When the other nominating bodies—at the Academy, for instance— realize you haven't been picked as a candidate, surely they will put your name on their slate," I ventured.

"Don't worry," Roald said soothingly, "I'll just say that I'm running through another organization. And in the end, when I haven't been elected, my enemies will get the credit for using tricky methods to stop me."

I doubted this would work. The government would then be under pressure to find a position for Roald and make him an offer he *really* couldn't refuse. I recounted again the surrealistic conversation I had had with Sergei Ivanov. "The very fact I was being questioned as I was indicates the state's interest in keeping you occupied. In fact, I rather felt like I was being interrogated."

Roald looked at me seriously, as if this word had triggered some deeper thought. "I could never and would never betray you, Susan, no matter what happens."

Despite these troubling questions, those January days were idyllic in many ways. Roald and I worked very hard on the book, and the intimacy and the freedom afforded to us at our "Belgrade" hideaway gave us the precious time we needed to confirm in our own minds that the step we had taken was the right one. "Those moments," as I was later to write in my journal, "were intensely happy, among the happiest in my life."

Occasionally I worried that Roald was giving up too much. But when I voiced this concern, he pushed the notion aside. "As long as you are confident in your feelings for me," he said, "I will never regret it. Remember what I said about the Nobel Prize. You are my greatest discovery. I don't need the Congress of People's Deputies or the Supreme Soviet or the Nobel Prize, I need you."

In fact, our work together on Roald's book had fulfilled an unexpected purpose. Hearing him speak eloquently and at length about his past not only reaffirmed my conviction that he was an extraordinary man but also reassured me that his desire to do creative science was genuine. I was moved by the reverence with which he spoke of his mentors in science. Recounting his early years in the controlled-fusion program and his relationship with such great figures as Lev Landau and Peter Kapitsa brought a shine to his eyes. I did not see that look at all when he spoke about political matters. The creativity of science fueled his passion for competition and for sharing.

Unlike in science, he would tell me, the best people in politics do not necessarily rise the highest and the fastest.

We did little else in those days but work on the book, with the exception of attending a foundation board meeting and a dinner with the Sakharovs for Moscow Tribune members. The Moscow Tribune was one of the first so-called non-formal political groups to blossom during *perestroika*, also, perhaps, the most radically progressive; Yuri Afanasiev, * Andrei Sakharov, Yuri Karyakin, an internationally recognized scholar on Dostoevsky, Roald, and others had given it form, and they met regularly to discuss politics and strategies for promoting a progressive agenda. There was deep concern in this group about the progress of *perestroika*, and more than a small measure of dissatisfaction with Gorbachev's political direction. All of them faulted him for flirting too much with the conservatives and for not decisively pursuing democratization and economic reform.

Seven of us sat around the kitchen table in the Sakharovs' apartment that evening. Although I couldn't understand everything being said, attending such a gathering was an unforgettable experience for any Westerner. Everyone talked at once, the telephone rang constantly, and conversation miraculously lurched forward amid the confusion. Emotions ran high, and each outburst was punctuated by satirical humor, usually directed at the authorities but always making light of the people's lot in life, however hard or tragic it was.

Elena Bonner and I spent some time alone in the kitchen when the others had retired to the sitting room. I admired her for her passionate concern for her country and for her unflagging devotion to Andrei. She complained about Gorbachev's unwillingness to listen to what the intelligentsia had to say. And she expressed dark pessimism about everything from the food shortages to the "appalling" handling of the Armenian earthquake.

Listening to Elena and watching the change coming over Roald, I began to sense that freedom, as we Westerners conventionally think about it, was not the driving force behind their political energies. They were fighting to build a civil society. Governmental restrictions, in their frame of reference, did not necessarily make a person unfree. The people I knew in the Soviet

---

* Yuri Afanasiev was one of the most radical reformers of the *perestroika* period. As rector of the Institute of Historical Archives, he used his platform as a historian to attack the Communist government for everything from Stalinism to the cover-up of the Molotov-Ribbentrop pact. In 1987, Afanasiev addressed a Carnegie Soviet Study Group, of which I was a member, and told us that the Soviet Union had done more to falsify its history than any other country on the face of the earth. In 1987, this was extremely radical indeed.

Union—particularly the Moscow Tribune crowd—had rich inner lives that had flourished even during the most difficult political times. In this inner life, you could think and feel anything that you wanted. This world was beyond the reach of the authorities, and as hard as they might try, they could do nothing that could take it away.

This was not an unarticulated concept for the Soviet people. They have a phrase for it, *vnutrennaya ssylka,* "internal immigration" or "self-imposed exile," to which they retreated when they could not participate, in good conscience, in state-sponsored rhetoric. They went into immigration inside of themselves.

I was deeply impressed by this notion. Roald and I often talked about the liberation that comes from being prepared to give up outside approval, even material security, in order to forge one's own way. And now those ideas had a very big effect on the emotional preparation I was making, within myself, for the months to come.

The problem in the Soviet Union remained that at the point you achieved internal freedom, the hand of the regime still, most regrettably, controlled your freedom of movement—and this issue was by far of greatest concern for us personally.

During one of my restless nights in Moscow, I wrote down a set of operating principles for myself, to guide me through our new set of circumstances.

- The U.S.S.R.'s "travel threat" to its citizens is like dangling the prospect of prison over people's heads. I can't condone having R.Z.S. in prison.
- If the U.S.S.R. wants to join the civilized world, it must adopt civilized policies.
- I am not going to live without protest in Moscow unless R.Z.S. is treated as a free person.
- If we go forward, R.Z.S. must trust that I will never give up on him and I will make fighting for R.Z.S. my priority.
- I am not going to think about the Eisenhower Centennial anymore.

My earlier idea to stage an engagement with one of my American friends was not on the list. I would have to find a more moral if less creative way to provide protection for Roald. I respected my male friends too much to drag them into this mess, and I would have to be solely responsible for my actions.

When I showed Roald my list, he loved my impassioned outburst. Taking my hand, he said, "So now we are rowing the same boat in the rough waters."

Roald's letter to the Party boss of Moscow did not stem the tide; as I had predicted, his name continued to be put in nomination all over the country. After Sakharov, he had the highest number of nominations, far exceeding the next largest.

Several hours before my departure, however, we learned that the Presidium of the Academy, authorized to cull the nominations and select a list for the ballot (which would be confirmed by the Academy's full membership), announced that they had rejected Andrei's and Roald's nominations.

The Presidium's reasons for eliminating Sakharov's name were easy to imagine, but the motives for rejecting Roald's were more subtle and interesting. Ever since Roald's tenure in Siberia at the Institute of Nuclear Physics at Akademgorodok in the 1960s, he was perceived to pose a political threat to Guri Marchuk, who had also been with him in Novosibirsk. As the current president of the Academy, Marchuk still feared him as a potential rival, and believed that his election to the Congress of People's Deputies would enhance his political position and perhaps serve as a stepping-stone to Marchuk's own job.

Roald believed that Marchuk had become more concerned about this possibility since he had relinquished his position at the Space Research Institute. For Marchuk, it would have been inconceivable to leave one's job for any other reason except promotion. So no doubt he worried that liberal Politburo members like Alexander Yakovlev would try to oust him and sponsor Roald for the Academy presidency.

I had the impression that Roald was quite relieved when he heard about his candidacy's rejection. It carried with it some honor or, if not honor, at least the comfort of not having to refuse the position directly.

I was on the airplane for London when I ran into a fellow foundation board member, Frank von Hippel, a professor at Princeton University. He had attended an election-related press conference before leaving Moscow. During it, Roald, whose respect for most members of the Academy Presidium I knew to be pretty low, couldn't resist getting his digs in—attacking the Presidium as a "dictatorship of mediocrities." He had then made the solemn pronouncement that he would not run for the Congress of People's Deputies from any other organizational or regional venue. He was a scientist, he said, and since the Presidium had rejected his candidacy, that was that.

I looked out the aircraft window. It was already dark, but occasionally I could see the lights of some distant Soviet city. Was I hearing Frank correctly? If Roald had done this, it seemed to me, he and I were at least in one respect "home free."

With Minister of Culture Vasily Zakharov (far right), with whom I tried to negotiate the Rostropovich concert

Giving a speech during the Institute's project on exchanges

Andrei Kokoshin (now Russia's first Deputy Minister of Defense), Sagdeev, and I in my kitchen. Would he launch a preemptive strike?

Evgeny Velikhov, chairman of the Survival Fund, later the International Foundation

Sakharov (at right) with Sagdeev and me

The dinner meeting on our first night in Paris, March 1988. Roald signed it later: "Please, Susan, take our *GLASNOST* more seriously, May 3, 1988"

Roald in a photo I took on our last morning together in Paris. I thought he seemed sad and aloof, and I learned later that he was already working on how to resolve our future

...gdeev in November 1988 with William
...bster, then director of the CIA. (I am in
... background.) Roald was overwhelmed
... the novelty of the encounter

...deev in the kitchen of "Belgrade I." It
... at this table that he told me about the
...leasant "warning" he received at a party

Gorbachev, speaking at the Nineteenth Party Conference in the summer of 1988, and responding to Roald's comments. Roald's advisory relationship with Gorbachev ended soon after

Evgeny Primakov (now director of Russian Foreign Intelligence) and I the Nuclear Free Forum in February 1987

...agdeev voting alone in the Supreme Soviet against the new anti-democratic law in October 1988

(from second on left) General Chervov, Arbatov, Sagdeev, Primakov, Velikhov, and others at a Geneva meeting before the 1985 summit

16 : Revolt in the Academy

I stayed in London for a few days to attend the unveiling of a statue of Granddad in Grosvenor Square, a very moving occasion at which Prime Minister Margaret Thatcher spoke. But events in Moscow were never far from my thoughts.

Within days I read that Sakharov was likely to accept the nomination of another constituency—a regional one, or perhaps one with another organization. As soon as that sank in, I knew immediately that Roald would be pressured to do the same. In fact, any moral arguments he might have used to avoid being nominated by another organization were weakened with the announcement that Sakharov had several under consideration.

When I reached the United States, I spoke to Roald on the telephone. He was uncommunicative about these unfolding events. When I mentioned that I had been surprised that Andrei, after his Academy rejection, had decided to run for the Congress through other channels, Roald replied dryly, "That was known while you were in Moscow."

Annoyed, I probed a little more, trying to get at his meaning. "There has been much activity since your departure and there are follow-ons to the developments that have taken place," he responded.

What was that supposed to mean?

Within twenty-four hours, at least three of my American friends, recently in Moscow, excitedly told me that Roald was now planning to run for Congress through non-Academy channels. Knowing that Roald and I were friends, no doubt each of them thought I would be thrilled. It was all I could do to keep my anxiety under wraps.

In the last days of January, Roald went to a conference in Davos, Switzerland, and when he arrived he called me to give me the telephone number of his hotel and make a plan to speak later in the day. Concerned that my telephone was not secure, I asked a close friend of mine, John Andrews, if he would let me use his apartment telephone. John had been immensely supportive of me throughout this nerve-racking period, and he graciously consented. Confident that Roald and I at least were talking on an untapped line, I raised the issue of these new nominations.

It was clear from Roald's voice that he was under great pressure to stay in the race, as Sakharov was. But he assured me that, despite this, he was sticking to his position that he would run only as an Academy candidate or not at all.

But things had become more complicated in my absence, he told me. A very active popular movement had formed in response to his situation: taking him at his word, an ardent and outspoken group of scientific workers were pressing the Academy to reopen their nominations procedure. Roald confessed that he was now backed into a corner. "If they succeed," he warned me, "I will have no option but to consent."

I gently assured him that I would do everything I could to support him, but I asked him about his desire to be a free international scientist—and a citizen of the world. I reminded him of the great tradition of his non-political mentors Lev Landau and Mikhail Leontovich. Our phone call was inconclusive, so we agreed to talk again.

I asked John if I could come to his apartment the following evening and call Sagdeev again in Switzerland. John, whom I trusted implicitly, agreed.

In our next conversation, Roald was mysterious, and his cryptic remarks made me upset and angry. It was our natural habit to talk in code, but it seemed very strange to do so when we knew the phones were not tapped. Roald told me, "Given the circumstances, the best scenario would be to base 'our project' part-time in Moscow."

My head was aswim with every possible interpretation of what he meant. We were presumably on an unbugged line, or were we? Was he telling me that he had been given a warning? Or was he hinting that he had decided to pursue a political career, that his followers had succeeded in persuading him to give up science and throw his full energies into the struggle?

"It will not be possible for me to co-chair such an important project in

Moscow with a Soviet official," I retorted firmly. But I was confused and miserable with uncertainty.

Nervously I scanned daily news reports from the Soviet Union. There were some interesting accounts of the battle raging within the Academy of Sciences over the Sakharov-Sagdeev fiasco. Most important was news of the internal movement to reinstate both men on the Academy ballot. As Roald had told me, the movement had emanated from Sagdeev's own institute, IKI, where radical young scientific workers had been the first to demand that the Presidium reconsider its final list. The Presidium had ignored the will of nearly half the members of the Academy of Sciences, using what the young scientists regarded as anti-democratic procedures. Despite more than forty petitions questioning the lawfulness of the election proceedings, the election commission appointed to investigate such complaints stated that the nomination procedure was "clearly an internal affair of the Academy."

Then, on February 4, an angry crowd of scientists staged a protest outside the Academy Presidium building. This band of nearly two thousand scientific workers was the first significant demonstration in Moscow during the *perestroika* era. The protesters carried banners that read "Send Marchuk to Siberia" and "Sakharov and Sagdeev for Congress," "We don't trust the Presidium," "We are the Academy too." The swelling crowd demanded that Marchuk come out to address the demonstrators. He was in the Presidium building at the time but did not appear, sending a representative to talk to the seething crowd instead.

This unprecedented demonstration frightened the Academy leadership, but Guri Marchuk stood his ground and refused to reopen the nominating process. But the radical young scientists had tasted the power of the streets, and they, too, were not to be deterred. Within days, they began a campaign to encourage Academy members to abstain from voting on the list of candidates that would appear on the ballot. If enough people abstained, the Presidium's candidates would not get more than 50 percent of the vote— the number needed to be elected to the Congress.

A little more than a week later, for some instinctive reason, I decided to call Louis Friedman, executive director of the Planetary Society and a personal friend. He had just returned from Moscow, where he had been part of the international team monitoring the results of Phobos.

"Despite a small case of jitters," Lou told me, "the backup craft is producing results, and everyone feels there's a chance that they'll still have a very successful project. Scientists from all over the world are in Moscow right now analyzing the data being transmitted back from space. Morale is high," he concluded, and then added, "It was helped greatly by the demonstration."

Mere mention of the demonstration and the election gave me an adrenaline rush. With an effort to sound calm and nonchalant, I asked evenly, "Has Sagdeev taken on another constituency?"

"No," Lou replied, "Roald's position is that he will not stand for Congress unless he is nominated by the Academy. Since they won't reopen the nominations, that means, I guess, he won't be going to the Congress."

But an article in *Moscow News* by Andrei Kuteinikov, entitled "How Will the Academy Vote?" made it clear that things were not so simple. It appeared that Roald's stand—intended to liberate himself from the election—might have done more than anything else to bring about this fateful confrontation between Soviet scientific workers and the Academy's leadership.

> At their meeting, most delegates from the Moscow-based institutes said they had been asked by their colleagues to reject all the candidates nominated by the Academy Plenum, i.e., to cross out their names on the ballot . . .
>
> If the representatives of research institutes reach agreement on this key issue, it is highly probable that the Academy will fail to fill the seats allotted to it. Even if one of the Academy's seats remain empty, as a result of the conference voting, additional candidates may be proposed, including those rejected by the Plenum on January 18.

Within days, newspaper headlines boldly proclaimed that Sakharov had declared that he would not accept a nomination outside the Academy of Sciences. Roald's position had obviously influenced Andrei's decision, which now upped the ante considerably and most probably assured an effective boycott of the election.

I was exhausted and tired of reading between every line of newspaper copy to come out of Moscow. Intentionally or not, Roald was journeying down a dangerous road—made all the more treacherous because of my presence in his life. Before long something would have to give.

The following week I made preparations to go once again to Moscow. I had business to transact, and as we had agreed, Roald and I were going to set aside four days to complete critical sections of his book. The night before my departure, I wrote in my journal:

> I am anxious that he do what he *wants* to do. But from where I am sitting it looks like he has boxed himself into a corner: he is challenging the Academy as a "legitimate way" to decline to participate. But what happens if the boycott is successful, and the action that he and Sakharov have taken forces out Marchuk? He will then have to put up or shut up. This is the part that makes me nervous. However, I have decided definitively that if he is nominated, our relationship will be put on ice—for who knows how long—maybe permanently.
>
> I feel the urgency to act because I think that conservative forces are gaining power and more and more people are getting the drift that there is something going on between us. Back before Roald took on the whole of the establishment, it might not have been the same worry. But now I am concerned that someone will use our relationship as a way to damage his reputation; to hurt him.

The day before I left for Moscow, I was so anxious to see Roald that I could hardly contain myself. But then it seemed I was punished for my impatience: my plane was delayed on the runway in Washington, and eventually the airline authorities told us we wouldn't be able to leave. Those of us in business class and first class were put up at an airport hotel at the airline's expense, and given tickets on the Concorde for the following day. We arrived in London in time to go to bed again, but despite the inconvenience, I was at least five time zones closer to Moscow.

Roald met me at the airport with Elena Loschenkova, and we all had our customary cup of coffee in the VIP lounge while waiting for my luggage. Both of them described the Academy fight in vivid and sometimes hilarious detail. As dusk settled in, we made our way to the mammoth Rossiya Hotel perched on the edge of Red Square. By the time we had reached it, the city was already dark.

Roald told Ivan to wait in the car, and he and Elena took me up to my room—a rather pleasant two-room suite—on the side overlooking Red Square. Just as I looked out the window, fireworks began miraculously to explode. Colors erupted over the onion domes of the Kremlin over and over again . . . brilliant blues, reds, and greens. Roald said to me proudly, "I ordered the fireworks for your arrival."

Despite the joy of seeing Roald and the amusement of this joke (the fireworks were actually for Red Army Day), there was nothing to celebrate.

I had arrived in Moscow resolute, and I told him so: if he was going to run for the Congress of People's Deputies, then I would have to end my relationship with him. This might seem harsh, but to continue was to court disaster. My presence in his life could only hurt him, and that was unbearable to me.

Roald listened carefully and said very little. "We must not make rash decisions," he said. "Stay close. Things will begin to clarify themselves."

I had my own meetings scheduled during those weeks, and I saw people I knew from before I'd met Sagdeev. On one of the evenings when I was busy, Roald went to the sixtieth birthday party of his good friend Fazil Iskander, a colorful Abkhaz writer. As Roald later told me, one of the intelligentsia's most well-known figures approached him warmly that evening. Obviously the worse for alcohol, this man—let's call him Anatoly Gleschenko—gave his loose tongue rein. Putting his arm tightly around Roald, he glowingly and emotionally spoke about how much their friendship meant to him. "Friends should look out for each other," Gleschenko continued. Then he dropped the bombshell: "My American friends tell me you are in love with Susan Eisenhower," he said softly but seriously. "Think about it carefully before you decide to marry. The cultural differences are too great, and she will find that she won't want to live here. It can't possibly work unless you intend to leave the country." This was his euphemism for defection.

Roald, unsettled, told me that he did not have much of a relationship with Gleschenko and thought it odd that he should take it upon himself to offer such unsolicited advice. Roald wondered aloud if the authorities had, perhaps, put him up to it.

Roald also confessed that he had noticed that we were regularly followed by a distinctive black car with a long, conspicuous antenna.

"Only the highest-level functionaries and the KGB have such cars," he noted. They were following him, and us, now on a fairly regular basis. Also during this time, the tires on Roald's black Volga had blown out or had flattened several times while he and his driver were on the road. Each time Ivan managed to stop the car smoothly. And each time the cause of the incident was suspiciously the same: a large rather rare screw was imbedded in the tire. Ivan and Roald were sure it was foul play. Such nails never would be routinely picked up on the street. Ivan expressed relief that he had detected problems early on. If the blowouts had occurred while they were traveling faster, he'd have lost control of the vehicle. Either these were KGB attempts to create a car accident or they were meant to be harassing "calling cards." Either way, they were dangerous signals, not to be ignored.

Roald and I did not know whether the warnings related to his political activities, our relationship, or both. We suspected probably both. Our situation seemed to be closing in on us.

With Roald's future—and ours—still so uncertain, our need to be together became more and more acute. Our brief visits to "Belgrade" gave us some privacy and a chance to talk, but the separations were nearly intolerable, and we decided to remedy the situation. Despite the obvious risks—and Roald's heightened visibility—we decided for the first time to say, "The hell with it." Solemnly promising "not to feed the monsters" anymore, we agreed that I would stay with Roald at his apartment. Unfortunately, this strike for independence did not alter the fact that we still had to cover our trail to do so.

For me to stay with Roald overnight at his apartment meant that I had to leave the hotel with my door key still with me, since keeping it would indicate to the hotel staff that my room was indeed occupied. I went through the motions of pretending to stay in my room, even though I was nowhere in its vicinity. But we had no illusions about how long that ruse could last.

In the mornings, when I came back to the hotel, I was always in a state of alert and terror, maybe like the feelings a guilty teenager has who has sneaked off in mischief and hopes to avoid a severe parental reckoning. But here the stakes were incalculably higher.

We were so frightened of arousing suspicion that one day I feared our luck had run out. We were in the kitchen of "Belgrade" drinking some tea and doing some taping when we heard the sound of a key in the lock of our door. Roald jumped up to see who was entering the apartment. He was gone a minute or two, and when he returned he told me, without comment, that it had been his landlady. He had somehow managed to get rid of her.

Apart from that one terrifying attempt at intrusion, in some crazy way those four days we spent together at "Belgrade" were worth the risk. It didn't matter that the little flat was cramped and dusty; we were making memories, something that no one could take away from us.

17 : Fear No Evil

Over Easter I took the children on a well-deserved vacation to visit my sister Anne in Florida. Happily we sat on the beach, gossiped, and watched the sun set over the Caribbean. I felt confident and strong, if a little anxious about the news that the Academy election had been a standoff. Sagdeev's scientific workers had managed to beat the system and persuade enough people to reject the official slate of candidates. That meant Sagdeev and Sakharov were back in the running.

Then, to my surprise, about halfway into my vacation my office telephoned from Washington to say that Roald had just phoned from Sweden. They gave me his number and told me he wanted me to call him.

Roald had been nervously waiting for his spacecraft's encounter with Phobos. The date had been postponed slightly to find the optimum moment to change the trajectory of the craft—and Roald had decided that keeping himself busy was a must. He rented a white tie in Sweden and joined his scientific colleagues at a gala bash to celebrate the two hundred and fiftieth anniversary of the Royal Swedish Academy of Sciences, of which he was a foreign member. I took it as good news that he was still, apparently, allowed to make such foreign trips.

Roald stopped me immediately from asking any questions about the Academy election. Instead, he told me that he had tragic news. On his way to Sheremetyvo, his institute had gotten word that electronic contact with IKI's second spacecraft, in orbit around Mars, had been lost. Alec Galeev, IKI's new director, told Roald to go on to Stockholm—nothing more could be done. It was important, he said, that Sagdeev hold his head up in the international community.

I could tell from Roald's tone that he was heartsick. I offered what support I could, but other topics would have to wait until we saw each other again. "Only four more days," he said before saying goodbye.

I spent the rest of that vacation deeply engrossed in Natan Sharansky's book, *Fear No Evil*. It was a riveting tale about his arrest and imprisonment for Zionist activities in the Soviet Union. For me, perhaps the most spell-binding part of his story concerned his relationship with the KGB. It had tried to break Sharansky in countless ways, to get him to compromise and contradict himself accordingly. I was shocked by all the tricks it had used to intimidate him—as well as the lengths it had gone to in order to tape his conversations and harass his friends. I was particularly troubled to read that his conversations with Robert Toth, a *Los Angeles Times* reporter, had been bugged in a car. Roald and I had always been very careful about what we had said in his official black Volga, but we had had many involved conversations in his own Lada—on the assumption that it was probably pretty safe. Then I remembered the incident a year earlier when his Lada had temporarily died at the top of Lenin Hills. I wondered if perhaps a device had been affixed to it at that time. A shudder passed through me.

There was a general belief in the West that *glasnost* and *perestroika* had brought an end to KGB surveillance and interference in ordinary domestic life in the Soviet Union. In fact, many members of the Soviet intelligentsia complained that the KGB seemed to be gaining strength, if anything. As one of our friends said to me with impeccable Soviet logic, "You don't think that Gorbachev would unleash all these [political] forces without knowing exactly what was going on everywhere in society, do you?"

Vitaly Korotich, the brave and innovative editor of *Ogonyok* magazine, told us that, just about this time, he went to his native Kiev to give a speech, after which he took the night sleeper back to Moscow. On his return, he was told that Gorbachev wanted to meet with him at the Kremlin. He arrived at noon for this unexpected tête-à-tête, to find that Gorbachev had in his possession tape transcripts of the speech and other conversations he had had while in Kiev. According to Korotich, Gorbachev, in a state of irritation and exasperation, said acidly, "You think I don't know what you say about me?" In typical Soviet style, Korotich displayed some humor on the subject, noting that some poor guy had to stay up all night processing the tape transcripts.

Our anxiety about the KGB was consistent with worries about the Soviet political struggle. Too much rested in too few hands. Gorbachev, no longer revered as the engine of change in the country, had become an unknown quantity—and one who caused a great deal of anxiety among those who were politically out on a limb.

I made a list of pros and cons, which I took on my next trip to Moscow. We were right back to square one with the elections, so it seemed to me we would have to revisit all the arguments and decide once and for all what Roald should do—or what I should do, for that matter.

I was no sooner on the ground in Moscow than I saw that the issue of Roald's candidacy was not the only thing I had to worry about.

After I had checked into my room at the Rossiya Hotel, Roald suggested that we take a walk. I knew he wanted to tell me something well out of electronic earshot. As we walked among the trees in a little park, ironically not far from the Central Committee building, he told me that the loss of Phobos had created a furor within the space community. Due to a technical error in the on-board computer, the spacecraft, like the one before it, had refused to respond to commands from the ground. Even though the loss of the two modules was the direct responsibility of the industry contractors, it was still a considerable blow to the prestige of the scientists running the project, and to their prospects for continued international cooperation.

Roald was bitter, all the more so since a wall of secrecy had descended on the records of the mission.

I listened carefully as we paced around the little square near the hotel. Roald told me somberly that a group of young engineers, working at the installations where the responsibility for the errors lay, had come to warn him that a cover-up was under way. "They told me everything—about how their installations had been falsifying the documents, and how this cover-up would give the complex's hierarchy the opportunity to use absurd arguments about the probable loss." (Meteors hitting the spacecraft were eventually "identified" as the cause of the loss—about as probable, Roald said, as colliding with an orbiting Loch Ness monster.)

"What did you say to these young men?" I asked calmly.

"I told them I would demand an international commission to investigate. We will have to provide an open framework for scientific cooperation or it will mean the end of the international collaboration I have spent so many years building."

The military-industrial powers in the U.S.S.R. would undoubtedly resist such an international commission strenuously. It was also perfectly clear that such a demand would bring down their full wrath on Roald's head. But I agreed with him: learning the truth was critical, not only so that those responsible would be made accountable, but also so that the scientific and engineering community could learn from their mistakes. Roald nodded with satisfaction that he had my support.

Making more enemies in this powerful sector of the Soviet elite would significantly increase the dangers to us, but it was Roald's moral and professional scientific obligation to pursue the truth. The fights over Phobos were not the first time he was in direct conflict with the barons of the complex. I knew the stories from our work on his book, the most sensitive parts always carefully taped in hotel rooms in third-country cities like Stockholm and London. Risks aside, there was a serious matter of principle at stake.

That afternoon we worked on the book some more, this time in his office. When we had finished, we had dinner and went to a concert. Afterward Roald and Ivan dropped me back at my hotel. Then, as had now become our habit since January, Roald was taken to "Belgrade," and after Ivan had gone, Roald came back to the hotel to pick me up in his own car.

The next morning, just before sunrise, we tiptoed up one flight of stairs to summon the elevator from the floor above—so we could avoid being seen by our neighbors. Then we took the elevator to the ground floor and silently closed the main door behind us. As was our habit, we tried to leave early so that Roald could get me back to my hotel well before I would be picked up for my morning meetings.

This morning, however, I noticed that the black car with the powerful big antenna was sitting in the circular drive of our building's inner courtyard. Roald walked quickly in the other direction, appearing not to notice the well-fitted vehicle. When we got into his orange Lada—after he'd put the windshield wipers in place and removed the steering wheel lock—I asked him if he had noticed the car. He nodded stiffly. "It is the car I have seen before," he said.

Within days tragedy struck again. On April 9, paramilitary troops killed a number of hunger strikers and demonstrators on the main square in Tbilisi, Georgia. News filtered in the next day, and that evening we had dinner with Yuri Osipyan, Elena Loschenkova, and Georgi Managadze. Although Georgi had not lived in Tbilisi for a long time, he was in constant contact with the Georgian community, and so was Elena, whose husband, Reso, was also Georgian.

Managadze arrived at the restaurant with his usual bottles of Georgian wine, but the atmosphere was somber around the candlelit table. He told us that he had learned on his most recent telephone call to Tbilisi that as many as twenty women had died, and hundreds more had been injured. Soviet troops under the command of General Igor Rodionov had used sharpened shovels to beat their victims to death. With great emotion, Georgi barely managed to add that there were rumors in Tbilisi that some kind of poisonous gas had also been used, not tear gas but something apparently more toxic.

Roald turned to me and took my hand. Tears were coming down his face. "Beaten with clubs and sharpened shovels, poisonous gas! . . ." he said with disbelief. As he spoke he wiped his cheeks, but the tears continued to fall.

Everyone at the table was stunned. How incongruous the horror of the Tbilisi massacre seemed with the democratic elections currently under way. We were sustained in some small way by the friendship and fellowship we all felt among us. There we were, as Managadze said with pride that evening—a Tatar, an Armenian, a Georgian, a Russian, and an American—"beloved friends." "And," he added, ". . . even when she is far away, we never forget Susan . . ."

As if all these incidents weren't enough, after dinner Yuri, as vice president of the Academy, went to find out about the election results. He came back and told the table triumphantly that as a result of the election rerun, Roald and Andrei had both been officially nominated by the Academy Presidium for the Congress of People's Deputies. Short of Armageddon, both men were assured election to the new body.

I joined everyone in toasting Roald. He lifted his glass tentatively. But he did not raise his eyes to meet mine.

These tumultuous events forced me in on myself. It was clear that Roald would be elected to the Congress unless his enemies made efforts to discredit him before the election. Would I be the tool they would use? I could take no more of this. As I carefully explained to Roald that very evening after dinner, it would be all but impossible for me to come to his defense if anything were to happen to him in the coming weeks. Even though he was separated, he was still legally married to someone else, so I would have only limited standing on which to protest on his behalf. All the delays in our plans had heightened the risk.

"If we are going to engage in increasingly dangerous activity, at least I want to be able to protect you if the worst happens," I said. He could always count on me, I assured him, but the time had come for us to back off for a while.

"All right," he said as we walked along the Moscow River near my hotel, "if you insist, I won't press you to come to 'Belgrade' tonight. But I will never give up. You will just have to start getting used to the idea of being married to a Soviet congressman."

I was silent.

"I want you to know that nothing has changed with me. And after the election is over, I will take whatever steps are necessary to fulfill the plans we have already decided upon."

I walked on.

"Don't forget you are my dearest friend."

I continued to walk.

He kept repeating, "You will just have to get used to being married to a Soviet congressman."

I felt a swell of internal resistance rise involuntarily in me. I wasn't so sure. Who said I had to get used to the idea? But I did not argue. I simply took my leave. This night, on my way to my hotel room, I collected my key from the floor lady and resigned myself to a fitful night's sleep.

The next day I left for Washington. Roald insisted on taking me to the airport. He talked most of the way, and I sat silently and listened.

"Look at what they did in Tbilisi, those bastards," he said with passion. "My country deserves more. If I am elected to the Congress, please try to look at it differently than you do now. The young scientists *demanded* that they be represented for once by decent people. I will serve a useful function if I can be that decent person—at least until their generation can take over. In the end it will be their revolution, anyway.

"We'll find a solution to this," he continued emphatically. "You are central to my happiness. We have reached the point of mutual necessity."

Those were the last words he whispered to me.

.   .   .

I saw Roald again in eleven days. By the time we met in Washington, in early May, he had already been elected to the Congress of People's Deputies.

During the days of our separation I had been tense and had felt under enormous pressure. My head was spinning. I seemed almost disoriented. In all their simplicity, Roald's words had stirred me profoundly. For once I was confident he was taking on this responsibility out of conviction, not coercion. This was deeply significant to me. No more ambivalence, no more waffling. The Tbilisi massacre seemed to have clarified his mind completely. He was right that the Soviet people deserved decency for once. They had earned it because they had not simply accepted what had been handed to them but had demanded something different. Roald's scientific constituency had demonstrated, even used persuasion, to change the outcome of the elections. Roald should be proud to serve them.

I understood that I would have to begin to make some changes in how I viewed Roald's new position—and how I would regard the consequences. I had carried my share of Cold War baggage in resisting the notion that I could be married to a Soviet legislator. But it appeared it was I who now lagged behind. In this Congress there would be Soviet legislators who were decent, honorable people who could stand proudly next to the most civilized and enlightened men and women anywhere. If I had now made that internal distinction for myself, couldn't I convince others? And if my own countrymen did not understand, should I care? Roald himself did not represent an ideology that the West abhorred. In fact, he was considerably more critical of his society and his leadership—indeed more anti-Communist— than vast numbers of respected people in the West.

What if the Soviet regime didn't approve of his marriage to me, should that stop us? With enough visibility and an unshakable faith in one another, wouldn't we eventually win?

Clarity slowly came to my mind. In my best moments I felt a sense of liberation. In my worst, only anxiety about the logistics of "getting there."

That evening I met him at his hotel. I couldn't believe that he was in Washington. After the scrutiny we had been put under in Moscow, I feared that perhaps they wouldn't let him leave, but now he was here. When we saw one another we hugged tightly, clinging to one another. Then I gave him a brown leather briefcase I had bought—to match the one he had given me in London. He was thrilled with the gift, and seemed to attach more importance to it than I ever would have imagined. He set the lock combination to the same numbers I had on my case.

"Let's go somewhere quiet where we can catch up," I said as we piled into my car. I had already made reservations at a quiet restaurant near Dupont Circle where I thought we could talk without interruption.

" 'Belgrade' is hell without you," Roald said to me as he fastened his seat belt. "I've been away from you for eleven days and I barely survived."

As I sat across from him at a small corner table, I thought it was funny seeing Roald in Washington—I had just been reading about him in the newspaper. Days before, he, Sakharov and others had proposed the establishment of a congressional commission to investigate the "Tbilisi massacre." He had a transcript of his proposal and a videotape of the massacre with him. Roald asked me to have it converted to the American format and distributed to the press. I took the tape and put it in my big shoulder bag. "It's important that there is a copy of this in the West," he said seriously.

Things were getting progressively more and more dangerous in the Soviet Union. The country was entering a pre-civil-war state, we surmised, and the level of hatred between groups was rising. This was an ugly and an unfortunate side effect of *glasnost*. No one was exempt from even the most outrageous accusations. Roald told me that during the election leaflets had been distributed saying: "Vote against Sakharov and Sagdeev: members of the Jewish Mason Mafia." Who knows who had been responsible for this? Roald had racked up an impressive list of enemies: the less progressive of Gorbachev's circle, the Academy hierarchy, the military-industrial complex, and now the army, because of this proposed Tbilisi commission.

Roald made an important point that evening. "We must go on as we were," he said confidently. "To stop would feed the monsters. They would be only too happy if they thought they were depriving us of our rare and precious moments together."

When we said good night, he put his arms around me and gave me an enveloping hug. As he held me, he whispered, "This is circle defense. When we are this way, no one can hurt us."

That night I wrote in my diary:

I have no doubts about what Roald means to me. It's odd but I *have* to be with him . . . However, I have no illusions about the dangers. I am sure that his position on the "lists" is getting more and more prominent. But it is clear that he is determined to do what he is doing . . . And now to figure out how to manage the next few months, and to clarify what I should do about my business and getting the book substantially under way.

The book tapes were now virtually transcribed. I had found, as I worked feverishly to complete them during those months, that they created some real emotional difficulties for me. Hearing Roald's voice all day long had not been particularly comforting. It made him seem so far away.

Now we were going to do one more tape, but this time it would be a video. When Roald had signed the book contract, he had agreed that he would promote it when it was published, but given recent developments, we decided we should take one more precaution before he left America. I arranged with a friend, a television anchorman and producer named Tim White, to do a videotape of Roald talking about the key stories in his book. This would be available if he were denied permission to leave the Soviet Union in the future. The seven-hour interview was both fascinating and poignant; in it Sagdeev talked about the future of his country, at times with a sense of hope and at times in near-despair. At the end of the session, all of us, including the cameramen, clapped. As we left, Tim gave me the videos and I put them in the safety-deposit box where I was keeping everything related to Roald's book.

This precaution was not unjustified. While in Washington, Roald and Vasily Aksyonov, a well-known Soviet writer and Roald's childhood friend, had talked about the peculiar conversation Roald had had with Anatoly Gleschenko at the Moscow party in February. Aksyonov was most interested in this tale and thought it was clearly a serious development. Gleschenko, he said, had been the one who had issued the "warning" to him before he was completely discredited and stripped of his citizenship in the late 1970s. But, as I noted in my journal, "it does not seem to be a warning that Roald intends to heed."

When I spoke to Roald on the telephone not long after his return to Moscow and asked him how things were, he said only that he was "sitting on top of a volcano." That was the last time I talked to him for almost a month. The Congress of People's Deputies—and coverage of it—put such a load on the few international telephone lines going in and out of Moscow that it was impossible to make a connection. We were totally cut off.

I read as much as I could about the Congress, and it seemed to me that the most significant aspect of it was that it was televised in its entirety. Apparently everyone in the U.S.S.R. was glued to their television set, watching the spectacle of live political debate. The deputies openly called for accountability for the Tbilisi massacre. Forthright criticism of Gorbachev and his policies was also aired, uncensored, for the first time. Accusations were even made openly that Gorbachev had built a luxurious dacha for himself in the Crimea during a period of severe national hardship. This was heady stuff for the new legislators, and by the end of the Congress few could have doubts about the power of television in transforming the national agenda.

In early June I went to London on business to visit one of my clients, a London-based shipping company. During my stay in England, I managed to get through on the phone to Moscow without any difficulty, and somehow Roald and I managed to talk twice a day. During one of those calls he conveyed to me—still in code—that he would be in Italy for a few days. I decided to go there on my way back to the United States.

It was a brief stop—less than twenty-four hours—but we were both delighted that I had managed to work out the visit and we basked in the five hours he managed to steal from his work. It was hard for me to tell what Roald's new status as a member of Congress really meant to him, but he was ebullient and full of what seemed to me to be self-confidence.

We ordered dinner in my hotel room and turned on the television to see if there was any news from Moscow on CNN. Instead, to our horror, the cameras took us to Tiananmen Square and dreadful scenes of Chinese armed forces in battle with student demonstrators. Roald and I watched transfixed. Comparisons were unavoidable between the tragedy in Beijing and the one in Tbilisi.

"April 9 and that terrible law that Gorbachev put through the old Supreme Soviet was the start of it all," he remarked. "Gorbachev uses the conservatives to implement what he wants—so he can blame *them*," he added with sudden bitterness. We wondered what those conservative Soviet forces would make of the instability in Beijing. "It will only strengthen the hand of those who think that things in the socialist world have gone too far," Roald sadly surmised.

These events underscored the necessity for us to act on our plans fairly soon. The timing of our wedding announcement would be very important. Roald suggested that it should be in the fall. "Our wedding," he said seriously, "will be a very big test for M.S.G."*

---

* M.S.G.—Gorbachev's initials.

18 : The Project Is Launched

Within a week of my return from England and Italy, I began to look for an apartment. In addition to the Soviet political situation, I was also worried about American attitudes. The depth and sincerity of America's new enthusiasm for things Soviet had not been tested. Was the Cold War really drawing to an end, or was this a period of détente—a breather in a longstanding hostility between the United States and the Soviet Union? I had made my commitment and was determined that we would overcome the political obstacles, even if I wasn't sure how my American friends, associates, business colleagues, let alone the press, would react. Would I be discredited? Would even my security be jeopardized? Would I, as I sometimes thought, find a burning cross on my front lawn?

It seemed to me prudent to rent an apartment during this period. My daughters and I would continue to live in our house in Bethesda, but I could use the apartment as a studio for writing and for putting up guests. It would always be available in case I felt the girls and I—and Roald, if he was with us—were no longer secure in our home. I found just the place about five minutes by car from my house.

Roald and I affectionately referred to the new apartment as "Belgrade II." But unlike our "Belgrade" in Moscow (now "Belgrade I"), this one came with a doorman and a security system if things went unfortunately sour.

This year, for a change, I was not unhappy that the girls would be spending their summer vacation in Rochester. I had always used their absence to do the bulk of my business traveling, and this year my schedule was arduous. In less than a month I went from Brazil to Moscow, with many points in between. Roald and I managed to see one another for a few brief days in the South of France, while he was doing a two-week stint at the observatory in Nice and I was in transit to London. I had been uncertain about turning up in such an illogical place, wondering if my arrival would pique suspicion. But Roald argued that we could finalize the plans for "our project" and finish any last-minute taping that needed to be done for the book. I reluctantly agreed.

When I arrived in Nice, I wondered how I could even have hesitated. I was stunned by the countryside, its interesting topography and its glorious colors. I had a room at a small hotel at the top of a mountain overlooking the Mediterranean Sea—not far from the observatory. In the morning, bells could be heard on the mountainside as the herder rounded the goats up for the day's grazing. The surrounding peaks were ablaze with bright flowers. Against the azure sea, one could see bleached villas and distant sailboats. Being in the South of France was a kind of culture shock—far from the pressure and the tension of Moscow and Washington. Being so wrapped up in the unfolding Soviet political drama, I had forgotten that people live this way: in serene settings, in quiet pursuits. But as soon as Sagdeev and I had the chance to sit down and do our final taping, all the frustrations and worries of Moscow returned.

Roald had been distressed by Gorbachev's performance during the Congress. The Soviet President had been bossy and determined to maintain control over everything. "But he couldn't hide it from the millions of viewers watching it on television," he said.

Roald had overheard Gorbachev tell one deputy, who'd gone to the microphone, to "sit down and shut up." "And a small share of his irritation was focused on me," he continued. "When I asked for the floor, Gorbachev said to me: 'What are you flashing? [It was his voting card.] Go back to your place and sit quietly.' "

Roald was already disillusioned with many of the decisions that had been taken with respect to the congressional committees. Vladimir Lapygin, head of the company that had made the on-board computer responsible for the loss of Phobos II, had been given the important chairmanship of the Committee on the Armed Forces and the KGB. This crucial committee was now effectively in the control of Lapygin's mentor, Oleg Baklanov, who had just been promoted from the Ministry of General Machine Building to the highest post in the military-industrial complex, Secretary of the Central Committee for Defense Industry.

Roald had had some serious confrontations with both Lapygin and Baklanov over the future of the Soviet space-shuttle program, Soviet SDI technology, and most recently the stonewalling of the Phobos records.

Roald lamented Lapygin's promotion, particularly as it had come at the expense of Evgeny Velikhov, who had been his friend for thirty years. Velikhov had been assured the chairmanship of this powerful committee, but something had gone very wrong. Gorbachev, who had once promised Velikhov the post, either could not or would not deliver it to his loyal but progressive supporter. Liberals suspected that he simply chose not to honor his pledge. But the appointment of Lapygin demonstrated that in these matters Oleg Baklanov had now gained the ear of the General Secretary and President.

All this was ominous enough, but the worst of it, from my point of view, was that oversight for the KGB and the armed forces was under the authority of a single committee, run by a major figure in the military-industrial complex. It was like putting the fox in charge of the chicken coop. The man was also one of Roald's most ardent adversaries.

Roald speculated that this new committee would try to impede the work of the Tbilisi commission, which, according to Roald, had been a real "eye-opener." Perhaps the worst part of this tragic story was that the government had consistently refused to tell the doctors treating the massacre victims what kind of chemical weapon they had used on the crowd. Any release of information on the substance's chemical composition would violate state secrets, they said. Even Foreign Minister Eduard Shevardnadze, himself a Georgian, could not pry this information loose.

Roald had missed one commission meeting during those hectic summer days, but he had assured the Georgians that he would make a special trip to investigate the events in Tbilisi personally. He was crucial to this process since he had voted against the law that had created the paramilitary forces eventually used against the Georgians. Several opposition groups said he was the only commission member they'd talk to.

When we met again, several weeks later in Moscow, Roald begged me to come to Georgia with him. He knew that I had business to do in the capital, but he persisted. "You can be the commission's international observer," he coaxed. "After all, you are on the human-rights committee of the foundation."

Although time was pressing, I could not refuse this opportunity. The

April events had deeply polarized the population of Georgia, radicalizing many of those who had initially supported the maintenance of good working relations with Moscow. As the victims of the massacre had been mostly women and young girls, the sense of violation was keener. It was as if a father had suddenly learned that his most precious daughter had been cruelly and intimately defiled. The collective reaction was nothing less than outrage and determination for revenge. As we would see with our own eyes, the impetus for Georgian statehood was resurrected from the deaths of these female martyrs.

As Roald had come to Tbilisi as an official of the commission and the Soviet Congress, we were put up at the Communist Party guest house—a modern stuccoed mansion set back in the hills beyond Tbilisi. Apart from the predictable pool table in the downstairs salon, this guest house had a luxurious roof deck that overlooked a well-stocked pond and a lush summer garden. This patio divided my room from Roald's, which was located on the other side of the mansion.

The first thing we did, after settling into our rooms and freshening up, was to go into Tbilisi and look at the main places associated with the massacre. At a makeshift table near the site of the beatings, volunteers were collecting signatures to support Georgia's independence. All along the wall of the building where the victims had been attacked rows and rows of flowers had been laid. (Some weeks after the massacre, when the flowers were removed, the clean-up crew had become ill from the lingering chemical fumes.)

During our stay we met with opposition leaders who spoke in passionate terms about the events the night of the killings, among them Zviad Gamsakhurdia. As destiny would have it, he would become the country's first freely elected President and the target of a "progressive" later headed by Eduard Shevardnadze. I interviewed him during that time, and he was anxious to have Western exposure for the massacre, this act of Soviet barbarity. He gave me his home telephone, but asked me if I ever called him, to do so from a public telephone. This was perhaps a precaution he was accustomed to—having spent three years in jail as a political prisoner during the Brezhnev years. But it was also an indication of how he viewed this national crisis.

After a lengthy session, we were taken by government car to the hospital, where we met with the victims of the gassings. It seemed ironic, we noted later, that on the way there we passed a large gardened area where a statue had been draped in canvas. Our driver explained to us that it was the image of Sergo Ordzhonikidze, the early Georgian Bolshevik who had come to his homeland after the October Revolution to consolidate territorial gains for the Soviet Union. He later became one of Stalin's victims. As we approached, the canvas was being lowered by local engineers and they were putting a large chain around Ordzhonikidze's neck. When we passed, they were affixing "the noose." One had an eerie feeling that one had just seen a public hanging.

The hospital was modern and clean. Our meeting took place in the hospital chief's office, where we sat around a modest conference table. One by one, young women came into the room and each one described what had happened that fateful night. Occasionally the doctor would encourage a woman to show us her blisters from the poisonous gas. Inflamed welts could be seen all over their necks and sometimes inside their throats. The women told us how Soviet troops had held them by their hair and pushed back their heads to spray the chemical substance directly into their faces. Many of the women noted that the soldiers who committed these brutalities were drunk.

All of us were chilled by the sights we saw and the stories we were told, a revulsion compounded later by seeing amateur videos of the incident itself. The whole operation had been clearly thought through, and the soldiers were obviously acting under specific orders. No one could avoid being deeply moved and disturbed.

Later, Roald told me that one of the most heroic acts in the terrible months that followed came from a group of chemists at the Georgian Academy of Sciences. They took the time, and risked their safety, to analyze and identify the chemical substance that had been used on the victims— in direct violation of the military security order.

That night we dined with a few Georgian officials in what turned out to be an impromptu celebration of American independence. Indeed, it was the Fourth of July, the significance of which was not lost on the Georgian guests. They lavishly toasted the American holiday and the notion of self-determination and independence. How extraordinary it was that these sentiments were being voiced in the Communist Party guest house.

I slept badly that night, either because of the sizable meal we had had or because of the bizarre setting in which I found myself. The images of the day danced in my head. At about 5:00 in the morning I could stand it no longer, so I threw on some clothes and crept silently across the tiled roof patio to the hall leading to Roald's room. I knocked softly on his door and whispered to him that I couldn't sleep and I needed to walk. "Please come with me," I begged.

Several minutes later Roald joined me on the roof patio and we quietly made our way down the front staircase of the house. As soon as we had gone through the main door and were beyond earshot of the mansion, I apologized for getting him out of bed at such an early hour. I told him that I couldn't reconcile all that I had heard and seen with where we were staying. I was sorry that we had allowed ourselves to be put up in this symbol of Communist Party power.

"Roald," I said, "you mentioned it to me before, and now I am going to raise it with you. After what you have seen, don't you feel you should do something about your Party card?"

Roald seemed uncomfortable with the reference, and made a sign indicating that he did not regard any part of the grounds as a safe place to talk.

"I had a bad night, too," he said, as if to say that his mind had been working in many of the same directions.

We abandoned this attempt at openness and walked instead for a few more minutes, making unimportant observations. The early-morning light could be seen on the eastern horizon and the birds were beginning their morning serenades. We had some lighter recreational outings planned for this day, but we both knew that we—like Tbilisi—would never be quite the same.

The night we returned from Tbilisi to Moscow, Roald and I decided that I would stay with him again at "Belgrade I." As the old elevator cranked up seven flights, we got out onto the landing, and as usual, the neighbor's dog began to bark. I barely noticed the dog's announcement of our arrival; I was, instead, fixated on the appearance of Roald's front door. In place of the old padded brown door was an oak one with metal reinforcements and several sets of locks.

I was silent until we had entered the apartment and were safely behind the closed door.

"What happened to the door?" I asked.

"Someone broke in and I had to replace the whole thing."

"Did they take anything?"

"Not really. They rummaged through my papers and took my shortwave radio. That's about it."

"Why didn't you tell me before?"

"I didn't want to worry you."

I was alarmed, knowing that the chances were very high that it was not a normal break-in. Roald knew that I would surmise exactly what he had: the break-in had been staged by the KGB to have a look around and to intimidate him. Unlike the KGB theft of Sakharov's memoirs in Gorky, no papers of value had been found in this flat, since I had all the materials relating to Roald's book in the West. Later, we wondered if they had planted a listening device in the flat to get a better idea of what our plans were. Whatever their purpose, I was deeply unsettled by the discovery.

The political situation in the U.S.S.R. was unraveling very quickly. A coal miners' strike in Siberia had been called and it was now escalating beyond the initial mines; the walkouts had spread to Kuzbass in Russia and Donbass in Ukraine. Liberalization had emboldened everyone. Only one question remained: how long would the old guard put up with the threat to their power? As we watched the evening news from Elena Loschenkova's house, everyone sat in tense silence. The only other strike in Soviet history—during the Khrushchev era—had been broken up with force and several dozen people had been killed. Everyone wondered if the government would use this strike as an excuse to crack down.

Roald and I were genuinely alarmed by the rapidly deteriorating situation, and we could not forget the extensive list of powerful enemies Roald had made. In the event of a crackdown he would not necessarily be singled out for his radical positions but swept up with *everyone*. On such a scale there would be nothing anyone could do for him personally.

We were not alone in assessing the situation as we did. One evening some weeks later, Roald and I dined in New York with Seweryn Bialer, a distinguished Sovietologist, and Nicolai Shishlin. Shishlin was in the city as Bialer's guest at Columbia University, to work together on a book of Gorbachev's speeches. Roald and I had just come from a conference in Sundance, Utah. Bialer was morose about political events and predicted that the coal miners' strike would bring catastrophe on the Soviet Union. We all knew that strikes had been one of the Bolsheviks' most effective measures for bringing down the Kerensky government. Shishlin and Bialer were not comforted by their analysis of Gorbachev's speeches either. They were skeptical of his desire and ability to bring about the necessary reform. Bialer recognized Gorbachev's deep belief in Communism, and he shared our exasperation with the many Western observers who seemed to read into Gorbachev what they *wanted* him to believe. Shishlin, disturbed by the leadership's tactics, voiced the same opinion.

Bialer thought that a crackdown could come at any moment. As Roald and Nicolai walked ahead of us on a narrow stretch of sidewalk, Bialer said to me softly, "I love these two men, and I would use all the influence I have on their behalf if the worst happens."

On August 23 the political crisis deepened when more than a million people in the Baltic republics formed a human chain to protest their incorporation into the Soviet Union in 1940. In response, the Central Committee issued a sharp statement accusing the independence movements in the Baltics of "exploiting the atmosphere of Soviet reform to 'disintegrate the cohesion' of the country." Baltic nationalist leaders condemned this statement as "imperial" interference in their affairs and asserted that they had "no intention of softening their demands for independence."*

Roald told me he would be filing his divorce papers as soon as he returned to Moscow, and it would take six weeks for the formalities to become final. After the papers were registered, we guessed our larger intentions would be obvious. Amid this political turmoil, anything could happen.

"This is a test. Today is August 28, 1989."

"It sounds fine," I said.

Roald cleared his throat.

"One, two, three, four, five." I motioned to Roald with my hand.

Susan, my darling, I think it absolutely essential that I am leaving you tomorrow with this statement on video, because I don't know what kind of problems we are going to have. Every day one can expect an unpleasant surprise. I think that while everyone is asking if Gorbachev is stable, if *perestroika* is irreversible, in general the same question could be asked about those people who are known as promoters of *perestroika*. I helped Gorbachev a great deal and I think I was a faithful follower of *perestroika*. I was also proud to be able to help Andrei Sakharov, at several important instances, and that definitely made a few more enemies for me. And it is with great pain I observe that old thinkers—old guys—around the Politburo and in almost every high echelon of power are still there. So please keep this video and let's hope that it will be just our family souvenir, a memo of the history of our family. But if something dangerous should happen, I would ask you to use it without any hesitation.

* David Remnick, *The Washington Post*, August 28, 1989.

I stopped the video camera, and Roald shifted in his seat slightly, his face still somberly set. He raised the sheaf of papers he had in front of him, and I steadied the video camera on the pile of books I had assembled as a tripod. I counted to five—cuing him for the second segment, this time his prepared statement.

The coal miners' strike of July of this year has brought into sharp focus the staggering difficulties that are being experienced by the Soviet Union on its road to economic and social reform. I am returning to my country tomorrow for the first time since that event. Throughout the weeks of my stay in the United States I have been watching with growing concern the dark clouds forming over *perestroika*.

Yesterday reportedly the Central Committee issued a sharp and threatening rebuke to rising national self-consciousness in the Baltic republics. The unwillingness to adequately recognize the rights of ethnic groups by central authorities only aggravates the situation. Today it was also reported that 300,000 people were demonstrating in Moldavia, to demand restoring its native language, thus decelerating the process of Russification. This process was never admitted officially, but in reality it was going on in almost every ethnic republic or region.

The next months will be full of uncertainty as the government tries to weigh its response to mounting economic and ethnic troubles. This comes at a time when the Congress of People's Deputies, the newly found voice of the people, has barely found its footing.

I am speaking to you because I leave the United States with a great deal of uncertainty about my own fate. I have been known to stay on the liberal end of Soviet political life, among the most outspoken critics of stagnation. And I have been a consistent and resolute advocate for radical reform. While this stance is still not adopted by the majority, I think I have become particularly vulnerable, for two major reasons.

Before the establishment of the new Congress of People's Deputies, I was a regional representative of the old Supreme Soviet. During one of the final acts of that body, legislation was introduced that proposed a restrictive law on meetings and demonstrations, and the usage of paramilitary troops for crowd control and breaking up demonstrations. Because I believed that those measures were unacceptably harsh and potentially dangerous, I was the only one out of 700 deputies in the Chamber of Unions to vote against these proposed laws. For that time this was considered a public challenge to the authorities that introduced the measures. However, in strife-ridden areas like Georgia, my vote against these pieces of legislation were regarded as important opposition to these tools of government control. On April 9 paramilitary troops brutally killed twenty girls and women, with sharpened shovels and poisonous gas, and inflicting serious injury on hundreds more. My earlier stand against the use of such paramilitary troops prompted the Georgians to request my participation on the commission to investigate the Tbilisi massacre. The outspoken position I took on ethnic issues has made me a target for conservative forces who demand obedience and order at any cost.

But there is another matter, a personal situation that also has made me vulnerable to attack. Two years ago, while attending a conference on U.S.–Soviet relations, I met Susan Eisenhower, one of President Eisenhower's four grandchildren. We struck up a conversation, and before the conference was over, I believe we both knew that we would become uncommonly close friends. What we did not know, perhaps, is that we would form a deep attachment to one another which would be characterized by love, respect, and an unshakable trust in one another.

It was natural for me to attend such a conference in the United States. Through my scientific career in controlled fusion and space science, I traveled abroad extensively, for more than thirty years. And in more recent times I have spent even more time in the United States, working on projects related to international cooperation in science as well as on issues related to U.S.–Soviet bilateral relations. Susan, like myself, has dedicated much of her work and her efforts to fostering international cooperation and improving U.S.–Soviet relations. Because of our experience, we knew, as our relationship developed, that we were entering territory fraught with risk and potential danger. We spent a great deal of time evaluating the consequences of our feelings for one another. But despite the complex situation in which we found ourselves, we both needed to be together. In discussion with our children, we received their generous support, despite their obvious knowledge of the risks we were taking.

Our hope is that we will be able to marry this fall. However, our life together will be complicated by the need for special permission—to travel in and out of the country. Because of the age of Susan's children, we will need to spend the bulk of the school year in Washington. It is our deep desire, however, to continue the work we have been engaged in over these years. Despite the differences in our nationalities, cultures, backgrounds, and upbringing, we have forged an enduring partnership . . .

The forthcoming months are likely to be difficult. But Susan and I are committed to each other and to taking this step, no matter what the reaction from official circles. If, however, we are put in a position that would make an immediate marriage impossible, it is important for our friends and our countrymen to know that we have *de facto* taken this step and we are prepared to see it through, no matter what the consequences. We firmly believe that our choice constitutes no threat to anyone, either on a personal level or within the larger political context. Perhaps even more, we hope this step we are taking will send a hopeful message to a world divided by mistrust and fear.

The following day, as we had planned, I took the videocassette to the safe-deposit box. After that, I put a letter in my desk marked "Open only in case of accident or death." It contained instructions about where to find the key to the security box and an authorization for my sister Anne to use the videotape or the tape transcripts of the book—at her discretion.

That afternoon I drove Roald to the airport. We had decided on our course of action, and everything was settled between us.

As we said goodbye, we had no idea of what would happen, but we were utterly determined to follow through with our plans. It was not a false sense of courage or heroism that drove us. It was our deep need to be together, as well as some sense that in the end—no matter how long it would take—we would eventually "win."

What we didn't know that hot muggy day is how elusive "winning" would be. How could we have ever imagined that it would be another two years before we would draw our first free breath together?

19 : The Message Is Sent

By the time I put Roald on the plane for Moscow, we had been together for more than two months. On September 5, I wrote in my journal:

> We were connected to such an extraordinary degree that at times I can—even from this distance—feel him thinking about me. I called him today and he told me that he knew I would be calling, so he was waiting. Telepathy! It's funny, I knew he would be waiting for my call.
>
> Our experiences were so diverse and deep. From Tbilisi to Sundance, we were together in places halfway around the world. And the same closeness and connectedness only grew stronger.
>
> Perhaps the most important development is that we have stopped talking about the future and we are now living it. We made no bones about being together either here in Washington or in Moscow or in Tbilisi.
>
> Now I am filled with his presence here in "Belgrade II." We spent a month together cooking, working, sharing. And then as time drew near we dealt with the contingencies straight on, with a plan in hand and a clear eye on what might be required of us. I noticed after he had gone that he left some clothes in the closet. He also left the briefcase I gave him and the video camera that has come to mean so much.

Several days later I received a letter from Roald:

Susan, my darling,

I hope in Gander* there would be a chance to send you this message. I am so overwhelmed with our being together, "Belgrade II" and the Sundance trip, that it is difficult to talk about future arrangements and work. Coming to my small "Belgrade I" asylum would give me a lot of time to reconstruct in my memory these incredible weeks. Maybe we did not do our best for the main book or for other projects. But the more I recall our "jam session" the more clearly I realize that it was not the main shortage. I should have been speaking much more about my love, we had to dance the two of us just a bit more, I had to sing . . . If you would allow me next time, I will.

I have to tell you after reading today's *Pravda* (August 29): "Ethnic boiling is approaching the critical mark." On the second page is an article on how Lithuania joined the U.S.S.R. in 1940 (of course, with great enthusiasm!). On the first page, indignation of Russians about "Baltic excesses." On the last, a long story describing the events in Moldavia. I will start collecting materials on ethnic issues. One can suspect a lot of happenings to come.

Izvestia comments on everything in a slightly different way: instead of blunt condemnation in the spirit of the Central Committee's statement, it calls for moderation in order to avoid extremism and blood, so much desired by the conservatives. It even gives a chance to some voices to criticize the language of the statement.

I hope you would already be back from Ohio to receive this letter. Please kiss the kids for me and do not forget my small calculator for Amy. It's on your desk at "Belgrade II" in a black envelope. Take care of yourself and remember in moments of desperation, please remember, we shall overcome!

It is about 7:00 p.m. East Coast time. However, the stewardess is already giving Moscow time. At "Belgrade II" we probably would be thinking about dinner. I believe we have not had a pilaf† for quite a while.

Before our plane lands let me tell you again how much you mean for me.

Love, Roald

Business took me to Moscow several weeks later. As soon as we managed to reach the privacy of "Belgrade I," Roald told me he had bad news. He had gone to file his divorce papers and the bureaucrat at the appropriate

---

* The refueling stop for Aeroflot flights to Moscow.
† This was a reference to Pilaf Tatar, a dish that Roald makes. It is a Muslim tradition that the male cooks it—a tradition not very faithfully fulfilled, because Roald tells me he learned how to make it from his mother. I don't want to spoil a good thing. From the beginning I assured Roald that his secret recipe was safe with him.

agency had told him that they had just changed the rules: new regulations stated that a mutually agreeable divorce now required a three-month waiting period, not the six weeks Roald had been told earlier.

Both of us were close to despair. The situation in the Soviet Union was spinning out of control, and both of us suspected that some stabilizing measures would be adopted soon. We could only imagine what those measures would be.

Our problems were further compounded by the gossip mill. Roald told me that several well-placed people had told him they had heard that there was something going on between us. Paul Michel's advice of "openness" had been right, of course, but now we felt as if we were in a race against time.

We had a day-long marathon, brainstorming our options. We finally decided that we would notify the Politburo of our intention to marry. "We should get to Gorbachev before the KGB does," Roald said, "if they haven't already."

Roald had always said that the only way one could deal with "these guys" was to negotiate with them from a position of strength, but we were no longer in such a position. We would have to make a virtue of necessity and adopt a different strategy. We decided to approach the question as if there were no reason why we *shouldn't* marry.

"Let's treat them like human beings and see if they have grown to fit the description," Roald joked.

I was in strong agreement—perhaps because both of us knew that we really didn't have any other options.

The first problem was to find someone who would convey our message to the Politburo sympathetically, someone who could serve as an advocate for our cause. After lengthy debate we decided to ask Nicolai Shishlin, who still served as Alexander Yakovlev's closest aide.

We made arrangements with Shishlin to come to "Belgrade I" for dinner. Roald told him we needed to see him urgently.

I went over and over our scenario, wondering if indeed we were doing the right thing. It was a considerable gamble. Once we had told the authorities definitively, anything could happen. But something else bothered me. I would have preferred to go through all this after Roald's divorce was final, so that he could resolve his legal status with a minimum of outside pressure. But this, unfortunately, was now a luxury.

Shishlin was late for dinner. Each minute that passed was agonizing; I was convinced he simply wouldn't turn up. Nearly an hour later, the doorbell rang. Nicolai was standing at our door with a handful of carnations and dressed as if he had just come from the office.

He apologized profusely for the delay. Urgent business had come up at the Central Committee and he had been unable to get to a telephone to call us. It wouldn't have mattered: our telephone had been mysteriously dead for the last twenty-four hours. Such blackouts had been happening more and more frequently, most probably another KGB trick.

We began a rather hurried meal. Again Shishlin apologized, saying that he had to return to the office before long. The shortness of time was made worse by the fact that Roald couldn't seem to get to the main subject. We talked about the forthcoming Eisenhower Centennial and Evgeny Primakov's promotion to the Politburo. Not until Shishlin said he had to go did Roald finally get to the point.

"Kolya, Susan and I want to enter into a closer association."

Shishlin looked at us blankly. There was silence for a moment or two.

"We want to get married," Roald clarified.

Shishlin hesitated and slowly began to shake his head. He did not respond right away.

"I think there could be problems . . ." he finally said ominously. He paused again, this time for even longer.

"What would be the difficulties?" Roald asked, somewhat impatiently.

"Well," Shishlin said thoughtfully, "how would you fulfill your social responsibilities, such as your obligations to your 'dear' Academy—and, of course, to the Congress? The state would also be concerned about your family."*

It was frustrating to hear them both talking around the real issue, which was Roald's status as a former director of an institute within the military-industrial complex.

Roald assured Shishlin that his divorce was by mutual consent. Then he added, "But listen, Kolya, I wouldn't be leaving the Soviet Union for good. We want to divide our time. I have my children here and my grandchildren."

"That's right. We'll go back and forth, I have business here," I piped in. "But you should know that I am a mother with three children and I can't travel any more than I do currently. In fact, I should slow down."

Roald leaned forward, trying to press his ideas home. "This must be seen

---

* In the Soviet lexicon "families" were frequently a big issue. A person could not emigrate without the permission of his parents, no matter how old he might be.

as a positive thing," he said passionately. "We live in an interdependent world. Here is a tangible example. It could be a confidence-building measure. And it should be treated as such. It is certainly not a tragedy."

Shishlin was silent, then he conceded, "It could give my country an opportunity to be better. We learned a lot from Sakharov. For years he wasn't allowed to travel because of the military secrets he knew. But they were not breached when he did finally go abroad . . . Still, there may be difficulties."

Roald, in growing defiance, suddenly said, "I could have taken the easy way out and defected. And you should tell Yakovlev and Gorbachev that we stayed here and did it this way as an act of good faith."

The two men rose and went into the kitchen for some minutes.

When they returned I was in tears. It was as if a dam had burst. The tension and anxiety connected with this moment had been too much, and suddenly it occurred to me that we might have adopted the wrong tactic, that we had possibly just dug our own graves.

I covered my eyes with my hands. I tried to gain control over myself, but the tears wouldn't stop.

Nicolai and Roald went on talking in Russian. Suddenly Shishlin leaned down and said gently, "I am sorry, Susan, I have to leave."

Wiping the tears from my eyes, I stood up and joined Roald and Nicolai at the door.

"I will make a preliminary inquiry and I will call Roald on Monday," Shishlin said. And then, as he kissed me on the cheek, he whispered, "Be brave."

The door shut behind him. I was terribly upset about the whole encounter, especially about how I had handled myself. I told Roald I felt humiliated that I had been unable to avoid crying. "It was just all the built-up tension."

He came over and put his arms around me. "We must stay in circle defense," he whispered. "We did a good thing, we saw Nicolai together. It sent a strong message. Our comments were fine. They were strong. And they made it clear how much we care about each other."

Roald and I washed the dishes and he prepared to take me back to my hotel. As he had a congressional subcommittee meeting the next morning, Elena Loschenkova would have to take me to the airport, and we agreed that it would be better if I was at my hotel. It was regrettable that this night of all nights we could not be together.

Just as we were leaving the flat, the telephone, which had been dead for at least a day, suddenly rang. Roald picked it up and spoke for several minutes. After he hung up, he seemed troubled and distant. As we got into the car, I tried to find out what the call had been about, but I was unable to wrest anything from him. Roald's mood had changed so rapidly that I was crazy with concern. What had been said on that phone? Or had *I* done something to upset him?

I couldn't bear the powerlessness of it all, of never knowing what to expect. I told him that the uncertainty was the hardest part. Suddenly he responded with alarming pessimism. "Expect the worst," he said gruffly. "No more travel. Or maybe I'll be hit by a car."

I knew well that a "car accident" was not a desperately farfetched possibility. Roald had had his tires mysteriously punctured and during just one year, Boris Yeltsin was said to have had at least four car accidents, one of which was serious enough to put him in the hospital.

We rode through the streets of Moscow in unhappy silence. At my hotel Roald told me he loved me and kissed my cheek in a business-like fashion. I did not see him again before my departure for Washington.

Since the Politburo would soon know of our intentions, on an extremely limited basis we had decided we should also tell our families and a small number of others whose critical support we needed. I called my father and asked him to come to Washington so that we could have lunch together: I needed to discuss something important, I told him. I also called Roald in Moscow to see if he had heard anything from Shishlin. Unfortunately there had been no word, though the Monday date had long passed. "No news" was compounded by the maddening simplicity of our telephone exchanges. The specter of the tapped telephone still stood between us.

Given the way circumstances were developing, it was clearly time to discuss my plans with my father. We had become very close over the years and I admired the honest directness he always brought to every subject. It was best that he be told now what I had undertaken. Roald would be in the United States for about a week in October, and if all went well, I planned to have him meet my father then.

I decided to invite my father to "Belgrade II." In addition to giving us privacy, I thought the location would underscore the seriousness of my situation.

Daddy arrived punctually at noon and for some minutes we made small talk about the progress of Roald's book. Then I summoned the nerve to get to the point.

"Daddy, I am planning to get married."

My father looked utterly stunned. "To whom?" he asked, obviously struck that something so important in my life could have transpired without his knowledge.

I explained that the reason he had known nothing was not because I had wanted to exclude him but because I was trying to protect my husband-to-be.

"He is Soviet," I said evenly. "It is Sagdeev."

"Wow," my father said slowly, "wow." Then he added, "Isn't it wonderful that such a thing is possible in this day and age?"

We weren't sure such a thing *was* possible, I told him, but we intended to get married anyway.

"Wow," he said once more, this time more thoughtfully.

Ironically, Daddy's main concern was not about me but about Roald. He questioned me closely about Roald's long-term professional interests and suggested that it could be very bad for us both if Roald was "giving up everything" for me. I could only tell him what Roald had told me about his desire to do science and be a citizen of the world. I explained that we planned to travel back and forth between the Soviet Union and the United States—to continue the work we had already started, to serve as a bridge between both societies. I tried to allay his concerns by assuring him that Roald and I shared an extraordinary love, a kindred bond held together by trust.

My father did not need to be sold on the subject of Roald as a son-in-law, it seemed. He was worried only about the cultural adjustment that Roald would have to make if we chose to spend our lives mostly in the United States.

I was proud but not surprised that my father, the son of an American President, expressed no concern whatsoever about whether or not my actions would cause a family or even a political scandal. The subject never even came up. In fact, when I told him that Roald felt it was necessary that we marry in Moscow to demonstrate that he was not defecting, Daddy agreed without question to come to Moscow for the wedding.

As the Politburo had already been notified, I thought it was perfectly appropriate for at least one American official to be in the loop, so I called the State Department to see how best to contact Ambassador Jack Matlock. I had known Jack since he went with us to Latvia for the first Chautauqua conference in the U.S.S.R. Since becoming ambassador to the Soviet Union, he was getting high marks throughout the Sovietology community, and it was fortunate that there was someone I knew so well in that post.

I felt that Jack would lend a sympathetic ear. He greatly respected Roald. Perhaps even more important, his son had married a Russian woman and he had gone through at least some of the same issues we were about to face—although Matlock's new daughter-in-law had no military-related or official connections.

It was my luck that apparently Jack and his wife, Rebecca, were on home leave in Tennessee. I left a message for them, and he returned my telephone call within hours. When I told him I was phoning about a family situation not unlike his son's and asked him to keep our conversation entirely to himself, he responded like the old Moscow hand he is. He never asked me for a name, though I could tell he knew to whom I was referring, and we conversed in the cryptic way people do when they think they may be overheard.

"It will certainly be news!" he said immediately.

"Do you think there'll be a serious problem?"

"Well, the fact that we have two big names here will help. The problem might be with his ties—though they might not be considered as sensitive as they used to be. It may depend on his security clearance." Then he added, optimistically, "Nothing is insurmountable."

I appreciated his help more than he could have imagined, and told him that I would need his advice about how things could best be done on the American side, particularly if the situation got complicated. We agreed we would see what the next month would bring and that I would call on him at Spaso House, the American ambassador's residence in Moscow, during my November visit.

Ten days later I had a curious overture from Yuri Osipyan, who was in Canada, headed for the United States. He insisted that we have dinner when he arrived in Washington. I agreed, but I could tell by the way he talked that something was up.

Yuri's star had risen dramatically since the election of the Congress of People's Deputies. With the establishment of a presidential system, Gorbachev had also instituted a twelve-member Presidential Council, to which Yuri had been appointed. This body met about once a week and had authority over the full range of Soviet affairs. Although it was like a cabinet, a number of members, like Yuri, served without portfolio.

We settled next to the fire at the Polo Club at the Ritz-Carlton, and Yuri began almost immediately with the subject most on his mind.

"I met Roald recently in Moscow and tried to persuade him to run for president of the Academy of Sciences. He could win and we need to have him in this important position," Yuri said, watching me intently. "You know, Susan," he said as his gaze narrowed, "he turned me down."

I understood where this conversation was leading, and immediately felt uncomfortable under Yuri's intense focus.

"It doesn't add up," he said softly, "unless it has something to do with you."

"I can't lie to you, Yuri," I said, finding it hard to meet his eyes. "Roald and I want to get married, and it would be quite impossible for him to take on more official positions under those circumstances."

Yuri sat back in his chair. He was impassive at first, then a smile slowly came to his face. "I'm very pleased for you both," he said. "I have watched this relationship develop over a long time, and I am very happy by what I have seen."

Yuri's response was like gale-force fresh air. Relief blew over me. I poured out all my doubts and worries—about the authorities and the restrictions they might place on Roald.

Yuri volunteered to talk to Gorbachev about our situation. "Now, about the Academy presidency," he added, "I think Roald could still take it on if you would agree to live in Moscow."

I said nothing to that suggestion; it was hardly my place to speak for Roald or to give Yuri even an off-the-cuff response to this unexpected notion. But Yuri's general support kept me going during the hard times ahead.

Roald was a different man when he spoke to me from Stockholm. His arrival in Sweden, beyond the ever-present ears of the security services, made a big difference to our conversations, and as was typical when he was on a foreign trip, we talked two or three times a day.

I asked him again what had gone wrong the evening of my departure from Moscow, and he explained that the telephone call had been from Tema, his estranged wife, who had said that she did not have all her documents in Moscow. This meant that they would have to file their divorce papers later in the week, when the bureau was opened.

"To tell you the truth," Roald said, "after Shishlin left I was trying very hard to be cheerful, but I, too, was anxious and upset. Then when it appeared that we had another bureaucratic snag, it was the last straw. I felt suddenly overwhelmed."

He apologized and confessed that he had waves of panic. But, he said, he was feeling much better now that his papers were filed. He told me that the three-month waiting period would culminate on December 29. If everything went as we hoped, he could be with me by my birthday on December 31.

When I told him about my conversations with my father and Yuri, Roald was jubilant. Before leaving Stockholm, he wrote me a letter describing his feelings. It arrived nearly a week later.

My dear,
Even the weather is different now in Stockholm, after my mood has completely changed. Two days ago when I arrived it was raining, heavy lead sky. Tell me please, confess, how could you influence it from such a distance, sending to me such a sunny bright morning. And the air is so transparent and pure as only in Nordic countries . . .

On serious issues: The Tbilisi commission goes well. We have adopted a baseline for the draft—it blames the Moscow authorities, local bosses, and the army. I would expect now that the bad guys would try to change the language peace by peace [sic].

As a by-product we now have a very detailed reconstruction of the event. I will tell you about it when I see you in October.

I was very outspoken on a recent television program, from Afghanistan to ethnic issues . . . combined with my avoidance of the interregional group meetings, I believe it is the most appropriate (independent) conduct. I heard during the last interregional meeting Yuri Afanasiev precipitated as an open adversary to M.S.G. [Gorbachev]. Sorry for mentioning all of these stories without giving detailed descriptions. I will accumulate them for an oral account in less than ten days now.

You are the only person I wish to share all I have with. In every way I dream of the time when I will be talking to you during hours, days, weeks, years . . .

Take care of yourself. Hugs and kisses to the kids.

Love, Roald

P.S. I enormously enjoyed your story on dinner with Yuri.
8:15 a.m., September 30, 1989

I joyously greeted Roald in New York, days later. He was receiving an award from the Citizens Exchange Council for his contribution to U.S.– Soviet relations; then we planned to go to see my father in Pennsylvania and visit the Institute for Advanced Study in Princeton.

To save time, Roald and I met my father at a small colonial tavern not far from his house near Valley Forge. At first conversation was stilted, but my father heroically moved beyond his natural shyness to make Roald feel comfortable—entertaining him with stories that even I had never heard before. He told us about my grandfather's visit to Moscow in 1945 and his own impressions as the son accompanying the wartime commander. There were tales about dinner at the Kremlin with Stalin and Beria, the Physical Culture Parade on Red Square, and Daddy's relationship with and impressions of Zhukov, and with Khrushchev. I listened dumbfounded. In all the years I had been traveling back and forth to the Soviet Union, he and I had never talked about these topics. Roald was charmed.

After lunch my father was only too aware that we had to push on to Princeton, so he suggested that he take us to the rent-a-car shop to pick up the car we had ordered.

I let both men sit in the front seat so that they could continue to talk in what little time was left. My father told Roald he had learned some Russian folksongs while in the American army of occupation in Austria after the war. Daddy started to sing "Stenka Razin" and Roald joined in. How strange it was to hear my father and my husband-to-be singing Russian folksongs. I took enormous pleasure in this front-seat display.

Even though my father could sing them in Russian, he confessed he didn't know what the words meant. "What about 'Stenka Razin'?"

"Let's just say the song's about the perils to a foreign princess of marrying a Russian," Roald quipped.

If we had reasons for optimism, we were still disquieted by the fact that Nicolai Shishlin had not contacted Roald. Neither of us had heard anything from Nicolai since our meeting at "Belgrade I" nearly two months before. But I discovered through the grapevine that Shishlin was coming to Washington at the end of October, as part of the 1989 Chautauqua conference, and I decided to confront him. I knew he would be staying at the Savoy Hotel, across from the Soviet Embassy compound. With nothing to lose, I decided to contact him there to see if I could find out from him what had happened with his approach to the Politburo.

I planned to drop into the hotel for a brief chat, and to drive some of my secondary points home, I decided to take my youngest daughter, Amy, with me. At eight years old, she was an irresistible little girl with dark hair and large gray-blue eyes. I thought her presence might inhibit conversation, but it would certainly remind Nicolai that I had considerable family responsibilities in the United States.

On the way to the Savoy, Amy and I stopped by the liquor store and I bought a bottle of Nicolai's favorite whiskey, Chivas Regal.

"Hello, Nicolai? This is Susan, Susan Eisenhower, calling from the house phone downstairs. I wanted to say hello and I brought you a little souvenir I wanted you to have."

Several minutes later Shishlin emerged from the elevator and I introduced him to Amy. I gave him the Scotch and we stood around, aimlessly chatting. It was as if nothing had gone on between us. Then, without warning, he kissed my cheek, thanked me for the Scotch, and disappeared again behind the closing elevator doors.

I was disappointed not to have gotten even a small hint about what was going on. But the next evening Shishlin telephoned me. It was quite late, about 11:00, but he wanted to thank me for the Scotch and to ask me how I was doing. He was with Sergei Ivanov, from the Embassy, he said. Conscious of Sergei's proximity to the telephone, I tried to keep the conversation on unimportant topics.

A few days later I had to go to Chicago on business. In a phone booth at O'Hare Airport I learned from my office that a Mr. Shishlin had called and asked me to give him a ring at his hotel in Washington sometime in the evening.

All day I anxiously waited until I could call him. It was not until 10:00 p.m. that I was finally able to make the connection.

"Susan my dear, I am so happy to hear your voice," Shishlin said—this time he sounded more accessible, friendlier.

After chatting amiably for some minutes, I finally asked him directly if he had any news about the matter we had raised in Moscow.

"Susan, it is not certain yet, but there are some developments."

Shishlin warned me that he had had only a preliminary response. Alexander Yakovlev had hesitated for some time, he told me, apparently in deep conflict about Roald's intentions. "I said to him, 'Alexander Nicolaiivich, ever since the beginning of time a boy has had the right to choose his girl.' I think that argument finally worked," Nicolai said proudly.

"What did Yakovlev say to that?" I asked.

"Alexander Nicolaiivich was very sorry about Roald. He told me, 'I love this man, but this means he is going to leave us.' " And he confirmed that

Yakovlev had intended to support Roald for the presidency of the Academy.

"I hope you told him that the Soviet Union wasn't losing Roald but gaining a daughter-in-law," I said defensively.

"Never mind, my dear Susan. Be happy."

"And the others?" I asked anxiously.

"Well," he said slowly, "our Evgeny Primakov said, 'We should support Roald, he's our friend.' "

Nicolai's news had constituted some progress, but we knew only what Roald's friends and supporters thought; we had no reaction from Gorbachev or anyone more conservative. Knowing the Soviet system as we did, we could not indulge in optimistic confidence until there was some word from the General Secretary himself. Shishlin had nothing to say about that, or if he did, he was not passing it on. It was Gorbachev who would decide our future, and whichever way he leaned would say volumes about who had his ear during this turbulent phase of *perestroika*.

20 : The World Standing on Its Head

During Roald's visit to the United States he had had strong indication from the Institute for Advanced Study in Princeton that he would be offered a position there. The news filled us with hope, but political events seemed to be closing in on us. Even as we had sent our message to the Politburo outlining our intentions to marry, the world had started to shake.

In August, East Germany had voted its Communist Party out of power, a development without precedent in any Soviet-bloc country. Not long thereafter, Hungary opened its borders and East German refugees began pouring into the West. By mid-October, in Leipzig and other East German cities, tens of thousands of demonstrators were regularly taking to the streets to demand democracy and freedom.

As foment gained force in Eastern Europe, it seemed that Mikhail Gorbachev was losing his nerve. In mid-October he called together the leading editors of the progressive press, who had been his most vocal critics, and accused them of being "irresponsible" and "inflammatory." At that Kremlin meeting he singled out our friend Vladislav Starkov, editor of the popular *Argumenti i Facti*, perhaps because the previous week the newspaper had run a public-opinion poll indicating a critical drop in Gorbachev's popularity. Gorbachev announced that Starkov had exceeded his mandate and he fired him on the spot. (Roald likened the Soviet President's behavior to the wicked queen who smashed the looking glass when she got a negative answer to her question "Mirror, mirror on the wall . . .") In no time at all, a standoff between Gorbachev and the newspaper ensued. Starkov went back to his offices, solicited the support of his staff, and then resolutely refused to "resign." Within a week it was clear that Starkov was untouchable.

The news of the rapid changes taking place in Eastern Europe was received strangely in Moscow. I was in the city in early November when the Berlin Wall had been breached and had fallen. This news was carefully downplayed in the Soviet press. Gennady Gerasimov, Foreign Ministry spokesman, summed up the regime's position on *International Panorama,* a television talk show.

> The events in G.D.R. [East Germany] could not but revive talk about the unification of Germany, but it is . . . precisely idle talk which ignores the realities of European politics today. The G.D.R. is, in fact, a member of the Warsaw Pact Organization and our strategic ally. We have troops there. So what are they talking about? . . . At the same time this idle talk is politically dangerous; it rakes up nationalist aspirations and brings us back to confrontation between the military blocs . . .*

Within a few weeks a kind of depression spread over Moscow. People seemed a little unglued, disoriented. Perhaps, too, there lay the residual fear that the Communist Party of the Soviet Union would have to make some decisive move to save itself. These events coincided with the November anniversary of the Bolshevik Revolution. The huge red banners of Lenin in Red Square belied the collapse of his legacy throughout the Communist bloc. People wondered how the enigmatic and unpredictable Gorbachev would react. The whole country seemed to be on the verge of an emotional breakdown.

Roald's determination to marry in the Soviet Union took some time for me finally to accept, not because I didn't understand his concern about the appearance of defection, but because I was uncomfortable about what kind of response it would elicit in the United States. We finally agreed that we would marry in Moscow but announce our engagement in the United States. That way, if the Soviet reaction to our plans was terrible, we could reconsider the site of our wedding.

During my stay in Moscow, I met with Jack Matlock at Spaso House to discuss all this. Jack recognized my concerns about how the news of this marriage would be received in the United States and of my desire to wed

---

* Moscow Television Service, November 12, 1989. Reported in FBIS, November 13, 1989, p. 32.

"symmetrically." Roald and I would have our civil marriage at Wedding Palace Number 1, the only registry office where Soviets could marry foreigners. To restore the balance, Matlock graciously offered the ambassador's residence, technically on American soil, for a religious ceremony. He could make no predictions about the outcome of our approach to the Politburo but said that he would send an "eyes only" message to Secretary of State James Baker to brief him about our plans. I left Spaso House deeply grateful to Jack for his understanding and support.

When Roald and I met later that same day, we had some disagreement about whether or not I should have given Matlock the go-ahead to send the cable to Secretary Baker. Roald was apprehensive about having the information about our plans in writing. His anxiety was contagious; the two of us stewed about this small matter for nearly two days. But finally I pulled myself together. "Why shouldn't we put something in a confidential cable?" I wrote in my diary. "I am sure such memos are flying all over Moscow."

It was as if we were living in suspended animation, nervously waiting to find out what Gorbachev's position on our forthcoming nuptials would be. We assumed that by now the Politburo was doing background checks, assessing whether our union might create a breach of Soviet national security. We kept hoping to get some kind of assessment of Gorbachev's attitude, but it was not forthcoming. I left Moscow with everything up in the air, while political developments in the Soviet Union and Eastern Europe seemed poised for some kind of terrible showdown.

Roald and I decided that the two of us should meet one more time before the Second Congress of People's Deputies was to convene on December 12. In case we had to go through another communications blackout, it would be best to have all our scenarios planned in advance, just in case.

I was ambivalent about where we should meet. I swayed back and forth between going to Moscow again and meeting Roald in some third city. We decided finally to aim for Paris in early December. Roald had been invited to go to conferences in Paris and Lausanne, and he thought we could get together somewhere along the way. As chairman of the Committee of Soviet Scientists, he deputized someone whom I will call Boris Rumyetsky, a former Central Committee apparatchik, to make all the arrangements for his exit visas and travel documents.

When we had resolved our plans for Paris, we both remarked on the "coincidence" that during the very same days President Bush and President Gorbachev would be in Malta together. *Time* magazine's issue for that week was headlined "Super Partners." Roald and I liked that notion very much.

Despite being in Paris, we were still having troubles with "the monsters." Throughout our Paris stay, Rumyetsky and a man named "Ivan" from the Soviet mission to UNESCO seemed to be with us at every moment—incredible, I thought, that Roald and I could barely manage a moment to be alone. Worse, Roald seemed intent on inviting the two men to dine with us at nearly every meal. I couldn't imagine why he was so deferential to them.

I had suspicions about Rumyetsky. What kind of a man was sent to Czechoslovakia to work with "youth organizations" just after the Soviet invasion in 1968? Who a year later was sent to Vietnam for the same purpose? At first I was surprised at Roald's cordiality toward him and the amount of our time that Boris was allowed to monopolize. Then I got angry and upset. Like the "eyes-only" cable to Baker, why should we be concerned about what Boris and Ivan thought if the people who would decide our future already knew about our plans? Such logic may have been easy for me, but I had to concede that I had not grown up in a society where even small-time informers wielded tremendous personal power over those they targeted.

Within days Roald sent me a sweet and loving letter from Lausanne. I think, after Paris, he had sensed that I needed to hear some reassuring words.

> December 10, 1989
> Lausanne
>
> Susan, my love,
> How sad to return to the lonely place, which keeps so much of your touch! I hope that it is not going to be too long and at least one of the last times [that I come here alone] . . . I am going to implement the decisions we took in Paris, going to the Congress (now much less exciting) . . . I am so spoiled by you now—cannot stay, cannot live without you even a day, no a minute, a second.
>
> Your loving faithful serf,
> RZS

When we spoke several days later, Roald tried to tell me on the telephone that "Paris" had been part of "old thinking." Concerned, he said, that one or a number of the people who were with us reported to "other authorities," he apologized that he had naturally tried to underplay my presence in Paris.

I knew that we were on the threshold of making the kind of changes that would free us both for each other, so perhaps that is why I found the ensuing weeks nearly unbearable. I imagined that the authorities would "accidentally" lose Roald's divorce papers—thereby effectively forestalling our marriage. It was the kind of trick they had often used in processing visas, and I guessed it could perfectly well apply in this situation. The leadership could always blame the lack of resolution of Roald's marital status on "legitimate" bureaucratic snags.

Roald and I survived by talking on the telephone literally every night. I took it upon myself to call him at about 11:00 Bethesda time. That was one of the hours that offered a reasonable prospect of getting through, and it also served as Roald's wake-up call in Moscow.

One evening it took me nearly an hour to get a line. When I finally made the connection, I was in a state of total exasperation. "But you have reached me," Roald said brightly. "And I am so happy to hear your voice. I love you."

The words hit me like an electric shock. We had broken the sound barrier! The words "I love you" uttered over the telephone were utterly liberating. Let the monsters chew on that for a change!

On December 14 tragedy struck once more and plunged "our project" into a new state of uncertainty. That evening as I was preparing for bed and waiting to call Roald, my sister Anne phoned me from New York. "Sakharov is dead," she told me. "I just heard it on CNN."

As soon as we hung up, I began trying to dial Moscow. After ten or so minutes I could hear the ringing tone at "Belgrade I." When Roald picked up the phone, I apologized for calling him so early but, I told him, Sakharov was dead. He was shocked to hear the news. "I can't believe it," he said. "I saw him only a matter of hours ago." Roald and I spoke briefly, then said goodbye. He was intending to call some of their friends and colleagues for more information.

It was unbelievable that Sakharov should have died as he did. The Second Congress of People's Deputies had just begun, and Andrei had made an important contribution to its work by eloquently pushing for the abolition of Article VI of the Soviet constitution, which gave the Communist Party a political monopoly as "the leading and guiding force in society." It had been a dramatic moment indeed when Gorbachev turned off Sakharov's microphone while Andrei was speaking and he had been unable to finish his impassioned speech.

Sakharov had died at his apartment the evening after that very session. According to Elena Bonner, he had been working on a draft of a new constitution.

I could not imagine what Sakharov's death would mean for Roald. They had been personal friends for many years, but in the last two they had become closely identified politically as well. I knew there would be great pressure on him to assume Sakharov's mantle. This became more obvious when Roald was invited to serve on the funeral commission and was asked to write the eulogy for his old friend in *Izvestia*, *Literaturnaya Gazetta*, and *The Washington Post*.

I fretted a bit about Roald's new dilemma, but I had developed a kind of calm. This event went far beyond the two of us. I decided that I was willing to stay with him as long as he wished and that I would not press him about a precise wedding date. His future in Soviet politics had now assumed an unexpected new dimension. I felt that if I were to take him away from the reform movement, it might actually destroy the great love we had for one another. So I was fully prepared to go forward with him, or even let him go—taking all the risks associated with either choice.

I tried to tell him all this over the telephone in code, but to my surprise Roald was adamant: "The project will be launched as planned."

The tension of the final weeks of December was nearly intolerable. On the political front, the Lithuanian Communists broke from the Moscow-based national Communist Party. Vaclav Havel became the first non-Communist President of Czechoslovakia in more than forty years. And the conflict in Romania erupted into revolution; at Christmas a military tribunal executed the Party dictator Nicolae Ceauşescu and his wife.

Amid this turmoil, Roald told me on the telephone one evening that he had been unable to secure an Aeroflot seat for December 31. I immediately took this to mean that the authorities had been unwilling to give him a ticket. So, to cover our bets, I sent Roald a hard-currency ticket but told him that he shouldn't come to the United States unless his divorce became final. If it did not, then we'd have to think about what the next move would be.

As December 29 neared, I waited anxiously for word from Roald about his divorce. In desperate need to relieve the stress I was feeling, I sat down once again to write him one of those "letters" that I never sent but kept for him to read in our still unknowable future.

December 28, 1989

Dear

This is probably the last time I will write you before you face the final arrangements on your divorce . . . Before sitting down to write you I reread much of what I have written in my journals in the last few months. It is obvious that I have been under considerable strain—which has escalated over the recent past.

More and more I have become concerned that events and the physical distance between us have been driving the agenda. I am concerned that you are feeling obliged to move forward, when in fact you may need more time to adjust to a number of things. I am sure, for instance, that Andrei's death was a terrible blow and that it has given you more than a moment of pause about what you should be doing.

But I want you to know that I think our relationship is remarkably durable and that nothing could really jeopardize it, unless you have not been honest with yourself.

Above all else I love you as a human being. From the moment I met you I was drawn to you by your tenderness and your sweetness and all the lovable qualities I can't find words for. This is something that never goes away.

Then it happened that these feelings simply grew and developed into a deep desire to be *with* you and to bring to your life a joy that would make you genuinely happy.

I want you to know this because it is important that you understand that taking your time, and being sure about the two of us together, will not change the way I feel about you. But our future happiness together depends on our mutual knowledge that you came to this marriage as an emotionally free man—and that you are entering this new life without doubts. You would hurt both of us immeasurably if you were not honest about this . . .

As you know I have spent nearly seven years by myself. I built a rather successful life out of the ashes of two painful divorces. I am not frightened about making the changes that are necessary for us to be together, but it would grieve me, more than you could know, if for any reason you are fooling yourself and, in the process, fooling me as well. I felt utter assurance about "us" after this summer, but as I am sure you realize, we have been together only thirty-odd days in more than 130. It has been difficult to second-guess your feelings, especially with so little exposure to one another during this time. That is why Paris was so difficult for me to understand.

You have probably figured out, from watching me in action, that I can be pretty determined at times and fully committed to success. Having said that, I was interested to see an entry in my journal from just about a year ago, I was surprised by the clarity of the thought. Nothing has changed. The idea I articulated then is just as real now. I said something like: "I am prepared to fight for what you want with everything I have—but I could not live with the outcome of a compromise that was reached because of lack of courage." I was talking then about your race for the Congress of People's Deputies. Now I am talking about us.

Remember it was you who captured my heart some time ago. Whatever happens, you should know that you will always have it.

With real love,
Susan

I put this letter in the file with all the others which I had written to Roald but which he had never read.

That night rather than staying at my home—the girls were still on Christmas vacation in Rochester—I decided to go to "Belgrade II." Tomorrow would be the day that Roald would know one way or the other if the authorities had decided to block our marriage. I slept badly all night, wrestling with the anxiety of the last two years.

About 6:00 in the morning, the telephone rang. I got up and went to the adjoining room to answer it. There were two beeps on the line, which meant that it was a call coming through from Moscow. I held my breath.

"Susan?" I could hardly hear Roald's voice.

"It's me," I shouted back. The line crackled ominously. "It's me," I repeated.

"Can you hear me?"

"Just barely," I shouted.

"I am calling to tell you"—the line stuttered again—"I am calling to tell you I am free . . . to be your serf."

I cannot begin to describe the relief I felt at the sound of Roald's words. But I knew that I wouldn't be fully satisfied until he was with me—the political situation was still so dreadfully unpredictable. Within the last few days, particularly with the Ceauşescu execution, the world had turned upside down.

We planned that I would meet Roald's plane in New York and we would spend New Year's Eve with my sister Anne. The morning of December 30, I took the shuttle to LaGuardia and hailed a taxi for my sister's apartment in Manhattan. Anne and I had a quiet dinner that night, but I was agitated and distracted. After dinner I decided to call Roald, and after nearly half an hour of dialing we confirmed that I would meet him at Kennedy Airport late the following evening. As we spoke, he was packing and would be leaving in a few hours to go to the airport.

The next morning I rose early, unable to sleep. Out the window I saw to my horror that thick fog was blanketing the city. I searched the paper for news of a predicted clearing, and then I called a telephone weather report and turned on the television for some kind of update. But the fog, I was desperate to observe, only grew worse as the day wore on. I waited in agony, worrying about the worst and fussing about the best, unable to contain the anxiety and anticipation I was feeling.

I thought perhaps one alternative for watching the clock would be to go to the video store and rent a movie for the afternoon. For some reason which I still cannot explain today, I selected *Dr. Strangelove, or: How I Learned to Stop Worrying and Love the Bomb.* For the better part of the afternoon I allowed this black comedy to absorb some of the nervous energy that I had otherwise directed toward the weather and the prospect of Roald's imminent arrival.

Anne had called a car company well in advance to reserve a car to take me to the airport—a wise move. The fog did not relent, a steady drizzle had started to come down, and most taxis in New York were tied up taking partygoers around the city for New Year's Eve. Anne had invited a number of friends over to see in 1990, so I joined her guests until 9:00—the hour I had set to leave for Kennedy Airport. Excusing myself, I found my coat and went out onto Park Avenue, where the car and driver were waiting for me.

We drove through the dark shining streets of New York and onto the fog-shrouded highway. It seemed like the longest hour of my life. When we reached Kennedy, I discovered that the Pan Am flight from Moscow had been delayed, but at least they made no mention of diverting it. I paced back and forth, checking the board for new information every few minutes.

Nearly an hour later, the monitor showed that the Pan Am flight from Moscow had landed. I watched every passenger come through the customs exit doors, looking at their bags for some indication of which flight they had been on. Gradually I began to notice tags from the Pan Am flight, and I inquired of an elderly passenger if he had come from Moscow. He confirmed that, yes, the flight had arrived and that most of the people had already collected their luggage. I waited. And waited. There was no sign of Roald. I focused all my attention on that door, but he did not come through. My heart began to sink.

Suddenly someone touched my arm and I turned. There was Roald, standing beside me, with two bags firmly clasped in his hands. Dropping both of them he threw his arms around me. We held on to each other, unable to let go.

"Happy birthday," he whispered in my ear. "If we hurry we can be back in New York in time to see in the New Year. Nineteen ninety is going to be our year."

21 : Negotiating a Wedding

Anne flipped through the thick authoritative-looking book she held on her lap. "I don't know what to advise and I don't see anything about it here."

"Anne," I said, "believe me, *Emily Post* has nothing to say on this subject. I don't think any etiquette book in the world can give us advice about this kind of marriage."

I was resigned to "fly blind." We'd have to make decisions about all sorts of social matters entirely on the basis of what served Roald's and my concerns about our safety. The more visibility we gave our wedding, the more difficult it would be for the Soviets to act arbitrarily.

Despite the pressure, from the moment Roald arrived in the United States he seemed at peace. While Sakharov's death had been a big blow for the Soviet people, and for him personally, he had rejected the idea of somehow becoming Sakharov's political successor. "In no time at all," he predicted, "my generation will be swept away politically. That is the nature of revolutions." He was also convinced that the two of us together could play a much more significant role as interlocutors between our two countries. It would take many years for our countries to normalize relations, and we were in a nearly unique position to assist in that process. But all these dreams and plans were contingent on getting approval for our marriage, which still was not forthcoming.

Had the authorities thrown up their hands in resignation, or were they still making up their minds about the national-security implications? We feared that it was the latter, and I was uneasy about the effect of Roald's declaration of war against the military-industrial establishment over the loss of Phobos I and II. That issue was far from resolved, and Roald was still pushing for an international commission to get behind the iron curtain of secrecy that shrouded the true reasons for the spacecrafts' loss. The only thing we could do was to move forward until we were stopped.

In Washington, Roald and I decided that we would begin our preparations. Unable to leave each other even for a minute, we decided that he would come home and live with us. I told my children that I was marrying. Their reaction reflected the collegial way Roald and I had conducted ourselves. Although they all knew "Dr. Sagdeev," only Caroline had any idea that I had been involved with him. Amy was particularly thrilled when she heard the news. "You mean I am going to have another daddy?" she asked. "Who is it going to be?"

"Dr. Sagdeev."

"Oh goody!" she squealed.

I swore her to secrecy. She nodded and solemnly took her fingers and ran them across her mouth as if sealing her lips. However, I struggled with her for days as she persistently asked me if she could use the "w" word.

After Roald was safely with us in Bethesda, I started telling a number of my friends who worked in the government. I also asked them to keep an ear to the ground for gossip or any news that might affect the timing of our announcement. I had already contacted my siblings and parents with the same request.* And, to a person, they expressed support and promised to call me if they heard anything through the grapevine.

The confidential calls I made to the Washington establishment did not provide unanimous support for what we were doing; in a few cases I was a little saddened by the reaction I received. But in the main, support surfaced as we had hoped.

Richard Nixon phoned me to congratulate me, but said with some chagrin that the Soviet Union would be losing someone who was badly needed for *perestroika*. I had heard this many times, and I was able to assure him that Roald hoped to play a new role now as a bridge between our two societies. "There is so much in this respect to be done."

Senator Dole and a few others from the Eisenhower Centennial Commission also called. I was grateful to them because of the sensitivity I still

---

* I was particularly touched by my mother's reaction. For Christmas she had given me a silk and flannel nightgown that she had chosen for its warmth. "It is for a Russian winter," she said.

felt about the impact our marriage would have on the Eisenhower Centennial, whose year-long celebrations had already started.

When I rang Brent Scowcroft, National Security Adviser, he thanked me for the information but seemed a little noncommittal. Then about a half hour later he called back and apologized. "Did you say that you are going to marry *Roald Sagdeev?*"

I told him that it was so.

"Oh well, that's wonderful," he exclaimed. "I couldn't say that about some of the people I have worked with there, but I have known Sagdeev for years and he is a very fine man. I wish you both all the happiness in the world."

Several days later, one of my friends told me he thought we should go public as soon as possible. "I went to a party the other evening," he said, "and a man from German intelligence asked me if I had heard the rumor that a prominent Soviet and a visible American were about to wed. He told me Helmut Kohl wanted to know who it is."

The "heads up" was well taken and Roald and I began to step up our timetable. We decided to announce our engagement as soon as we reached President Bush with at least a message. In his own sphere of reference our marriage was small potatoes, but I understood the potential for embarrassment if there was a bad public reaction, especially since he had been so gracious to me at Kennebunkport and at the White House.

I decided to make the approach as informal as possible. So one late afternoon, I called Bucky Bush, the President's younger brother, whom I had met at Kennebunkport the previous year. Bucky listened attentively to my news, and I tried to fill him in on who Roald was in Soviet society.

"Listen, Bucky, I'm going to leave this up to you. If you think this is something the President should know about, I'd appreciate it if you would tell him. If you think it's unimportant, then keep the information with you and brief him later if necessary." Bucky said he would do so.

When I came home from the office a couple of hours later, my housekeeper, Delores, told me the White House had called and the operator had said the President would telephone again when he came out of a meeting.[*]

At 7:30 the phone rang again and President Bush came on the line. "Bucky says you're getting married. Bar and I send our warmest wishes. I

---

[*] I discovered later that the meeting was on the invasion of Panama.

understand you have an exceptional man there, and we wish you all the happiness in the world. Where are you planning to live?"

I was stunned by the question. For some reason it had never occurred to me that anyone in the United States would ask it, let alone the President. Had the country progressed faster than I had thought? I told the President that we wanted to divide our time between Washington and Moscow and that we intended to continue to work hard to improve U.S.–Soviet relations.

"Well, I think it's just great," he said.

The President's words impressed me deeply. It meant a great deal that he had such confidence in us that he was prepared to go on record with me while the social-political jury was still out. I don't know whether President Bush knew it or not, but his simple gesture cast a halo of optimism and protection over our union.

Still, Roald and I were exhausted by the combination of anxiety and fatigue. Things were not helped when Ella Orlova, a friend of ours in Moscow, called to say that all our friends had read the news of our engagement in a brief article in *Pravda*. Ominously, she said, it made no independent comment about the forthcoming event but had simply quoted a *France-Presse* story word for word. They were concerned because the Soviet press had taken this same damning approach to try to discredit Boris Yeltsin. At the tail end of his first trip to the United States, *Pravda* had quoted, without comment, an Italian newspaper report on Yeltsin's behavior during his American visit. This hands-off commentary by the authorities made our friends wonder whether it was safe for us to come back to Moscow or not.

To add to the confusion and the abundance of mixed signals, a huge bouquet of flowers arrived later that day. It was from Soviet ambassador Yuri Dubinin, sending congratulations and warmest regards for many happy years together.

"Poor guy," Roald mused, "he probably hasn't received instructions from Moscow yet on how to handle this situation."

Enough was happening in the U.S.S.R. to make us realize just how many crises were preoccupying the very people whose decisions we were awaiting so eagerly. The political situation between Moscow and the republics was rapidly deteriorating. Gorbachev made a disastrous trip to Lithuania in an effort to dissuade the Lithuanian Communist Party from breaking with Moscow, and when he returned to the Soviet capital, a new outbreak of violence erupted in Azerbaijan in which more than forty people were killed. The situation in Azerbaijan looked as if it would continue to escalate dangerously.

With most of our legwork done, Roald and I responded favorably when a friend called and suggested the story be given to *Time* magazine. Strobe Talbott, editor-at-large, was a friend of ours, so it made some sense.* Later that morning Strobe called, greeting me warmly if slightly bewilderedly. "I must say I pride myself on being pretty close to these things, but your marriage is something I would have never guessed."

Within an hour a photographer had been dispatched by *Time*—and we hastily contacted the rest of the press, to avoid excessive favoritism.

I was fascinated by the way our story was handled. Most journalists reported it as a "Cold War is over" human-interest story. *The New York Times* ran an article on the front page, but *The Washington Post* put it in the "Style" section. I was surprised that so many people I talked to seemed to take the possibility of such a union for granted. Many people predicted that Gorbachev would come to our wedding and offer the bridal toast. These new indications of wishful thinking were only underscored when we discovered that almost no one remarked on the significance of a marriage of a Westerner with a member of their Congress, a scientist with high-level security clearances.

Several days after Roald and I announced our engagement, the First Lady's social secretary, Laurie Firestone, told me that President and Mrs. Bush wanted to give a small dinner in our honor.† We were deeply touched and hoped that their gesture would have its effect on the Kremlin. In the choreography of the Cold War, symbolic initiatives were usually reciprocated. If Gorbachev accepted the idea of our marriage, he would be free, indeed impelled, to respond to something so visible and official as a White House invitation. And if Gorbachev reciprocated in this way, his official recognition could keep Roald's enemies at bay.

The dinner that January 15 was held on the second floor of the White House in the "family quarters." In one simple evening all the elements of

---

* Strobe Talbott became Under Secretary of State in the Clinton administration.
† They were interested in knowing whom we would like to have at the dinner. I, of course, mentioned my siblings who lived near the Washington area, but I left the others pretty much up to the White House. A day later, the White House called again and said that Brent Scowcroft, National Security Adviser, Administrator of NASA and Mrs. Truly, and Bob Gray, prominent Republican and former Eisenhower administration member, would be coming. Laurie Firestone said that Ambassador Yuri Dubinin had also been invited.

my life seemed to be brought together in perfect harmony. Having Roald and Yuri Dubinin with me at the White House—indeed on the second floor—was, in a sense, like introducing them to my past. I think the Bushes sensed this.

The President said to Roald, in a fatherly way, "Susan is very special to us and we want to know that you are going to look after her properly and be a good husband."

There were a few toasts to our happiness, and a few more toasts to improving relations between our countries. Indeed, after President Bush had raised his glass to us, he spoke of his respect for Mikhail Gorbachev and his current dilemma. Earlier in the day, the media had reported that Soviet troops had been sent to Baku to quell the rioting in the Azerbaijan capital.

Looking at Dubinin, he said he understood the challenge that Gorbachev was facing today and the necessity to take measures in Baku—to put down senseless ethnic hatred and internal conflict. "Tell President Gorbachev that I support his action," he added.

After dinner the Bushes offered to show the guests the other rooms on the second floor. Ambassador Dubinin was the first Soviet ambassador who had ever been in the private quarters of the White House, so when the Bushes suggested that we all go up to the third floor, where the children and grandchildren traditionally stay, Dubinin could barely contain himself.* He was most impressed by the Bushes' openness and hospitality, but he was also desperate, as we guessed later, to get back to the Embassy to send a coded message to the Foreign Ministry and to Gorbachev conveying his astonished discovery that President Bush would support Gorbachev in doing "what had to be done" to put down ethnic violence and confrontation in the Soviet Union.

At the end of January Roald and I boarded a plane for Moscow together. It seemed odd to enter the Soviet Union *with* Roald, instead of waiting to see his smiling face at the end of the jetway. After the long trip we were greeted by a sizable group of friends, all of them carrying flowers and giving us affectionate hugs. Most of the people there hadn't known that Roald had gone to the United States with the intention of announcing plans to marry. When I asked him why so many people were there to greet us (some

---

* This area is traditionally off limits even to American dinner guests.

of whom I didn't even know), he said they had all read the article in *Pravda* and were concerned that we were walking into trouble. "They came to the airport to express their support," he said.

Not long after our arrival we were given a pile of letters that had come in our absence. What was striking about them was that most of the cards had come from non-Russians. From their inscriptions, we understood the root of their support: many of the Estonians, Tatars, and Georgians who wrote us applauded us for standing up to the Kremlin or for our bravery. Another category of letters emphasized the importance of this union as a demonstration that Christians and Muslims could live together in the same household. Very few of those who wrote said anything about the "end of the Cold War."

The day after our arrival, we had to present our "papers" to the chief wedding bureaucrat at Wedding Palace #1, a middle-aged, matronly-looking woman. She told us to come back in two weeks. Then she gave us a little blue card that entitled us to go to a special wedding store. There, a bride could buy a white dress and a groom could buy any one of a few models of suits. Gold rings could also be purchased there, as well as special food items for wedding receptions.

This card was a very valuable commodity. In a society suffering from greater and greater consumer shortages, it would have been impossible for the average bride to prepare for her wedding without the special protection these stores placed on the goods. Roald and I noticed that our "wedding card" also allowed us to buy a refrigerator and other appliances. On a list with several consumer items that most brides would need to start a new home, more than half the items had been crossed out. "You see," Roald said, shaking his head, "this is indicative of the times we live in."

The next ten days were a whirlwind. Roald and I met with the Protestant chaplain who had agreed to perform the religious ceremony at Spaso House; we made plans for flowers to be bought at the open market and arranged; I authorized the making of a cake, with ingredients purchased and driven to Moscow from Germany; and we persuaded Metropolitan Pitirim to send us a Russian Orthodox choir to sing during the ceremony.

The question of hotel rooms was most difficult for many reasons. It was suggested that the fourteen wedding guests we had invited to come from the United States should stay at the Oktyabriskaya Hotel, where security would be tight. But when Boris Rumyetsky checked the availability of rooms, the manager said it would be impossible to accommodate so many people. A day later Roald told me it had been done. "How did Boris do it?" I asked.

Roald laughed. "This is indeed a country of miracles. The manager told Boris that he would 'find the rooms' on the condition that Boris get him an invitation to the wedding."*

From the beginning of our wedding preparations, we were engaged in a dialogue with Valentin Falin. I had known him for some time, and regarded him as one of the most interesting men on the Soviet scene.† As former ambassador to West Germany, later chairman of Novosti Press Agency, and currently chairman of the International Division of the Central Committee, Falin was a very tough negotiator whose political sympathies were becoming less progressive and more conservative by the day. Despite this, there was something about our wedding that struck a sentimental chord with him,‡ and he tried hard to smooth the way as best he could.

Falin advocated a special Foreign Ministry luncheon in our honor. With Secretary Baker and Foreign Minister Shevardnadze negotiating the START and CFE treaties in Moscow during these days, it would be natural, he thought, that this symbolic wedding receive their attention. I don't know whether he was being enlightened or simply practical. He probably knew that Roald and I had been honored at the White House and figured that the Soviets might as well get some mileage out of our marriage, too. Nevertheless, the idea was nixed, by whom we never found out.

Political tensions in the city were mounting. On the Saturday before our wedding there was a huge demonstration that nearly overwhelmed Moscow. Despite the cold snowy weather, 250,000 people gathered near the hotel

---

* The Central Committee Plenum was convening in Moscow and many Party members were staying at the hotel. We noticed them when we came in for meals. They had been assigned to the dining room next to ours and we would often see them in deep discussion. At the Plenum, Gorbachev called for the Party to give up its "leading role" in society and agree to a multiparty system. Many of those we saw in the hotel looked glum and serious.

† It was under Falin's watch that the Soviet Union was accused of disinformation in spreading rumors that the AIDS epidemic had been started by U.S. biological-warfare research. And it had been Roald Sagdeev, in 1987, who had publicly debunked the accusation, exclaiming that no serious person could believe that the United States would do such a thing.

‡ When Yuri Osipyan told him in November that Roald and I were planning to marry, he predicted that Americans would not be ready for such a marriage and that it would seriously undermine my standing in the United States.

where our wedding guests were staying and marched toward the Kremlin, on the other side of the Moscow River, demanding the repeal of Article VI of the Soviet Constitution. Momentum had been furiously building for this reform since December, when Sakharov had called for its elimination and, with his death, had become a virtual martyr to this cause.

The old guard was sure to have been unsettled by this vehemence— moral leaders like Sakharov often turn out to be even more powerful in death than in life. Only months before, when Chinese students had gathered in Tiananmen Square to mourn the death of reformer Hu Yaobang, blood had been tragically shed. Would the Soviet authorities attempt something similar here?

The night before our wedding, *Moscow News* asked to come by our hotel for an interview. We had just finished speaking to CNN when the reporter arrived. He seemed perplexed, even somewhat uncomfortable, about his assignment. He began by saying that he simply did not understand the nature of a love that would expose itself to such risks. Roald and I tried to explain how much we wanted to be together and how much our relationship had come to mean to us—but he persisted. "Couldn't you jeopardize everything, even the love you have?" he asked.

It was hard to know how to respond. "People," I answered, "win if they don't lose faith, if they can hold on and rally others to their side. In such cases, the state inevitably finds that it is not a productive use of energy to persist." I cited Andrei Sakharov and his release from Gorky.

But the reporter still remained troubled. After a half hour he shrugged, wished us well, and went out into the dark February night.

Certain images of our wedding day have stayed firmly in my memory. I remember flowers, flowers, and more flowers. I had never seen so many beautiful bouquets before. When we arrived at Wedding Palace #1 well-wishers were there with even more flowers.

I think the chief wedding bureaucrat knew that our wedding was going to disrupt palace routines. When we arrived it was obvious that ours was the only wedding scheduled that morning. Unlike the other Soviet newlyweds, we did not stand in line waiting for access to the wedding hall. In fact, the press had staked out positions all around the entrance of the palace. Inside, there were also crowds of reporters.

Roald and I spoke with them briefly and went into the wedding hall, where the chief bureaucrat waited for us to present our passports. It was on these documents that the authorities wrote the particulars of our wedding.

Several minutes later we proceeded into a larger hall. As we approached the door, one of the palace coordinators asked us if we wanted "pop" or "classical" music. The quartet, whose job it was to play all day long for the succession of couples who came through the door, were waiting for a decision. I said, "Classical." I was so distracted by everything that was happening that I didn't really hear the music, but my sister Anne told me later that they played a selection from *Cats*.

Our friends stood around us, and at the end of the hall, the matronly official lectured us about our responsibilities to the state. But in what I thought must be a departure from her usual speech she spoke about the additional responsibility Roald and I had in showing the world "another way." She spoke eloquently about the senseless divisions that separate people—and that in inhabiting an interdependent world, people would have to learn to live harmoniously together.

During parts of her speech, several newsmen tried to move in for closer shots. Elena Loschenkova moved forward to block their intrusive move and very nearly started a full-scale scuffle in the process.

Roald and I exchanged rings. Elena told me later that she feared that a reporter would knock one of the rings off the plate. If that had happened, she said, it would have meant bad luck.

After the ceremony, Roald and I left through the front door. By this time a sizable crowd had formed—a number of people appeared to come from the neighborhood. As I settled into my seat on the right-hand side of the *chaika*, I noticed that several *babushkas* were peering in the window. I rolled it down and gave each of them some flowers from my bouquet.

Planning the wedding had brought all kinds of unexpected concerns. When a reporter from *Paris Match* wanted to photograph us, the considerations were very complicated. Would we have the picture taken in front of the Kremlin? I vetoed that idea. Would we do it in front of the Tomb of the Unknown Soldier? Both of us were hesitant.* St. Basil's? Roald balked. The ornate cathedral had been built to commemorate the Russian

---

* The practice of having brides pay their respects to the Tomb of the Unknown Soldier had become tremendously politicized during the Brezhnev period. I was happy to do so if it had resonance with the most important cultural traditions, but both Roald and Nicolai Shishlin advised against it.

sacking of Kazan, his native city. "They'd never let me go home," he quipped.

We had the same kind of dilemma after the wedding ceremony. Tradition had it that the bride and groom make a kind of pilgrimage to a few patriotic places where the bride would leave her flowers. Most of these spots had ideological overtones, however, so were out of the question for us. All the same, there was nothing wrong with the tradition itself.

So after some thought, Roald and I decided to leave my flowers at the wall of Novodevichy monastery. It was around the monastery pond that we had walked so many times in deep thought and concern for our future together. It now seemed a miracle that we were here—at this very place —together as man and wife.

Later in the afternoon, at 4:00, we had the religious ceremony at Spaso House. We were happy that some of the most glittering intellectual talents in the Soviet Union attended it. Yet despite their "liberal" bent and familiarity with spiritual issues and Western traditions, the service was for most of them the first religious wedding they had attended. We had the service translated into Russian so they could follow what was being said.* But the concept of making vows *to each other* was unknown to them— indeed, in sharp contrast to the Soviet ceremony, where the state lectures one about one's responsibility to *it*.

By far the most exotic of our wedding guests was the Mufti of Moscow, the spiritual leader of Tatar Muslims. He had told us in advance that he could not come—presumably because he understood that it would be a Christian ceremony. But just before the nuptials began, we had word that he would be coming to the reception. So I was surprised, as I walked down the aisle, to see the Mufti, in his splendid white turban, seated in the front row not far from the Russian Orthodox choir, in glorious song. (When I asked about it later, I was told that the Mufti had stood outside until his curiosity could stand it no longer, then he ushered himself in and took a seat in the front row.) Later, he presented us with a copy of the Koran as a wedding present.

Roald and I recognized that it took courage for our Soviet friends to come to our wedding. As the leadership had not given our union their blessing, no one really knew how to react, and while some senior government officials came, others were conspicuously absent. Despite the presence

---

* Roald and I each said our vows in our own language. We thought it was important for both of us to fully understand what we were committing ourselves to.

of Susan Baker, wife of the U.S. Secretary of State, none of the other spouses at that level turned up. Nor were we invited to anything that could even be remotely regarded as a reciprocal gesture to President Bush's dinner. On the contrary, my father—who had been received by Stalin, Khrushchev, and Brezhnev—was not invited to the Kremlin to see Gorbachev, although Falin had apparently made an effort to set up such a meeting.

From the quiet off-the-record messages of congratulations and warm wishes we got from Alexander Yakovlev and Evgeny Primakov, it was clear that Gorbachev himself had balked.

Despite this, we had to turn many people away for lack of space. No one, except for officials at the highest echelons, waited for instructions anymore. If people wanted to come to the wedding, they did. It was the surest indication yet that things in the Soviet Union had begun, fundamentally, to change.

At the end of the day, Roald showed me a letter that had been delivered from Foreign Minister Shevardnadze and his wife. The emotional note showed that he was not only the most liberal man in the Politburo but probably its most romantic:

Dear Susan and Roald,
Congratulations on the festival of your love, the victory of feelings and wonderful impulses, a veritable name-day of the hearts.

Your union is like the birth of a new bright star—the star of a faith in the eternal drive for happiness, the star of a never dying hope for the triumph of love.

The lives of both of you confirm the wisdom discovered by the ancients: one's happiness is an indispensable part of the happiness of others. You are undertaking the resolution of the most noble task—to provide the survival and prosperity of all humankind, to pull it out of the chains of disconnectedness and distrust.

You came to the right decision: it is easier to achieve if two big hearts, open to the anxieties and concerns of others, are brought together.

From this very day, our countries will be united not only by the ties of interdependence, by the direct telecommunication line of Vladimir Posner, but by the strong union of Roald and Susan. With such a union, we believe, all of us should be confident in the fate of civilization.

We wish you the happy joint flight in the space of love and mutual understanding.

Sincerely yours,
E. Shevardnadze
N. Shevardnadze

The day after our wedding, Roald went to IKI to tie up some loose ends before our departure for Kazan to meet Roald's parents, who were not well enough to come to Moscow. Despite the Foreign Secretary's effusive and heartfelt good wishes, his letter did not constitute permission for Roald to live abroad, nor did it give him an exit visa. To get around this, we had chosen Budapest for our honeymoon, since Roald didn't need an exit visa for Hungary, and once in Budapest he could leave for the West without a problem. As a wedding present, the American Embassy had rushed through a U.S. entry visa for him.

We knew that the ambiguity of his legal status would make him vulnerable on future trips to the Soviet Union, particularly if there was a crackdown. Nevertheless, we had decided to proceed until we were stopped. We could think of no other way. Although we were nominally leaving the Soviet Union for only a short while, neither of us really knew when and if we would return.

In his tiny one-room apartment I cleaned up and prepared for the coming weeks. I had only several hours to complete a mammoth job. First I wrapped up an evening snack for the night sleeper train to Kazan, and then I set about packing what I could of Roald's belongings.

Going through Roald's things was an emotional experience. Most of the photographs, books, papers, and gifts were connected to me in some way. The rest of them were about people and places that had consumed my imagination from the moment Roald shared with me his colorful stories.

As I went through his papers a kind of sadness seemed to cling to the silence in the dusty flat. Why can't people be everywhere at once, with all the people who need them and love them and want them to stay? It was hard for me even to fathom that we had actually taken the step and married.

Disbelief came naturally in the environment of "Belgrade I." I knew and loved every inch of that funny apartment, with its peeling wallpaper and buckling linoleum floor. Despite its size and deteriorating condition, some of the happiest moments of my life had been spent here. The personal connection and closeness between Roald and me had been so powerful that nothing about the little place could have seemed even remotely inadequate. It had been our refuge from Roald's powerful enemies and from the prying eyes of our neighbors—who had existed for us only as a threat to our sanctuary. I had certainly thought of them as a threat, and yet I'm not sure I ever really saw any of them. It seemed that they rarely left their own apartments, preferring instead to watch television and shout orders to their barking dogs. Occasionally we would hear someone on the landing emptying vodka bottles into the communal trash chutes near the elevator.

I was deep in thought when suddenly I was startled by the chirping of the doorbell. Adrenaline coursed through me; my ears began to throb and burn. I had always been under strict instructions from Roald not to open the door to anyone. But now I thought perhaps Roald was returning without his keys . . .

"Hello," I said. There was no answer through the door.

"Hello," I repeated.

I offered a few clumsy sentences in Russian.

Then came a reply. It was the landlady.

I felt I had no right to deny her entrance, so I timidly opened the door.

From what I could tell with my limited Russian, she had read about our wedding in the newspaper and had come to see the "foreign wife" for herself. As we exchanged awkward pleasantries, she eyed me intensely, cocking her head and pressing her long chin forward. She stayed for several minutes and then left as suddenly as she had appeared.

I closed the door behind her with relief, but then another feeling overcame me—a peculiar sense of confusion, almost dizziness. Roald and I had had many people at our wedding, we had given interviews, and we were together for everyone to see. Yet there was something unsettling in this visit: the landlady had at last intruded on our haven, where we had been together only for ourselves and sheltered what we were becoming from the world.

It took me a few minutes to collect myself before our new circumstances began to sink in. Now we could summon the elevator to our own floor, and we could speak English together in the courtyard. Let the whole building find out that I'm an American, *babushkas* be damned—tell anyone you like. Nobody can hurt us now. If the Soviet authorities make trouble for Roald, they will be making trouble for *my husband*. Nothing they can do can divide us. We are husband and wife.

PART
FOUR

There are only four ways in which a ruling group can fall from power. Either it is conquered from without, or it governs so inefficiently that the masses are stirred to revolt, or it allows a strong and discontented Middle Group to come into being, or it loses its own self-consciousness and willingness to govern. These causes do not operate singly, and as a rule all four of them are present to some degree. A ruling class which could guard against all of them would remain in power permanently. Ultimately the determining factor is the mental attitude of the ruling class itself.

—GEORGE ORWELL, *1984*

22 : Letting Go

It was already dark as we edged our way down the long, crowded platform to the first-class section. There, a stout uniformed woman took our tickets and pointed us in the direction of our sleeping car. I wrestled with a shoulder bag and a large wedding bouquet I had brought for Roald's mother. The conductress disappeared to find us a vase for the flowers. This she did with a sense of mission. Flowers were given respect in Soviet Russia, a deference they never gave the bearer.

The clacking and swaying of the train were monotonous but relaxing. Roald and I talked for hours about the wedding and everything that had happened in the last days. He seemed lighthearted, though I could sense some drag on the liveliness, which I did not ask him about. I, too, had vague, inexplicable feelings about the magnitude of what we had done— so complex that I couldn't have put them into words even if I'd wanted to.

After a short light sleep, the public-address system roused us with Tatar music. I groped for my clothes in the hope that I could get to the end of the corridor, and the bathroom, before the other passengers. According to a man smoking a cigarette just outside our compartment, we were an hour away from Kazan.

When I returned from the lavatory, Roald had opened the curtains and our compartment was flooded with light. Early-morning sun glistened on the patches of snow that covered the rolling brown hills of Tatarstan. The conductress brought morning tea, and we sat opposite one another, silently watching the countryside pass by.

"We are nearing the Volga River," Roald said suddenly. "Look there!" He pointed to a wide snow-covered river basin.

"Volga Volga, Mother Volga," he started to sing, softly at first.

"Do *you* know what 'Stenka Razin' is about?" he asked brightly, his eyes dancing.

Like my father, I wasn't sure what the words of the song meant.

"It's about a Cossack named Stenka Razin who marries a Persian princess. When he realizes that his shipmates are grumbling and angry because he's married a foreigner and has neglected his friends, Stenka Razin makes his choice. He lifts up his wife, the Persian princess, and delivers her to the approaching wave. Volga Volga, dear Mother Volga." He started singing again in a low ominous tone.

"You mean he throws her overboard?" I asked.

Smiling broadly, Roald stood up and with a sweeping gesture pretended to pick me up. Then he stopped and looked out the window. "It's a shame," he said. "The Volga is frozen solid. You have been saved!"

Kazan, established at a beautiful site where two rivers join and enter the main Volga stream, was built by the Bulgars, successful thirteenth- and fourteenth-century merchants who spoke an ancient Turkic language. As our train crossed the river, I could see the Kazan kremlin in the distance, sitting high on a bluff commanding the landscape above the river, its painted white battlements and onion-domed spires sparkling in the sun. It was one of the oldest kremlins, or forts, in Russia.

The Bulgars, neighbors of the early Russian or Slavic tribes, were the first people to be stormed by the "Mongol hordes" of Ghengis Khan, before they conquered large parts of Eastern Europe. Roald told me it wasn't until his early adulthood that he discovered, with relief, that his ancestors had not been part of the Golden Horde but, like the Russians, had been victims of their rule.

Two centuries of Mongol dominance brought a Russian invasion of Tatarstan, led by Ivan the Terrible. In the centuries that followed, Russification reduced the native Tatar population to only 46 percent of the region's total. The Tatar language was now spoken by only a small fraction of the people, and virtually all the schools were Russian.

Like the Soviet Union's other non-Russian ethnic groups, the Tatars were afraid of becoming culturally extinct in their own homeland. With nationalist disturbances in the Baltics, in Georgia, in Moldavia, in fact, everywhere in the Soviet Union, one could only wonder how long it would take before such sentiments would grip this city as well. We had sensed the impulse for independence growing already: only a week before we'd received a telegram of congratulations from the Tatar Popular Front— hailing our marriage as a valuable step in "strengthening the ties between the Tatar and American peoples," making no reference of any kind either to the Soviet Union or to Russia.

Roald's uncle Hannan was at the train station, waiting to meet us, with a handful of red carnations. He had dark graying hair and a heavily lined round face. His whole persona exuded good-natured humor, and even though Hannan spoke no English, we understood each other at first sight. After introductions were made, we climbed into his car.

While Roald and Hannan exchanged local gossip, I gazed at the passing cityscape of Kazan. Despite the appearance of neglect, the remaining old city was a jewel of eighteenth- and nineteenth-century architecture. We drove through picturesque snow-covered streets of wooden houses with gingerbread window frames—apparently unaltered since they were built by prosperous merchants, who had flourished on Volga River commerce.

As we drove, Hannan told Roald about how "the news" had been broken to his family. His parents' initial reaction to our wedding plans had been shock and genuine upset. They had stewed about it for days, but Hannan, and Roald's younger brother, Robert, had explained that times had changed and they would simply have to adjust.

Whatever it was they said, Roald's parents had clearly "come around." That morning when they opened the door of their apartment off Dostoevsky Street, my mother-in-law looked at me with startled surprise, but I could tell instantly that she approved. A short energetic woman with vibrant blue eyes, she threw her hands into the air and planted a kiss firmly on my cheek. My father-in-law, less lively because of his difficulties in walking, nonetheless gave me an equally warm greeting: a genuine Tatar bear hug.

At lunch he offered a toast. "I am an old man," he said, his champagne glass wobbling in an unsteady hand, "and I am going to die soon. And when I go to heaven, the first thing I am going to do is to find President Eisenhower and tell him that now we are relatives!" Everyone laughed, and I could see that his comment was his way of welcoming me to the family.

More food was put on the table, and the flurry of serving went on for some minutes. Mama, Papa, and all the cousins wanted to hear the details of our wedding. Roald, I could tell, was beginning to warm up.

Roald, of course, knew that his father, an old Party man, was a conservative. As he described the details of our wedding, he obviously relished reciting the names of the many radical reformers who had come to it. I could see Papa's displeasure grow by the second. Then Roald leaned over to me and, like a naughty boy, whispered: "You see, my father doesn't seem to mind that I have married an American. But he can't stand the fact that we invited Yuri Afanasiev to our wedding."

With that meal over—and many more to come—Roald announced that before the "midday dinner" he would take me out for a walk to see Kazan on foot. We bundled up and escaped into the bracing February air.

Walking through Kazan was like venturing into Roald's past. All the stories of his childhood and his family's history came immediately to life. He showed me the sanatorium where his father had been hospitalized in the 1930s, and I saw two of his childhood homes, small wooden structures barely large enough to accommodate two people, let alone six. We had been out a considerable time when suddenly I noticed a woman carrying two very heavy buckets. Not far away, several people were standing near a pump.

"Don't they have running water?" I asked. The temperature was well below zero.

Roald admitted that a substantial part of Kazan was still without running water. Kazan, the capital city of one of the Soviet Union's oil-rich regions—which had pumped more oil than Kuwait in the last forty years —had houses with no running water just off the main street!

Local residents filled their buckets and returned to their wooden houses, with windows crooked from age and glass that no longer fit the frames. These ordinary people didn't have plush dachas and state-owned cars. They had outhouses in the dead of winter and long lines to buy rancid meat.

I shuddered slightly; in part from the sight before us, but also from the cold, which was beginning to penetrate my inadequate cloth coat. Roald put his arm through mine, and we briskly walked back to Dostoevsky Street.

The night before leaving the Soviet Union we had a private unofficial dinner with Evgeny Primakov. He had earlier been sent to Azerbaijan to serve as a political intermediary there, so the subject of the interethnic strife in that part of the world dominated the conversation. The subject of "what next" for Roald and me never came up. (Primakov probably didn't *want* to know our plans.) Any discussion about our new lives was confined to a progress report on the construction of our dacha outside Moscow. Located in one of the privileged compounds reserved for full academicians of the Academy of Sciences, this project had been subject to many delays and work stoppages. Both of us dreamed that the political situation would stabilize so that we could use this house in the summers, as we had planned.

The next day we left for Budapest. Everything went smoothly when we left, except that something about the documentation on *my* visa was "irregular." Roald and I nervously waited for twenty minutes while the KGB border guard disappeared for instructions. We nearly missed our plane.

Roald had many friends in Budapest, most of them connected to the Academy of Sciences, of which he is a foreign member. They thought we should move to Budapest, the only acceptable solution, they felt, to Roald's problem of "no permission." I had once supported the idea of living for a few years in Budapest. It would give the Soviet authorities a chance to get used to Roald's living abroad, and it would be a fascinating time to be there as an onlooker. It was certainly still an option, as both of us were filled with apprehension about what moves the authorities might still make.

Once we reached the city, Roald and I tried to relax, to have a real honeymoon. But the stress of our last year, of our engagement and wedding, was so great that both of us got ill. Suddenly more than two years of pent-up anxiety and separation took its toll on our bodies. We were quiet for no more than two days when we both developed intestinal bugs and very bad colds. It was as if our bodies—which had been in a state of constant alert—had finally let down their guard.

We came back to Washington sick and worn out—but also unable to leave one another's side for even the shortest number of minutes. When we both began work again, Roald, to a temporary job at the University of Maryland, and me, back to my company, the hours away from one another were near-hell. Roald called it separation anxiety. We talked several times a day to assure each other that we were safe and sound.

As for the girls, I could tell they found it strange to have a man in the house again. For almost a decade we had been a women's dormitory, my three daughters, my housekeeper (a widow), and me. A new atmosphere now pervaded our home. Girls would come flying out of the shower half-dressed, suddenly to remember that now there could be no more running around without clothes. These occasional awkward moments were made up for by Roald's own sweet nature, and by the respect the girls had for our relationship. They could see how good he was to me, and deep down they knew how elusive that had been and how precious it is when it is found.

For myself, I brought a little defensiveness to this new form of parenting, accustomed as I was to shouldering the entire burden myself. I tried to smooth over the ordinary consequences of life with teenage daughters. Loud music and other forms of nighttime noise would prompt me to corner them with pleas to let my new husband sleep. The girls always apologized for these lapses, for they knew that life had really fundamentally changed.

We had not been in Washington more than a week before Soviet friends began calling to tell us that Roald and I were under increased attack in the Soviet Union. Several times a week these well-meaning Russian friends would ask when we were coming again. We were alarmed by the urgency with which they said this. It was extremely complicated to figure out how we would manage the summer with the children, and how we would arrange work and money-earning, and still fulfill our plans to spend four months a year in the Soviet Union.

After weeks of painful debate we had to ask ourselves if we weren't still trying to feed the Soviet monsters. The problem was that the monsters didn't have faces we could see, so we didn't know how big their appetites might be. I worried that they would never get their fill and that we might have to feed them ever bigger helpings indefinitely.

The Budapest option was still on the table—a promising possibility for two people still trying to satisfy the beasts. We asked Yuri Osipyan what he thought about us living in Budapest one evening when he was in Washington. "Hungary isn't a fraternal state anymore," he said ruefully. "Frankly, if you leave, you leave. So you might as well be in the United States, where you already have ties."

Yuri's response was very telling. "This is the Soviet culture," Roald remarked grimly. "As Stalin used to say, 'He who is not with us is against us.' The feelings persist."

Within a month Mikhail Gorbachev called for an extraordinary meeting of the Congress of People's Deputies to consider Article VI and to elect him President of the Soviet Union. Should Roald return for this hastily called meeting? Now the calls from Moscow came almost daily at 6:00 in the morning. The pressure on Roald to attend this Congress was considerable. Nevertheless he hesitated. "What am I going to do? Go all that distance just to vote against Gorbachev?" After considerable debate, he decided to stay put in Washington.

Roald was not alone in his suspicions about Gorbachev's new demand for increased power. Given the developments in the Baltic republics, he and many of his colleagues were certain that Gorbachev's new authority would be used for no good.

In addition to the strain of making this decision, one evening before the Congress, the man I have called Boris Rumyetsky came with another of our colleagues for dinner at our house. They were pessimistic and worried about our situation in the Soviet Union. Boris went further. He said that he had gone to see Valentin Falin before coming to America, and when Boris told Falin he would be seeing us, Falin had shrugged and said that Roald was under attack in powerful circles for making such an "extended visit" in the United States. According to Boris, the military-industrial barons and the KGB of that sector were irritated and angry: if the wedding hadn't been so visible, they would have "never let Sagdeev go." They complained that people of less significance were barred from such freedom.

Then, Boris ominously told us, the KGB had said that if the American space program made any significant strides in the next few years, Soviet intelligence would "hold Sagdeev personally responsible."

After they left, Roald paced around the kitchen. His face was furrowed with worry. "Perhaps we shouldn't go to Moscow this summer," he suggested anxiously. Suddenly he began talking in the gloomiest terms about "car accidents" and other ways the KGB might try to "get rid" of him.

That night when we got into bed, I was rigid with stress and fear. "We got in just under the wire," I said softly. "But we probably should've known that we'd be continually plagued by these problems." Then I added, "It doesn't matter. We are together. We are in circle defense."

Roald was quiet for some minutes. When he finally spoke, his voice was hoarse. He cleared his throat and said, "I will not go back to the Soviet Union without you, but I can't be with you every hour of the day, so there is inevitably some risk we can do nothing about."

We both said no more. Roald rolled over and put his arms tightly around me. That night we clung to each other as if we were holding on for dear life.

23 : Too Little Too Late

Once the Berlin Wall had come down in November 1989, the Soviet leadership was in disarray. Tass reported that Eduard Shevardnadze had rejected the idea that Mikhail Gorbachev was responsible for the end of Communist power in Eastern Europe. "It has been destroyed by the will of the people, who wished no longer to tolerate coercion," he said.* Tensions were mounting all over the Soviet Union, especially in Lithuania. Gorbachev reminded me of a dominating and rigid parent who lectures his children about behaving themselves and showing more parental respect when the children have already grown up and left home. By now, even the Communists in Lithuania understood that the only way to survive was to break with Moscow.

In an interview around that time, a Latvian was asked how it felt to have the pressure turned up from Moscow. He said in effect, "We are not frightened any more. We are more frightened by the prospect of giving in. We don't want to go back to what we were before. Independence may be difficult and there may be great hardship, but we want to make our own mistakes now."

With sentiments for independence growing everywhere, we feared that Gorbachev would be either co-opted by the conservatives or ousted by the hard-liners who wanted to stop the disintegration of the U.S.S.R. The Soviet President had used force in Baku, but it was clear that this policy had not worked. After the election of a non-Communist, Vytautas Lands-

---

* *The Wall Street Journal*, February 28, 1990.

bergis, to the Lithuanian presidency, and the adoption of a declaration of independence, relations between Lithuania and Moscow deteriorated almost completely. Moscow escalated its harassment of the country: armored cars were seen in the streets of Vilnius, central authorities seized factories and Party buildings, Lithuanian draft dodgers were rounded up, and an oil and gas embargo was imposed to bring the rebel republic to its knees.* Moscow would continue its policy, it warned, unless Lithuania went through the Soviet Union's procedures for secession. In reality, as everyone knew, these lengthy legal procedures were so rigorous, the period of qualification so long, and the level of trust so abysmal that secession would ultimately be sabotaged by political reality.

Many people in the United States made the argument by analogy that we had to be sympathetic to Gorbachev because "we did, after all, fight a civil war of our own." But I kept remembering the words of the Georgian independence activist Merab Kostava,† who had told us in Tbilisi that since the Soviet Union was the last colonial empire, it was historically inevitable that it would break up. The question was whether Moscow would have the wisdom to adopt the peaceful British approach, which paved the way for the Commonwealth, or whether it would make the bloody mistakes that other imperial powers did, trying to stop a predestined process.

Roald and I had watched developments in Lithuania apprehensively. Could there be another Afghanistan? If the Soviets underestimated the likely American reaction to a Soviet use of force, that would be the end of détente.

We felt that we could not speak freely on the crisis for fear that his children, who were still living and working in Moscow, would be harassed or targeted in some way. It was typical in Soviet times for families to be punished for the behavior of one of their members.

Although we felt restrained from speaking out, behind the scenes Roald suggested a compromise in the Soviet–Lithuanian showdown to National Security Adviser Brent Scowcroft. He felt that if the international community, perhaps the United Nations, would serve as the ultimate guarantor of Lithuanian independence, conditions could be created to allow Lithuania to go through the arduous legal process for secession. Scowcroft listened politely, but we knew that the Bush administration would continue its tacit support of Gorbachev and his policy.

That spring, when Shevardnadze came to Washington to negotiate some

---

* Kaiser, *Why Gorbachev Happened*, p. 441.
† Kostava died in a car accident, not long after we saw him in Tbilisi.

of the details of the forthcoming summit meeting between Gorbachev and Bush, we were struck by the fact that the freewheeling Foreign Minister was, this time, accompanied by Marshal Sergei Akhromeyev, the Soviet Union's most famous general.* It became clear that the arms-control concessions that the Soviet Union had agreed to in Moscow at the Foreign Ministers' meeting, at the time of our wedding, were now unacceptable. The Soviet military saw the measures as disadvantageous to the Soviet Union, and—against the backdrop of the East European events and the probable unification of Germany—they were digging in their heels.

On March 28, the anniversary of Granddad's death, the White House gave a luncheon in his honor to mark the Eisenhower Centennial. The gathering was held after a joint session of Congress. I went to these proceedings at a slight disadvantage: I had completely lost my voice—a combination of overwork and the continued process of letdown and renewed anxiety.

Roald and I had been particularly worried about what Ambassador Dubinin, on more than one occasion, was saying about the situation in Lithuania. Dubinin persisted in pointing out that during what he called the "historic" dinner that the President had given in our honor, Bush had expressed support for Gorbachev's sending troops to Baku. "Isn't it wonderful there is such understanding?" Dubinin now said again to me at the White House luncheon.

"The Lithuanian situation will be regarded quite differently from Baku," I warned him. But I got the strong feeling that he had probably sent more than one cable to Moscow reiterating that the Americans would understand if the Soviet government "did what it had to do." Although accounts written since indicate that the Soviets had already taken note of the American objection to force in the Baltics, my diary indicates that Dubinin persisted in making these remarks.

Not long after, Yuri Osipyan came to our house for a drink. I was shocked by his appearance. He had lost weight and his eyes seemed to droop with fatigue and unhappiness. Since his appointment to the Presidential Council, he told me, his life had changed completely. His family was very upset about his decision to sit on the council, and now he had two bodyguards all the time. "This is the end of my private personal life," he told me

---

* Once chief of the Soviet General Staff, Akhromeyev was a close military adviser to Gorbachev. After the aborted coup attempt in August 1991, he died, an apparent suicide. While remembered as a progressive on certain arms-control matters, he was regarded within the Soviet Union as a hard-line pro-Communist reactionary.

glumly. I think he also knew that the Soviet Union was at a turning point, and that he would be called on to take some very unpopular positions, sharing in decisions that could undermine all the gains that had been made in the last few years.

Yuri, like Roald, was hoping that a compromise could be found with the Lithuanians. He had suggested to Gorbachev that he contact the Lithuanian legation in Washington, to propose some areas for discussion. According to Yuri, Gorbachev's advice was to "stay out of the dirty business."

That night I wrote in my journal: "Yuri wears a certain sadness that clings also to me."

Meanwhile, Roald and I were trying to put our own lives in order. We rearranged the furniture in the house in Bethesda, closed "Belgrade II," and moved my office. We were also touched that so many of our good friends gave parties for us.

That spring Roald was appointed to a tenured position as Distinguished Professor of Physics at the University of Maryland at College Park. The decision to forgo the offer from the Institute for Advanced Study in Princeton was based largely on geography, since for family and professional reasons we needed to stay near Washington. After all we had been through, we couldn't see ourselves living the commuting life, apart for several days a week. Still suffering from separation anxiety, it was hard enough for the two of us to say goodbye when we left for work in the morning. Also, in Washington we could continue our almost obsessive focus on the Soviet scene. Motivated perhaps by both guilt and fear—and an overwhelming impulse to be seen as a positive force—we were engaged in around-the-clock work with our Soviet colleagues in science, business, and bilateral policy.

Despite this level of near overactivity, we inhabited a political no-man's-land, and this reality only pushed us harder. The twilight zone of our new circumstances was readily apparent during the summit meeting that June.

I had an invitation to go to the National Academy of Sciences to meet the Soviet delegation, but Roald had not been included, which was awkward, since he had been among the Academy's first few Soviet foreign members. The Academy apologized but said that if Roald were to be included, his name would have to be put on the list by the Soviets. This was eventually arranged, but the whole process was strangely unpleasant.

We faced a similarly perplexing problem regarding Gorbachev. Some days prior to his arrival, I received an invitation from the Soviet Embassy for a luncheon to meet him. Billed as another gathering of "American intellectuals," it seemed to be similar to the event that I had attended during the December 1987 summit. In conversation with the Soviet Embassy coordinator, I asked if this invitation was also extended to my husband. He said flatly that only Americans were being invited.

Husband-wife solidarity, I thought, particularly with the signals we had gotten from Moscow recently, was more important than ever. But Roald insisted that I go alone, and he made plans to be in Boston.

Around midnight, just hours after Gorbachev's arrival, someone called from the Soviet Embassy. "President Gorbachev has just arrived in Washington and he has asked me to convey an invitation to Academician Sagdeev for the luncheon tomorrow." I managed to reach Roald on the phone in Boston and he reluctantly agreed to leave his meeting a little early and come back to Washington. As we had suspected that Gorbachev had withheld official support for our marriage, this encounter would be full of significance for us, and we were curious about how we would be received.

The next day, at the Soviet Embassy, the room was crowded with big names from Washington, Hollywood, and New York literary circles. Roald and I mingled with the guests for a while, then suddenly we were summoned. "The President wants you to come through the receiving line first."

Mikhail and Raisa Gorbachev were standing side by side, next to the new ambassador, Alexander Bessmertnykh. Raisa Maximovna was talking animatedly to someone on her right when Gorbachev caught my eye and exclaimed, "Susan!" Then, "Roald Zinnurovich! I want to offer my congratulations! I heard about your wedding, and I am now happy to have the opportunity to give you my best wishes personally."

He grabbed both our hands and pressed them together. "I unite you both in the symbolic union of our two great countries!" He held our hands together and raised them, in an almost religious way.

Raisa had not seen his gesture. When we moved to greet her, she repeated it, and declared our wedding a "symbolic union."

Later Roald told me that Osipyan had been responsible for his being invited to the luncheon. On the plane from Moscow, Yuri and Gorbachev had reviewed the invitations to the party, and Yuri had pointed out that Roald was not on the list. As Yuri described it, to get the Soviet President to add Roald's name required more than an hour's discussion and what he termed "the reeducation of Mikhail Sergeiivich."

Perhaps Roald and I should have been excited and relieved by Gorbachev's behavior to us. But he was three months late. More than gratitude or irritation, we saw his gesture as symptomatic of his great and tragic flaw: he was sadly behind the events caused by the historic processes that he himself had unleashed. Only after something had actually occurred was he able to accept it as done—and then, if he could, he tried to take credit for it. Although this trait was understandable, it lay behind almost every mistake he made before his final loss of power—including his failure to support Boris Yeltsin's election, only days earlier, as president of the Russian parliament. Yeltsin's popularity had grown significantly. He was perceived by the populace as a courageous advocate of their interests. But rather than make common cause with the more progressively minded maverick, Gorbachev backed Yeltsin's conservative rival, Ivan Polozkov. As much as any other decision, this revealed to everyone that Gorbachev could no longer shape events but only react to them. And when he did, most often it was too little too late.

Roald and I were both conscious of how long we had been away from the Soviet Union. My daughters were going to spend the summer with their dad in Rochester, and we both felt that going back to Moscow was a risk we should take.

Roald wanted to see his children and grandchildren—he had just become a grandfather again in March, when his daughter Anna had given birth to her first child, a son named Gregory. It was important for our family and friends to know that we had not deserted them.

No sooner had we landed in Moscow that June than we discovered that a campaign of press attacks had been launched against Roald, including a strongly worded rebuke in *Izvestia*. We were puzzled. *Izvestia* had gained the reputation of being a progressive paper; indeed, it was *Izvestia* that had printed Roald's early attack on the administration of Soviet science.

Speculation was rife about who had sanctioned the attacks. Many of Sagdeev's friends seemed to concur that it was an effort by the military-industrial complex to discredit Roald once and for all. It was said that the articles had been endorsed by the tsar of the complex: Oleg Baklanov, the man with whom Roald had had so many serious disagreements, particularly over the cover-up of the Phobos investigation.*

One evening, after the last session of a conference we attended in Len-

---

* Baklanov was to organize the attempted coup a year later, in August 1991.

ingrad, we found ourselves on the same night sleeper with Georgi Arbatov, who had chaired the meeting. We had the privacy and the time to talk about the situation. As the train picked up speed and the lights of Leningrad disappeared, we met Georgi in his compartment, where he got out a bottle of Scotch and some cheese and bread he had brought for the journey. Our conversation centered on the changes we had seen in the country since our arrival, especially the growing power of the military.

"What is the difference between a moderate and a radical?" Roald asked. "Six months!" he exclaimed, without waiting for Georgi or me to guess.

Known during the Cold War days as one of the Soviet Union's chief spokesmen, Arbatov himself had been through his own process of radicalization. Roald told me that in December 1989, at the Congress of People's Deputies, Arbatov had acted like a kamikaze pilot. During discussion of Prime Minister Ryzhkov's budget, he had attacked the military appropriations—and after the two-week session was over, he wrote scathing articles about the Soviet military-industrial complex and its insatiable appetite for money and resources. Since then Arbatov had become a visible target of the military. In fact, Arbatov and Roald were often linked. One military magazine had published a vitriolic assault entitled "Children of Arbatov,"* where Roald was of course characterized as one of them. Given how much Roald had done in Arbatov's electoral campaign to the Congress of People's Deputies, we took more than a passing interest in his on-going battle with the armed forces.

We asked Arbatov about his dealings with Gorbachev's chief military adviser, Marshal Akhromeyev. "When you see Akhromeyev these days are you still civil?" Roald asked impishly.

"Of course," Arbatov responded, "outwardly everything is quite normal with the army. In fact, I saw Akhromeyev at the Kremlin the other day and he greeted me in a perfectly cordial way."

This was indeed surprising, given that the two men had been exchanging vicious accusations in the news media for some months.

Arbatov then recounted a remarkable story. He told us that he had just had a birthday celebration. When he returned to the office one afternoon after lunch, his secretary was in a state of high excitement: Marshal Dmitri Yazov† had personally stopped by to deliver a "birthday present"—a care-

---

* A play on the famous novel that had just been published, *Children of the Arbat*, by Anatoly Rybakov.
† Then Minister of Defense. He was later charged as one of the leaders of the August 1991 putsch attempt.

fully wrapped package containing a leather-bound volume, which outlined Arbatov's distinguished military career beginning with his record as a young officer during the Second World War. The volume included beautifully mounted photographs of young Arbatov and copies of all his military citations and evaluations.

"Of course," Arbatov added with a realistic relish, "one has to ask oneself why they bothered to do such a thing for my birthday. Huh! The guys got out my file and wanted to see if they could 'get something on me.' And what did they find out? That I really *was* a wartime hero. When they realized they couldn't use my record against me, they probably thought, We might as well make the material up into a nice book and give it to him."

Arbatov confirmed that *perestroika* had perilously stalled. We ourselves had heard people speaking urgently of the looming harvest failure of that year's bumper crop, and for the first time there was hushed talk of civil war. Rumors said that the KGB and the army were conspiring to bring authoritarian rule back to Soviet life.

Some days later we had dinner with Yuri Osipyan and his wife, Luda. Yuri looked no better than he had when we had seen him in Washington. His responsibilities in the Presidential Council still weighed heavily on his shoulders, and his mood was grim. "The country cannot go on like this for more than a couple of months, maybe a year," Yuri said. Luda, equally alarmed by the increasing hardships and political divisions, seemed to punctuate everything she said with "If something happens . . ."

Roald and I found distressing scenes everywhere in Moscow. Stores were empty, and specialty shops for vodka and consumer goods had lines of anxious buyers snaked around full city blocks. When we asked one woman what she was waiting for, she said that she and the others were waiting to put their names on the list kept by volunteers at the door, self-appointed watchdogs who double-checked that only people whose names had been listed—in proper order—got into the store. This was the public's only defense, they said, against people who were ready to jump the queue and pay bribes to buy the limited goods.

One could see the origins of a popular Moscow joke at the time: A lady who has been standing in line for several hours announces that she is fed up and is going to the Kremlin to kill Gorbachev. The people standing around wish her well, and she leaves. A half hour later she returns and asks for her old place in line. The people agree and ask her what happened. "Did you kill Gorbachev?" they inquire eagerly. "No," the woman says. "I got there and the line was even longer."

Aside from material difficulties, society was showing deep and sometimes ugly fissures. One of Roald's scientific colleagues, who was a Jew, told us with great trepidation that a woman had telephoned him at home and said that she was calling from the Prime Minister's office to get his home address so that they could mail him an invitation. When nothing ever came in the mail, our friend began to ask around. A number of other people had received similar calls. Through a small private investigation, they discovered that the calls had been part of an effort launched by the radical right-wing group Pamyat to compile a list of names and addresses of Jews and "other enemies." The speculation was that this list would be used for specific acts of terrorism—perhaps pogroms. Many of the press attacks on Roald also had ethnic overtones. Innuendo implied that his unpatriotic behavior had something to do with his being a Tatar.

Everyone we talked to seemed fatalistic about the country's prospects of coming out of this period without bloodshed. One of our friends proclaimed that violence would be inevitable. "A country built on the blood of forty million deaths will never make this transition without cataclysm."

Another friend of ours said that people were behaving irresponsibly, predicting a similar inglorious end. "It's like watching passengers drink and make merry, in wild frivolous abandon, while the *Titanic* slowly sinks." As she said this, I wondered how she could see things so clearly and then grab a glass of vodka and join in? But as Roald said to me, Russians think that looking for lifeboats is shameful; the culture tells them that everyone should go down with the ship.

Roald's "no lifeboats" theory was a product of Russian fatalism, related to an impulse he called "co-suffering," a kind of equality and egalitarianism of grief and despair. If Ivan or Masha is happy or miserable, you should be, too. As in the economy, where government policy had been aimed at making everyone equally poor, the same instinct governed emotional matters.

When we saw Roald's parents again toward the end of the summer, however, we sensed none of that demand that we "co-suffer" with them. (Perhaps it is not a Tatar phenomenon.) What tension existed came from my father-in-law, who asked Roald what he had done about his membership in the Communist Party. Roald said that he had, effectively, left the Party at the time of our marriage. Hearing this, Papa grabbed his walker and, in a state of fury, got up from the table and hobbled into the adjoining room.

Hannan, Roald's uncle, arrived some hours later. Not knowing anything about what had gone on earlier, he entered the apartment in a cheerful and joking mood. "What is the procedure for leaving the Communist Party?" he inquired. Everyone waited for the punch line. "The endorsement of three non-Communists!"*

Everyone laughed except Roald's father, who glowered darkly. Then Hannan added, beaming, "Today is a great day. This morning I handed in my Party card to those bastards at the design bureau!"

Before he could utter another word, Roald's father, blustering under his breath, reached for his walker again and once more shuffled angrily from the room. Hannan watched him with astonishment.

It was not hard to see the pathos and poignancy in what these rapid changes must have meant for Roald's father and his generation. The suffering and deprivation that he and his family experienced had all been, it seemed, for nothing.

Roald and Hannan may have been among the earliest to hand in their Party cards, but the Communist Party was by now in deep crisis. The Twenty-eighth Party Congress, held that summer of 1990, threatened to block Gorbachev's efforts to continue his reforms. Expectations were that Alexander Yakovlev would persuade him to follow the lead of other reformers in countries like Hungary, and split the Party by establishing a progressive social democratic offshoot of it. Hopes were pinned on Gorbachev's taking leave of the conservative elements in the Party once and for all. But at the end of the Party Congress, much to the disappointment of Roald, Hannan, Shishlin, and our other friends, Gorbachev was re-elected as the Party's General Secretary. †

The next day, Boris Yeltsin and Vyacheslav Shestakovsky, rector of the Communist Party's Higher School, handed in their Party cards in disgust.

More painful to watch than Gorbachev's re-election as Party chief was his indecisiveness on the economy. Throughout that summer and fall he wavered between the progressive "500 Day" economic plan and a more conservative one being put forward by Prime Minister Ryzhkov. When it

---

* No one could *join* the Communist Party without the endorsement of three members.

† Yegor Ligachev, his old rival, however, failed to become Deputy Party Secretary and the Congress revamped the Politburo, which would no longer have any real power over the running of the country.

was announced that he would support a compromise plan between the two, Boris Yeltsin observed derisively that it would be like "mating a snake with a porcupine."

Within days the Moscow jokesters were ready with their retort: "What is the offspring born when you mate a snake and a porcupine?" The answer: "Two meters of barbed wire."

Moscow black humor reflected the people's deep fear that the armed forces would intervene to stop the steady erosion of central power and the indecisive slide into the abyss. By mid-September, rumors were confirmed that, indeed, military maneuvers had been staged outside Moscow. When the army insisted they were only routine, even the denials fueled yet more speculation.

Roald and I encountered a symptom of the hardening situation and the growing influence of the military when we discovered on our return to Washington that the Eisenhower Centennial activities planned for Moscow were now in jeopardy. A conference for Soviet and American historians had been scheduled to take place in mid-November, organized by the Eisenhower Institute and Georgi Arbatov's Institute of United States and Canadian Studies. On September 26 we got a call from Arbatov's deputy, Sergei Plekhanov. He told us that there had been a protest in the Supreme Soviet, accusing Arbatov of spending vast sums of hard currency from the state treasury to send three hundred Soviets to an Eisenhower Centennial event that was being held in Abilene, Kansas. This was an outrageous and false accusation. Arbatov and I had had nothing to do with that particular project; in fact, no Soviet state funds had been spent to send any Soviet delegations to the United States for the centennial. We surmised it was all a staged fuss.

Our suspicions that this was simply a blatant personal attack were strengthened when we discovered that the deputy who had made the protest in the Supreme Soviet was an army major. The next day another deputy with the rank of general complained that the delegation was celebrating the birth of an American who as President had been an "enemy" of the U.S.S.R. Plekhanov said that the conference's organizing committee would have to decide whether or not to go forward. He told us that Arbatov would call us when he got back to Moscow from Japan.

I was prepared to agree to canceling the meeting, but I hoped Arbatov wouldn't suggest it. The centennial was now becoming just an excuse to discredit all of us. I felt that if we canceled, we would all seem vulnerable and that our detractors might later use this perceived weakness against us. I was delighted when Arbatov agreed that we should hold the conference as scheduled.

In November, when we arrived for the conference, Roald and I saw how much Soviet attitudes had polarized. To position himself as the guardian of army interests, Gorbachev met with the thousand military servicemen who had been elected to public offices the day before we arrived. During the five-hour meeting, however, the acrimony of Gorbachev's audience became abundantly clear as one serviceman after another complained of their recruitment problems, the threats against their garrisons, the indifference of local authorities, their poor living conditions, and the barrage of negative publicity about them in the news media. They demanded that he sign the Union Treaty immediately, thus codifying the relationship between Moscow and the republics and legitimizing the presence of Soviet armed forces in the outlying regions.*

The morning the Eisenhower Centennial conference began, Marshal Akhromeyev launched yet another attack in *Sovietskaya Rossiya* on Arbatov and another of our friends, Yuri Ryzhov, director of the Moscow Aviation Institute. In addition to rebutting their recent articles line by line, for the first time Akhromeyev suggested that "[in response to] actions to dismember our country or change its social system, the armed forces—by the decision of the Supreme Soviet and the U.S.S.R. President—could be used to ensure the unity of our motherland and preserve its social structure in accordance with the U.S.S.R. constitution."

I noticed that Arbatov's hand shook slightly as he held the newspaper and read the article to me. As a student of history he had to know what these words might mean for him, the target of Akhromeyev's frustration, if a crackdown were to occur.

The following week Marshal Yazov announced that the Soviet Union's armed forces were authorized to use force to protect military installations and personnel in areas disrupted by ethnic turmoil.

The U.S.S.R., it seemed, literally was coming apart. Russia had declared the sovereignty of its laws over U.S.S.R. laws, and a number of other republics had taken the same measures. As a consequence, most republics had ceased paying taxes to the Soviet central government, which further

---

* See Stephen Foye, "Gorbachev, the Army and the Union," *Report on the USSR*, December 7, 1990.

threatened the viability of the most centralized of all state organs, the military and its industry, the KGB and the government bureaucratic apparatus.

Reacting to a growing sense of panic in the country, the Supreme Soviet of the U.S.S.R. demanded that Gorbachev give a State of the Union address. On November 24 he gave a lengthy presentation, full of sermonizing generalities, and to his apparent surprise it elicited a tremendous show of hostility among the deputies. I will never forget those faces, some of cynical indifference, others of outright hatred; and Gorbachev's variously filled with humiliation and anger. As Roald and I watched the speech on television, we both felt we were witnessing another turning point.

When Gorbachev came back to the Supreme Soviet the next day, he was in a completely different mood. Roald and I speculated that he had been unnerved by the malevolence of the day before. After only twenty-four hours' consideration, he announced a complete reorganization of the government. The Presidential Council was abolished and replaced by a so-called National Security Council. Within days he also announced that he had empowered the KGB to work directly with workers' vigilante groups to "police" enterprises for illegal and corrupt practices and to crack down on black marketeers and "economic saboteurs."*

When Ukraine announced its intention to become a nonnuclear state, we hurriedly made arrangements to leave for the United States as soon as possible. Neither one of us wanted to be in Moscow when the crackdown came.

---

* From the earliest Soviet times, the leadership had blamed poor harvests on the weather and poor economic conditions on "speculators," "corruption," or "saboteurs." Foreigners, too, were often scapegoats.

24 : *Squeezing Out the Slave*

Before the end of the year, Gorbachev again summoned the Congress of People's Deputies. Roald decided, with virtually no second thoughts, that though he was still a deputy it was not safe for him to return to the Soviet Union. At the meeting in December, Gorbachev would again, for the third time in less than a year, ask for "extraordinary powers" to stabilize the U.S.S.R. But what was not completely clear in the West was that Gorbachev had already broken with his old progressive allies. Perhaps this is why Westerners were so stunned when Eduard Shevardnadze resigned on December 20, citing the possibility of an impending dictatorship.

By way of explanation for his departure, Shevardnadze told Moscow News that he could not support the use of force to impose discipline and order on society. To do so, he said, would make a mockery of the U.S.S.R.'s foreign policy and "new thinking." He also made it clear that the head of the "creeping coup d'état" (a phrase coined by another Congress member) was Gorbachev himself. *

Many analysts accused Gorbachev's progressive allies of desertion, but from what we had seen in November, Roald and I were convinced that it had been Gorbachev who had abandoned the progressives first, leaving Shevardnadze little option but to leave his post. While we were in Moscow, we'd visited Alexander Yakovlev at his Kremlin office. There were many small signs that he no longer had influence with the President. His desk

---

* See Kaiser, *Why Gorbachev Happened*, pp. 387, 388.

was clear, the phone didn't ring, and a feeling of inactivity hung in the air. He appeared to be a man marking time.

Then, in early December, the liberal Vadim Bakatin was fired as Minister of the Interior, replaced by Boris Pugo, former head of the Latvian KGB. At the same time, General Boris Gromov was appointed as Pugo's deputy—significant, we thought, because he was the first military man to take a position in this ministry, which was responsible for internal security. It seemed ominous that Gromov had more combat experience, as commander of Soviet forces in Afghanistan, than anyone else of his rank.

The last of Gorbachev's original group that had introduced *perestroika* was Prime Minister Nicolai Ryzhkov, but he would not survive the new year. Reportedly the victim of a heart attack, he was replaced by Valentin Pavlov, an unsympathetic apparatchik with inclinations toward central planning.* No one really thought Ryzhkov had had a heart attack. It was assumed that, like the other initiators of the Gorbachev reforms, he, too, either was fired or quit.

It was evident that conservative forces were unifying and that some kind of a campaign had been launched. During that same session of the Congress, KGB chief Vladimir Kryuchkov accused the CIA and Western interests of trying to undermine the Soviet Union and bring about "economic sabotage." He also said that the Soviet Union must "accept the possibility of bloodshed if we are to bring about order."†

Roald and I may have focused almost exclusively on Soviet affairs during these winter months, but the rest of the world was primarily gripped with fear and concern about the impending war in the Gulf. I had a suspicion that there was a connection between the events in the Soviet Union and the crisis in the Middle East, and a number of our Soviet friends agreed. Soviet cooperation—or at least neutrality—with the West in the Gulf crisis was vital for the success of Western policy there, since the Soviet Union had been a longtime ally of Iraq; timing an internal crackdown to coincide with this assured the Soviets of a milder Western reaction.

Every morning when we got up, there was a race to see who could get to the newspaper first. But American coverage of events in the Soviet Union often missed some of the most significant details. One example was an

* Pavlov was also central to the coup attempt in August 1991.
† David Remnick, "KGB Head Warns Republics," *The Washington Post*, December 23, 1990.

article that appeared in *Sovietskaya Rossiya* on December 22, entitled "With Hope and Belief—Appeal to Comrade M. S. Gorbachev." This was an unprecedented letter, for it was signed by fifty-three high-level military-industrial figures, most of them unknown outside their classified circles. Roald noted that they were the very people he had opposed during the Phobos investigation, the most senior of whom was the very powerful Oleg Baklanov.

> Having considered all the circumstances [it read], we request that you, as honored leader of the nation, halt the chaos and forbid the disintegration of the state using all the power and authority at your command . . . We propose that you introduce a state of emergency and presidential rule in zones of major conflict . . .

In early January 1991 it was reported that Soviet paratroop units had been sent to seven republics to enforce the military draft and to seek out deserters. That month, Roald and I had been scheduled to go to Moscow for the annual meeting of the International Foundation, and I also had some business to do there, but given everything, Roald again decided to stay in Washington.

His decision was immediately vindicated. While I was in flight to Moscow, Soviet army troops attacked and seized the television station in Vilnius, killing fourteen people. A rogue organization that called itself the National Salvation Committee was bent on asserting control among the rebellious republics, and the first step in that process was to control Lithuania and the other Baltic republics—it was anyone's guess which would be next.

It had become a tradition of the International Foundation to meet with Mikhail Gorbachev during these January days. From the moment I heard about what was happening in Lithuania, I was in a state of inward and outward protest about it. Gorbachev publicly insisted that he had not known about the use of force in Vilnius, but he seemed unrepentant.* This could mean only that Gorbachev either had no control over his government or he had tacitly approved the operation and its objectives. Not an inspiring thought in any case.

I recommended to my colleagues that we either decline to go to see

---

* This reminded me of the U-2 incident: One reason why President Eisenhower admitted openly that he had sanctioned the flights was that he wanted the country and the world to know that he was in charge of his own government and that he knew what was going on in it.

Gorbachev or draft a statement to present to him. I thought we could not go to the meeting without expressing ourselves on this most serious topic, if for no other reason than the press would be sure to ask us if it had been raised.

Several of the American board members balked at the idea. "Why ask him questions that he can't answer satisfactorily?" one of our distinguished directors asked. It was hard for me to persist with my opinionated stance or boycott the meeting altogether. I was among the youngest and least important people in the delegation. We had one former senator and one former Secretary of Defense. If they intended to go to the meeting, I did not see how I could refuse and also maintain my standing among them.

Given the impending UN deadline of January 15 in the Middle East, by which time Saddam Hussein was to withdraw from Kuwait, I was hoping that Gorbachev himself would cancel the meeting. When I came down to breakfast that morning, I was stunned to discover that the session with the Soviet President was scheduled, as planned, at the Kremlin at 11:00.

Still feeling rebellious, but unable to extricate myself, I went up to my room at the Oktyabrskaya Hotel and changed into a suit, which I purposely accessorized with a very large and striking necklace of Latvian amber and earrings to match. Perhaps this was sophomoric, but I felt defiant, and I hoped Gorbachev would notice. Considering protocol, I was unlikely to be given the floor to say anything.

As we gathered to leave for our meeting, several American delegates who had been silent earlier told me they agreed that someone should speak up at the meeting, and one even volunteered. I was confident that the Lithuanian crackdown would be mentioned.

We met Gorbachev in the same room where the board, including Andrei Sakharov, had met him three years earlier. How much had happened in the intervening years! On this occasion I received a warm kiss from several of the Soviet participants, including Vladimir Petrovsky, Alexander Bessmertnykh, and Alexander Yakovlev. And this time I spoke to Gorbachev in Russian.

From the outward look of things, it was very much like any other meeting we had had with the Soviet President. But I was amazed at the extent to which my American colleagues were once again completely captured by the famous Gorbachev charm. I could feel the determination to raise the Baltic question slowly drain away.

As before, Gorbachev began with a rambling soliloquy about the nuclear threat and *perestroika*, injecting from time to time such observations as

"Gorbachev clearly has the most difficult job in the world," using the royal third person.

My American colleagues nodded sympathetically.

"The only recourse we have not used," he continued, "is the recourse to God. God and *perestroika* . . .

"The left and the right," he said, "rise up against me. But they don't understand that Gorbachev has his own ideas, his own set of views . . .

"I will fight to the end for my goals . . . Those who accuse me of dismantling socialism I regard as reactionary. There are some forces who don't want renewal . . ."

And then he said the thing that struck me most, given the events that had just occurred in Lithuania: "As the Bible says, there are times to gather stones and times to throw them."*

There was a slight lull. We had been there almost an hour. Sensing that an opening had come, one of the Americans spoke up: "Mr. President, I have a very serious question to ask you."

There was a pause, a silence. The moment had come: perhaps we would now settle down to an honest discussion about the issue that everyone seemed to be skirting.

"Last week I saw Alexander Bessmertnykh in the United States, and I congratulated him on the birth of his son. Today I see Alexander Bessmertnykh, and I congratulated him for being named Foreign Minister. So my question is, what am I going to congratulate him for next week?"

There was embarrassed laughter. Suddenly jovial, Gorbachev quipped, "Oh, I thought you were going to ask me about Lithuania. Or maybe the Gulf!"

My mind drifted. All I could see was Sakharov. His head is bent slightly. His shoulders are hunched. From his pocket he produces a list of names —they are political prisoners of conscience. He refuses to be intimidated.

That had been only three years ago. In this very room. What would Sakharov think today of his "beloved" International Foundation, unable to say even one word about the people lying dead in the streets of Vilnius, with others anxious and threatened in Riga, Tbilisi, and even Moscow?

In my dizzy distraction I faintly heard someone ask Gorbachev what the West could do to help *perestroika*. Help *perestroika*? *Perestroika* was lying dead in the streets!

I looked at the clock near the door. We had been in the room more

* All these quotations are taken from notes I made at the meeting.

than an hour. No one had said *anything*. How could I leave this room? How could I go back home to the man I love and respect for the courageous positions he has taken in his life? Like Sakharov, Sagdeev, too, would be humiliated and ashamed.

My hand went up. Feeling awkward that I might be violating protocol, I decided to make my question as personal as possible. I had no mandate to speak for the group, but I had to say something.

"Mikhail Sergeiivich, as you know, my life together with my husband, Roald, is directly affected by the relations between the Soviet Union and the United States."

"*Ya znayu* [I know]," Gorbachev said, shifting the full force of his attention to me, his eyes boring into me.

"By the way," I interjected, trying to break the intensity of his gaze, "my husband sends his regards. He would have been here, but he was unable to come at this moment."

This friendly lob only brought a serious nod in response.

"Let me be direct," I said seriously. "Roald and I are terribly worried about the developments taking place in the Soviet Union, and we believe they could directly affect U.S.–Soviet relations. First, we are concerned about the nationalities issue, particularly about what has just transpired in the Baltics. Unless some nonviolent solution can be found, this could reassert the Cold War. Second, we are concerned that no clearly defined economic policy has been adopted in the Soviet Union. This jeopardizes U.S.–Soviet economic cooperation and the future of your country. And third, we are confused and concerned by the anti-Western rhetoric adopted by some of your government's senior officials.* Does this reflect a shift in government policy or does it indicate growing anti-Western sentiment among the population?"

Gorbachev, pooh-poohing the notion that anti-Western views existed in his government, pointed to Alexander Bessmertnykh's confirmation that day as the new Foreign Minister—a former ambassador to Washington. With this, he launched into another speech about how honoring individual freedom does not mean abandoning law and order.

I didn't really mind. At least I had done what I had set out to do. Nevertheless, I felt sorry for Gorbachev, who didn't get what he had bargained for with our group, he got a group of pushovers instead. But I felt

---

* I was referring to the KGB chairman's continued attacks on the West, including the most recent: an accusation that Westerners had sent rotten and contaminated food parcels as aid.

even sorrier for my American colleagues, who seemed to think that silence and acceptance were ways to help *perestroika*, if it still existed, in the Soviet Union.

Sure enough, when our bus returned to the hotel, a journalist, waiting for our arrival, asked me about the meeting with the Soviet President. "Did anyone say anything about the situation in Lithuania and the Baltics?"

"Yes," I said, "it was raised."*

That night I had dinner with Yuri Osipyan. His wife, Luda, was away, but his son Sergei was at home, ill with some kind of flu. In between rushing to his son's room and fielding a few telephone calls, Yuri ransacked the refrigerator for a bite to eat. In Luda's absence, and in the midst of tremendous consumer and food shortages, Yuri could produce only half a cup of borscht and quantities of kasha (a rice-like buckwheat pasta). We ate the modest meal on an elegant polished table. The television was running in the background.

At 9:00 we turned up the sound to listen to *Vremya*, the evening news. The program began with segments from Lithuania and Latvia. Bodies of the injured and dead were depicted, and man-on-the-street interviews strongly supported the Soviet military action. Within seconds the camera cut away from Latvia's barricades to our meeting with Gorbachev.

The blood drained from my face in shock and humiliation. As the names of the Western participants were read out, the camera—which I had not been aware of—captured only the moment after my American colleague had offered his joke about Bessmertnykh, so the group was seen laughing with Gorbachev. Then the announcer said, "But in answer to Susan Eisenhower's question, Mikhail Sergeiivich said . . ."

Why was I surprised that they gave only his answer without my question?

Yuri and I watched in silence. After the hard news was over, we turned down the sound so that we could talk again.

"I feel so ashamed," I said. "I should never have gone to that meeting. I feel absolutely humiliated and used. I warned my colleagues that this might happen. What a powerful personality that man has! Imagine: Gorbachev took a serious group of people and turned them into putty. How do any of you guys ever say no to him?"

"We don't," Yuri said somberly.

I understood almost immediately that Yuri had reached one of those

---

* The next day, irritated by press coverage of the Baltics crackdown, Gorbachev called for the repeal of the new press law, which would mean the imposition of the old restrictions on the press. He later retreated from this.

defining moments himself. Ever since the Presidential Council had been abolished, Gorbachev had pursued him to stay on his team in some capacity, but Yuri had deep reservations. He was a progressive man, and like Alexander Yakovlev, he struggled with the question of what Gorbachev would do if no one but conservatives surrounded him.

Yuri commented on how hard it was to deflect Gorbachev when he wanted something. This was consistent with many other stories we had heard from other Gorbachev advisers. Yuri told me that he often got as many as three or four telephone calls a day from Gorbachev, using all his persuasive skills to talk him into remaining with him. Anatoly Lukyanov had also been calling persistently, saying, "We want to have you with us."

Yuri repeated over and over again that things were very complicated and difficult. It wasn't clear exactly what he was referring to. He just went on saying, "The situation is so difficult."

It was obvious he was under excruciating pressure. I tried to offer reassurance, and also to bolster his inclination to stay away from the presently configured Gorbachev government. "Now is the time to stay true to your own voices," I said.

Such advice would prompt him again to repeat, "I must be strong, I must be strong. Things are so complicated."

I was convinced that the recent events had been especially disturbing for Yuri. Maybe he understood that they were part of a larger campaign being waged and that widespread repressions were in store. Maybe not, but he spoke darkly of the influence of Valery Boldin and how the only person who could stand up to Gorbachev—Vadim Bakatin—had been fired.

That night, as he called his driver to take me back to my hotel, his goodbye was especially poignant. He kissed me on the cheek and gave me a hug. But his hold lingered. The pain and the pressure he was under turned to tears. He sobbed quietly, whispering to me, "I am so alone in this, so alone."

I held him hard and said softly, "You may think you are, but we are with you. You have the love and support of Roald and me."

After several minutes of protracted goodbyes, I descended the stairs and got into the waiting car.

I was shaken, reflecting on what this terrible moment in history had done to this decent, if indecisive, man. I knew Yuri felt trapped. But only he knew in his darkest moments what personal issues he faced.

Like many others, Yuri had begun to understand his own emerging free

At the White House dinner in honor of our engagement (*official White House photo*)

(above) After the civil ceremony on February 9, 1990, at Wedding Palace #1 (*copyright by Stills*)

opposite) The day before our wedding at St. Basil's Cathedral, built to commemorate the Russian onquest of Kazan, which led Roald to quip that after this picture, his fellow Tatars would never let im come home again (*copyright by Stills*)

The religious ceremony at Spaso House the same day: with Roald (left) and with my father (below) (*copyright by Stills*)

The kiss stolen under Lenin's gaze (in front of a huge painting at the Communist Party guest house) on our wedding night

From *Krokodil*, a Soviet satirical magazine

In Kazan, two days after the wedding: (left) with Sagdeev's mother; (below) Aunt, Papa, I, Mama, Roald, and Hannan. My wedding flowers are in the vase on the table

Yuri Osipyan and I, just days after the "re-education" of Mikhail Gorbachev

Arbatov, Sagdeev, Shishlin, and I after the June 1990 summit

I, Sagdeev, and Starovoitov in Tatarstan just after the abortive 1991 coup. When asked how I'd feel if Sagde were drafted to become Tatarstan's new president, said, "I'm ready"

Our "circle defense," December 31, 1990, one year after our union. Both of us knew that if we hadn't acted when we did, our marriage would have been impossible: by then, Gorbachev was surrounded by conservatives and the political situation in the U.S.S.R. had changed dramatically will and choice, and like many others in the Soviet Union, he had begun to trust his instincts and his friends as never before.

Two days later I went to visit Roald's son Igor and his wife, Tanya, and their children. Roald's daughter Anna and her family were out of the city, but this get-together in their cramped little kitchen gave me a chance to see the Soviet political developments from Roald's children's point of view. To my astonishment Igor told me that he could stay only for an hour because he had to go into the city to deal with some documents. He told me that he and his family were moving to Lithuania.

If I was surprised that they had decided to go to Vilnius two days after the crackdown, I didn't show it. I offered Igor my full support and told him I thought it was a very bold move.

"They won't be able to hold back the tide," Igor said with conviction. "Lithuania will get its independence and I want to be there when it does." I admired his noble if romantic reasoning. Igor's grandfather on his mother's side had been born in Lithuania, and Tanya had family living there. "Anyway," he added solemnly, "the Soviet Union is doomed."

I told Igor that Roald and I had been reluctant to speak up publicly in Washington about the situation because we were worried about what the repercussions might be on him, Anna, and the rest of the family.

Igor immediately dismissed that concern. "The best way you can help us," he said, "is to tell Washington and the West what you have seen while you were here. You must speak out about everything. A lot could depend on it."

In fact, I sensed that a consensus had now formed among people in Moscow. The general belief was that the Lithuanian and Latvian events were intended as a dress rehearsal for something larger—for a union-wide crackdown. "They wanted to see if the army would hold," one Russian told me.

Much of this was confirmed by Andrei Kozyrev, who had become Russia's first Foreign Minister. He told me that the Russian ministers were worried that the crackdown would extend to Russia. Confidentially, he said, many of them had sent their families out of Moscow. I also heard some had obtained permission to carry handguns. They expected a "knock on the door in the middle of the night" at any time.

On January 19 the National Salvation Committee, the secret organization of anonymous members, announced that they had taken power in Latvia. The next day four people in Riga were killed by Soviet Internal Ministry troops.

Yeltsin, in the immediate aftermath of this bloodshed, moved boldly and decisively by declaring that the central government had violated Russian sovereignty with its attempted crackdown in Lithuania, and he called on Russian recruits there to put down their arms. Prior to the crackdown he had appealed to Russian troops to observe Russian law:

> Before you undertake the storming of civilian installations in the Baltic lands, remember your own homes, and your own people. Violence against lawfulness and against the people of the Baltics will bring new serious crisis phenomena in Russia itself and to the position of Russians inhabiting other republics including the Baltic republics.*

The law stated in Yeltsin's own words that "boys called up on the territory of the Russian Federation may not serve outside the territory, even more so take part in army actions against the peaceful population for the resolution of any kind of conflicts."†

The morning of January 16, during Roald's daily morning wake-up call (we had reversed roles), he told me that the Gulf War had begun. "You had better find a way to come home right away."

I did not know which crisis to be more concerned about, the one in the Soviet Union or the one in the Gulf. When I met with Jim Kober, the Moscow representative of American Express, he was buried underneath a pile of advisories from the American Embassy and the KGB on how to manage during the Gulf crisis. "American-named" companies, it was said, had been targeted by local Iraqi terrorists, and the American Embassy, only a few blocks away, was closed most days by noon because of Iraqi demonstrations. I took these threats very much to heart, as I was in the city to work with *American* Express and scheduled to leave the country on Pan *American*. Roald and I talked every morning, trying to figure out the best way for me to return, via Japan or through Frankfurt, Germany. I was hopelessly indecisive.

* Reported in FBIS, January 14, 1991, p. 94.
† Radio Moscow, January 15, 1991, FBIS, p. 92.

The day before I left the Soviet Union, I went to visit Georgi Arbatov at his institute. The nineteenth-century building seemed empty, ghostlike, abandoned. But for a few people, Arbatov was alone. He invited me into his office.

For the first time during one of our intimate get-togethers, Arbatov kept a television running in the background, loud enough to drown out the specifics of our conversation.

Sitting right next to me at a small table, he whispered his assessment of the situation in the Baltics and of current developments in the Gulf. As we spoke, both of us stared at CNN's coverage of the air raids in the Gulf. Our eyes were fixed on the screen, while Arbatov lamented that he had alerted Gorbachev to the possibility that the military would make a move —but that the Soviet leader had declined to take steps.

Arbatov would occasionally point to something on the television. "You have to understand," he told me, "that this campaign in the Gulf will anger our military-industrial complex. You are bombing their watering hole. Iraq was the one place they could go to make arms sales in hard currency, in between sunning themselves poolside at some Western quality hotel."

After nearly two hours of penetrating discussion, he walked me out to the elevator. I didn't know what to say. The situation seemed so desperate.

"Be careful," I said, "we will be thinking about you. Let us know if there is anything we can do." And then I added something that really came right from the heart: "I am terribly sorry about what has happened. I really am. I had such hopes that everything could resolve itself peacefully."

"I am not sorry for myself," he responded, "I am an old man. But this poor country, this poor sad country."

Arbatov had, months before, broken with Gorbachev and had now associated himself with Boris Yeltsin. He had been outspoken in his battle with Marshal Akhromeyev, so it was clear that if the authorities were to round up enemies, he was now squarely on the list.

I had developed a real fondness for Arbatov. It was hard to leave our friends at this time, but when the elevator opened we said a simple goodbye. I waved to him as the doors closed.

George Orwell wrote in *1984*: "It was not by making yourself heard but by staying sane that you carried on the human heritage." The Soviets had now crossed the line, perhaps irrevocably. The columnist Albert Plutnik emotionally wrote of this national transformation, in an article entitled "No Way Back," which came out in *Izvestia* on January 16 during the Lithuanian events.

> Openness in society in the days of *perestroika* and *glasnost* . . . have brought into public life millions of people who were formally, so to speak, exiles in their own country, people who did not want to participate in the common lie and tried, if only through distancing themselves in silence, to show their loyalty to profound pan-human values. Millions of people lived not in cities, not in apartment blocks, but inside themselves . . . People felt a mass need for self-renewal only in recent years, when they recognized that internal voluntary exile means living nowhere. It is a form of spiritual slavery. The emergence of many informal movements, social organizations, and political parties, the ethnic awakening—all this is nothing but the result of the awakened human need to squeeze out the slave in oneself drop by drop. The era of politicalization of the masses is the era of mass honesty and openness. The polarization of political forces and the diversity of views and interests are returns to an honest society. People came out in the open, trusting the ideals of *perestroika*, its leader, its stance.
>
> . . . The dramatic time that the country is living through can be judged accurately by looking to see who is gaining confidence and who is losing it. No, yesterday's men, who were so frightened of *perestroika* when it was first born, should not have more confidence in the future than the people who were awakened by it and who put their trust in it.

I was deeply moved by this essay, and hoped with all my heart that a nation of questing souls would not be forced back into "internal exile" at gunpoint. Would Roald and I have to fear for our children's and grandchildren's future, from our own self-imposed exile in Washington?

25 : A Date with the Godfather

I wanted to hide that spring. Still raw from the revolutionary events in the Soviet Union—where the people were gaining courage to confront their past and to build a civil society—I had to watch an incomprehensible display of American jingoism in Washington. As the "evil empire" grappled with the moral implications of killing innocent civilians at the hands of Soviet Interior Ministry troops, the United States was having a victory parade to mark the end of the world's first videogame war.

I had supported the war, particularly once it had started. But I was amazed at America's excitement in glorifying a victory that had cost disproportionately so many lives.

I took the metro downtown the Saturday of the parade to get my hair cut. At the station I saw several young boys, around ten years old, dressed in army fatigues. I arrived at my hairdresser's quivering. "They've got advanced weaponry on the mall and kids are dressed up for combat. It reminds me more of Red Square circa 1983 than the world's greatest democracy," I said angrily.

I promised myself that I would be a well-behaved guest that night. I really did. I was even prepared to simply rise above all the silly remarks. But I'm afraid it proved to be too much.

I just couldn't bear to sit there and listen to people take things at face value; to give our policy toward the Soviet Union, for instance, no thought at all.

One tall, distinguished-looking man at the party, in a white starched shirt and tasseled Weejuns, said that he had read Gorbachev's *Perestroika* and that he had been most impressed. "You know, he is really talking about capitalism," he told me enthusiastically.

I promised myself I would behave, so I didn't say anything. But I did think to myself that we must have read two different books. Who could forget the most memorable line of Gorbachev's book: "What we need is not 'pure' doctrinaire invented socialism but real Leninist socialism."

A bit later in the evening I finally lost my composure. Someone suggested that the United States, with its SDI program, brought about the end of Communism.

"Why do we think that everything that happens in the world is the result of something that America did?" I said with exasperation. I knew from Roald that Gorbachev had rejected a straightforward SDI system, in favor of developing cheaper countermeasures. So it wasn't SDI per se that had bankrupted the Soviet system.

I continued hotly: "SDI is promoted by special interests in the U.S. that see increasingly sophisticated military technology as a panacea for peace. Now they want to credit it with the collapse of a seventy-year-old system. Soviet Communism failed because the system wasn't flexible or responsive. In fact, it was inhuman. The system was brought to an end, bottom up— by the Soviet people themselves." Looking for other examples, I cited the loss of a role for the Soviet central government with the end of the Cold War and the disappearance of an external enemy. The final blow was a crippling tax revolt, as the Soviet republics refused to pay taxes to Moscow.

"We could learn a few things from their system's demise!" I exclaimed.

There was utter silence at the table. It was as if I had dropped a bomb on Washington itself. Filling the awkward void, I said finally, "Can we talk? Can we discuss these things? We *are* in Washington, aren't we? Not Beijing."

It was ironic that I didn't say Moscow. Perhaps that was the hardest thing to adjust to: how much freer Soviet expression had become despite all the threats. Discussion about fundamental questions was now commonplace. But we Americans, for whom it all came so easily, were engaged in self-imposed censorship, busy throwing away what others were fighting to gain and codify.

Despite the awe I had for so many brave people in the Soviet Union, I had no illusions about the disappearance of the dark side of Soviet life.

Before leaving Moscow I had had a most unpleasant encounter one afternoon. A man whom I will call Pavel started asking me some questions in a very loud voice, loud enough to attract a great deal of attention.

"They say that your husband should resign from the Congress," he had said provocatively.

I retorted that Roald had already asked his constituents about this matter and that they wanted him to stay on.

This answer notwithstanding, the man continued in a more and more bizarre way. "They say that the reason your husband never comes back is that he has been given ten million dollars for his work and he doesn't want to return because he has to pay hard currency to buy the plane tickets."

"How absurd. Roald earns the salary of a university professor. And how can you say that he doesn't come back? He was here only six weeks ago." I answered the questions, but a feeling of revulsion swept through me.

When I told Roald about this exchange and reported to him who the "friend" had been, he nodded slowly. "I always had good reason to suspect that Pavel worked for the KGB. We must dismiss what he says. He was probably only interested in knowing what you would say. Or maybe he just wanted to create a scene."

Most of our Soviet friends were, of course, loyal and steadfast. But others were willing to assume the worst of us: that we had "checked out" and were now "living well" in rich America. It was disappointing, because they evidently had no idea how tirelessly we worked in Washington to help them in their relations with the United States. Even Evgeny Velikhov had dressed me down, castigating Roald for not coming to Moscow at this time. His language was so harsh, and my discomfort so great, that I had had to excuse myself and go up to my room. Velikhov, I figured, clearly reflected the frustration and anger that existed within the military-industrial establishment, of which he was an important part.

As I recounted these stories, Roald and I decided right then and there that we would not be sucked into the terrible atmosphere that prevailed in Moscow—especially from a distance of six thousand miles. It was difficult, but we would pay no attention to the rumors and the bad feeling. We wanted to keep a positive attitude about everyone, but we also had no illusions. Probably many of them, at one time or another, participated in the gossip, maybe even contributed to the lies. The search for scapegoats is one of the tools of survival in revolutionary times.

Yeltsin's adroit maneuvers over the next few months seemed to avert an over-all crackdown. His strategy was to get the republics to sign treaties among themselves, separate from the central government in Moscow, and then, and only then, to address their relationships with the center.

In fact, Yeltsin described it this way at a press conference, when questioned about the possibility of signing the center-sponsored Union Treaty.

> The actions [in Lithuania] seem to me to have inflicted a serious blow on the practicality of concluding a Union treaty, since no one is likely to sign a treaty with a noose around their necks. You won't find any takers in our country now among the leaders of all the republics. Here there is once again the desire to thrust on us from above, on a plate, a ready treaty approved by a Central Committee Plenum and approved by the Congress of People's Deputies: here is a treaty for you, sign it! But wait a moment: who is signing the treaty, who is making a treaty with whom? Presumably anyone making a treaty with anyone else should be the ones to work on this treaty, discuss it, and only then sign it. But the whole process is going not from the bottom upward, as we proposed, but from the top downward. *

The implementation of this strategy was in a race against the clock, as other serious measures were simultaneously being taken by the central government. Valentin Pavlov, the new Prime Minister, withdrew all fifty- and hundred-ruble notes, as a way to stymie speculators and black marketeers. But in reality it hurt little old ladies and students who lived on fixed incomes. Also around that time the army was authorized to patrol the streets of the U.S.S.R.'s largest cities, and the KGB's powers were expanded to maintain oversight and search privileges of all Soviet and foreign establishments to combat "economic sabotage."

Despite this, the numerous National Salvation Committees had met too much public resistance and were disbanded. It was widely reported that right-wing forces felt betrayed by Gorbachev because he had tacitly approved of their crackdown and then had distanced himself from the bloody business when it was clear they had not succeeded.

In May I had to go to the U.S.S.R. again on business. Roald and I did

---

* News Conference, January 14, 1991, reported FBIS, January 16, 1991, p. 93.

not think it was safe for him to return with me, and many of our Moscow friends also gave him the same advice. My project was pressing, so I decided to go without him. I talked to Yuri Osipyan on the telephone several times, and he told me he would meet my airplane.

Yuri's illness, ironically, had helped him avoid a deeper involvement with the Soviet government. Although he continued to serve as an informal adviser to Gorbachev, all his official ties to the regime outside the Academy of Sciences had been severed. I was anxious to see him and catch up on all his news, but after the long flight, I saw no sign of him when I arrived at Sheremetyvo Airport.

That evening Yuri told me on the telephone that he had waited for three hours for an earlier plane. One of our friends had simply failed to tell him that my flight had changed. I was touched that he had taken so much time from his already burdened schedule to try to see me. His health had deteriorated considerably since that evening we had spent together at his apartment in January. He was slated now for a pacemaker and was under a doctor's constant supervision.

Instead, Ella Orlova was there to greet me. As we waited for my luggage we discussed the terrible nerve-racking spring they had just been through. The Gulf War was over and the Soviet Union had lurched through three months of domestic resistance and democratic activism. As many as 500,000 people had filled the streets in defiance of the troops Gorbachev had deployed in Moscow to intimidate the Russian parliament. And now the Russian republic was deeply absorbed in the first direct election in its one-thousand-year history to select a chief executive.

But perhaps the biggest change from January was that frustration was being directed more and more toward the West. The Soviet Union was sensitive to the West's paltry response to their requests for aid, as well as their own decline of importance on the world scene. That's why I had watched, with real regret, as the United States so callously conducted itself right after the Gulf War. This American hubris was playing directly into the hands of the hard-liners there, heightening the Soviet sense of impotence.

Despite the continuing instability, the relative peace of the last few months had encouraged my clients to continue to pursue their projects in the Soviet Union. One was a high-tech cooperative venture that needed high-level Soviet support. Roald had suggested I try to see Oleg Baklanov about this—there would be no higher authority to go to on the project.

But I think Roald was also curious to see if I would be granted a meeting. I learned later that fewer than a handful of Westerners had ever met the man, and not many more even knew who he was.

After the "Letter of 53" that had appeared in December, Baklanov had been promoted to the deputy chairmanship of the State Defense Council, founded by Joseph Stalin at the start of World War II. As Gorbachev's new right-hand man, Baklanov supervised defense and all the military industry surrounding and supporting it. He had moved into a Kremlin office only doors away from the President, and not far from Gorbachev's chief of staff, Valery Boldin.

I did not understand the significance of requesting such a meeting until I asked Ella Orlova to try to set it up. She immediately passed my request on to her boss, Yuri Osipyan, who had Roald's old position as chairman of the Committee of Soviet Scientists. After several telephone calls, Osipyan told me that Baklanov had agreed to meet me and that I should be ready on Thursday.

"Be on time," Yuri suggested.

On May 26, at five minutes past the appointed hour, a long black *chaika* pulled up to the entrance of my hotel. Two men emerged from the car: one was Yuri and the other, with an armful of long-stemmed red roses, was Oleg Baklanov. I was immediately impressed by Baklanov's tall, imposing stature and his quiet, courtly manner. After brief introductions, the three of us climbed into the back of the limousine and headed for some undisclosed destination outside Moscow. As the official car streaked down the wide *prospekt*, smaller cars swerved to get out of the way.

I had assumed that we would meet at the Central Committee building or at the Kremlin, but before long we had reached the open road, lined on both sides by thick forests. The air was fragrant with the smell of damp grass and pine needles, and the sun cast a golden glow across the road. Despite the serenity of the Russian countryside, I was a little uneasy about where we were going.

On the outskirts of Moscow, the car suddenly made a left-hand turn that led down a smaller side road. After half a mile or so we stopped at the entrance of a compound. A huge iron gate, with thick reinforced doors, slowly opened, and I could just barely see the entrance of what looked like a modern mansion. Yuri whispered something to me about Brezhnev's dacha.

During dinner that night I could feel Baklanov watching me. From the moment he had picked me up at my hotel, he had seemed curious about me—the young Western woman who married the Soviet Union's leading space scientist and whisked him away to America. I had the impression that he was trying to figure out what had motivated Roald to resign his prestigious posts and undertake such a risk to his professional standing, and maybe even his life. Was this woman worth the loss of status, or worse?

But I, too, was just as curious about Baklanov. In a way, meeting him was like meeting the godfather of the Mafia, a man who later admitted to me that he had "held my husband's future in his hands."

From what our closest friends had told us the previous summer, it had most probably been Baklanov who had sanctioned and sponsored the press attacks against Roald, notably the one in *Izvestia*. (The paper had apparently received volumes of letters from readers protesting it, but the editor resolutely "stood by the story," hinting that the decision to publish it had been taken at a very high level.)

"Thank you for the greeting card you sent us when we married," I said to Baklanov at dinner.

"You were thoughtful to invite me to your wedding," he replied courteously. "How is your husband enjoying his vacation in Washington?" he asked me smoothly.

"I don't think he regards it as a vacation," I countered. "He is finishing his book, which he must do before he travels again. I know that he is sorry he can't be with us here."

The surface conversation was very polite, but I was all too aware of what we were really discussing. In fact, Baklanov confirmed it: Sagdeev was "enjoying life" as a free man in Washington because a thorough investigation had confirmed that, apart from the once classified controlled-fusion program in the 1950s, he had never participated directly in a military contract. In fact, he had once been in serious trouble for *rejecting* a contract from the Ministry of Defense. Still, Roald knew a great deal, and Baklanov gave me the impression that he was on some kind of probation.

Before the first course, a number of toasts were offered by the four men at the table, Baklanov, Yuri, a Soviet "businessman," and a German who was nominally helping out with the language: to our meeting, to beautiful women, to our children, and even one to my grandfather, whom Baklanov said he admired. The toasts continued through the second and third courses. Then suddenly Baklanov stood up and announced that he was taking me for a walk. He, the interpreter, and I got up from the table and left the mansion.

Deep dusk was upon us and the air had grown chilly. Baklanov took off his suit jacket and offered it to me. Despite my natural reluctance to accept it, I didn't know how to reject his gallant gesture. He put his coat around my shoulders.

For about half an hour we walked around the grounds of the estate, along a path that meandered through a pine grove. I explained the nature of the commercial project I was working on, and we discussed the prospects for U.S.–Soviet cooperation in some areas of space technology. Baklanov told me that, internally, he had been a supporter of technical cooperation with the United States, but, he complained, the United States government frequently didn't back up the proposals made by American companies.

"If you want to present this to me formally," he offered, "be sure to have at least some preliminary U.S. government approval first." He implied that he wouldn't go to the mat one more time for a project that hadn't been cleared on the U.S. side.

I assured him that we would have a progress report to present to him, probably by the summer.

"Very good," he said, "I am ready."

"Can I arrange to meet you when we come in August, or will you be at your dacha?" I asked.

"No, I won't be at my dacha, but August isn't a good month. Why wait? Why not bring it sooner?"

"I'm not sure I can get preliminary approvals sooner," I replied.

"Very well, but don't come in August," he repeated. "Come sooner if you can."

We agreed that I would stay in touch with him through one of the "businessmen" who was in the house with the other dinner guests.*

We returned to the mansion and Baklanov offered one more toast to our friendship, and then he presented me with a striking sequential photograph of Buran, the Soviet shuttle, being launched into space on the back of the world's largest rocket, Energyia. Roald and I laughed about this later. Buran and Energyia were the focus of one of the bitterest disagreements he and Baklanov had had.

Baklanov signed the bottom of the photograph, and so did the others who were part of the gathering. Then we all got ready to leave.

It was 10:30 by the time the *chaika* limousine pulled around the driveway

---

* I was later to confirm, as much as anyone can confirm any of this, that the "business" his colleague was in was typical of many other businesses established at this time: they were fronts for either the KGB or the Party. The KGB used them for information gathering, the Party for laundering money, property, and assets.

circle. Baklanov got into the back seat with me, and Yuri sat in the front, watching over me protectively. We set off again for Moscow.

I was struck suddenly by the sense of power and secrecy implied by this place and these people. My hosts seemed singularly distant from the growing social, political, and economic turmoil in the country.

As I peered through the window, the moon glazed the pines and the white birch trunks seemed to shine. Looking back one more time, I could see only the fading light from the clearing.

That night I wrote in my journal: "What will happen to these people when the depths of the Soviet crisis begin to touch their world? What steps will they take to preserve their prerogatives and their empire? Will they look for scapegoats or seek out enemies? And if they do, will we be among them?"

26 : Twilight of the Empire

Why did Baklanov let Roald go? It was not simply because Roald had never taken a military contract. Roald had much more valuable intelligence than that. He knew personalities, command structure, technological capability, and the internal politics of the Soviet Union's most powerful and secret sector.

Baklanov, we believe, let Roald go because he had no choice. The KGB associated with the military-industrial complex had not predicted that our relationship was as serious as it was. Perhaps in their frame of reference it could have never been more than a friendship or a sexual liaison. A Western woman, indeed an Eisenhower, could *never* fall in love with a *Tatar*, a man shorter than herself!*

But once we announced we were marrying, they had to cover up their careless miscalculation. If they admitted to Gorbachev that Roald's relationship with me, and our intention to base ourselves at least partly in the West, was a serious breach of security, they would have been open to criticism for not stopping us sooner. In these circumstances Baklanov had no alternative but to say that Roald had not been a very big loss. Then the only thing left was to discredit him through the news media. As they discovered to their chagrin, even that didn't work.

Soon, however, what Baklanov did or did not think, would or would

---

* There must be something about the intelligence mindset. Not long after Roald and I married we ran into General William Odom, former director of the National Security Agency in Washington. "Oh," he said, "I read about your wedding in the paper, but I didn't pay any attention. It was a no compute."

not do, became suddenly irrelevant. August 19, the day before Gorbachev was to sign the Union Treaty, the tanks rolled into Moscow.

Around midnight we were awakened in our Bethesda home by a telephone call from an émigré friend who lived in Washington. "Gorbachev has resigned," she told us. Radio Moscow was reporting that he had been taken ill and that some kind of committee of national emergency had been established to deal with the crisis. For several hours Roald and I took turns dialing the numbers of countless friends. The few lines into Moscow were interminably busy.

At 2:00 a.m. we finally reached Vasily Selyunin, a journalist and one of Yeltsin's economic advisers. He told us that he had tried to call Yeltsin at his dacha but that there had been no answer. "You caught me just in time. I am on my way to the White House [the Russian parliament building]. That is where people are gathering."

Roald asked him about the State Committee on the State of Emergency in the U.S.S.R. Selyunin said that Baklanov had been one of three who signed the letter establishing it, along with Vice President Gennadi Yanayev and Prime Minister Valentin Pavlov. Then he added, "I'm going to the White House. I am an old man, they can kill me if they want to. But we are not going to back down."

So "Big Oleg," as Roald liked to call Baklanov, was deeply involved in the putsch. "It feels strange to think about it," I said. "Baklanov was adamant that we not come to Moscow in August. He didn't give his reasons, but he was very clear about it." How ironic that because of Baklanov's lack of availability we had postponed our visit. August was usually the month we spent in Moscow.

We could not make any other telephone connections that night. So we went to bed at 4:00 a.m., to get some sleep before the phone started ringing again.

The next day I received an unexpected call from one of our friends at the Soviet Embassy. He said he needed to talk to me. During lunch he offered nothing but small talk, and I was puzzled. The warning he intended for me came only after he drove me back to my office and got out of his car. The Embassy was backing the coup plotters, he thought Roald and I should know. He had waited to tell me this until he was standing in the middle of a busy Washington street, afraid, he indicated, that his car was not secure. I wasn't sure what this would mean for us directly, but I reported his warning to Roald all the same. There was nothing we could do but wait to see what would happen.

Those three days were unimaginably busy. Roald and I were constantly on radio and television giving analysis on the crisis. I was also asked to write op-ed articles for the *Los Angeles Times* and *The Washington Post*, and we spent countless hours on the phone to Moscow. Roald and many others thought the coup would soon collapse, but I had at least a few reservations. I had just been in Moscow and I had sensed that many people would have welcomed some kind of resolution to the wearying power struggles and the escalating crime. What I couldn't gauge was how resolute the military would be. I always thought that there might be a chance that some units would follow orders. It wouldn't take many.

But gloriously, I was wrong. On the third day the "seizure of power" collapsed and the "plotters," including Baklanov, Yanayev, Dmitri Yazov, Vladimir Khryuchkov, Valery Boldin, and Anatoly Lukyanov, were put in prison. Gorbachev returned to Moscow, a tired but seemingly victorious man.

The people who had gone to the streets, however, had done so not to restore Gorbachev's presidency but to save Yeltsin's. They had reaffirmed their desire for *Russian* renewal, not Soviet. Less than two weeks later, the Congress of People's Deputies was called into session, and this time Roald thought it was immensely important that he go. It would be the last meeting before the Congress dissolved itself in favor of new government structures.

Nothing could have prepared us for the atmosphere when we arrived only a week after the putsch. As Roald would say, the Russian people had made a massive and perhaps permanent *sortie* from internal exile. Everyone was ready to let their feelings fly on every conceivable subject. The atmosphere was wild, abandoned, no-holds-barred. Soviet-era statues had been felled or decapitated, and graffiti and swastikas were painted on the bases of monuments where some of the more notorious Bolsheviks had once resolutely stood. It was eerie, though, that on the base of what had been the statue of the KGB founder, Felix Dzerzhinsky—where rumor had said that anti-Communist slogans had been spray-painted—it now said "Felix lives."

The political situation in the Soviet Union was in much more flux than the international news media had led us to believe. Government officials and political aspirants were moving with lightning speed to take advantage of the chaos, to discredit old enemies, to seize property for themselves, or to declare themselves in control.

People filled our heads with stories about our other friends' behavior during the August events. Labels such as "brave," "passive," or even "sneaky" would stick to them for some time to come. I tried to suggest to these friends that they shouldn't move to condemn people so quickly for not living up to all their expectations, and I was especially bothered by the judgments against those who had been inactive or, as someone said, "sinfully quiet." I finally exclaimed in exasperation: "You have to have some compassion. Not everyone is born to be brave. Not everyone is willing to take political risks that could cost their lives or the safety of their families. Passivity is a problem and a danger, but so is a society with no capacity to forgive."

At dinner parties there was incessant talk that Gorbachev had been a part of the coup himself. This was widely believed. From the moment he had taken power, he had played to the full range of the political spectrum in an elaborate but increasingly complicated effort to satisfy both ever widening political extremes.*

The prevailing theory was that while Gorbachev was negotiating with the republics on the new Union Treaty, he was at the same time giving the "coup plotters" the green light. In doing so, Gorbachev was implicitly or explicitly agreeing that if the coup was successful, he would "get well" and return eventually to power; if it failed, then he would distance himself completely and deny any involvement with them.

This was the only explanation that those who knew Oleg Baklanov and some of the other "plotters" could countenance. Baklanov was a cautious man, and no one could imagine him embarking on a suicide mission.† He was also no clown. It would be hard to imagine him involved in something without the *i*'s being dotted and the *t*'s crossed. As we were later to hear from those who visited him in his jail cell, his sense of betrayal was so overwhelming that he refused to allow Gorbachev's name to be used in his presence. He and his co-conspirators, we believe, had fully expected to get Gorbachev's signature on the emergency declaration when they went to the Soviet President's summer retreat in the Crimea.

The coup events dominated everything those weeks in Moscow, especially since there were three mysterious suicides in the wake of the events: Boris Pugo, Minister of the Interior; Marshal Sergei Akhromeyev; and Nicolai

---

* Even one of the early *perestroika* jokes was: "What are the political factions in the Politburo?" The answer: "There is Gorbachev and Yakovlev on the left side and Gorbachev and Ligachev on the right."
† One of his former colleagues told us that they thought Baklanov had been deeply influenced by Valery Boldin, Gorbachev's chief of staff, who was later imprisoned for his role in this conspiracy.

Kruchina, Secretary of the Communist Party in charge of Communist Party property and assets. When we heard of Kruchina's suicide, Roald was bewildered. They had both belonged to the same sauna club in Moscow and Kruchina's son worked for Roald at IKI. He said he didn't think that Kruchina was at all suicidal.

It was also strange visiting Georgi Arbatov then. Since we had last been to Georgi's apartment, a heavily reinforced door had been installed, a gigantic German shepherd dog had been acquired, and a supply of Mace was kept in the hallway drawer. It was an odd sensation to dine only a few floors above where Pugo had been found with a bullet in his head. The Arbatovs' stepped-up security was, in an odd way, a function of Pugo's departure from this world. During his tenure as Minister of the Interior, the building had been protected by ministry guards, but with his death they, too, had disappeared.

One evening Roald and I dined at the Metropole Hotel with the *New York Times* columnist Flora Lewis, who was briefly in Moscow. After we'd discussed all the tumultuous events in Moscow, in a completely unrelated way Flora told us stories about covering corruption cases in Europe and detailed, with some color, the way murder was made to look like suicide.

After dinner Roald and I walked across Red Square to the Rossiya Hotel, where we were staying. The square was shrouded in darkness, haunted by the anti-Bolshevik uprising and the strange undercurrent or backlash from those events. "Smoke" from the struggle could still be detected in the damp late-night air.

As we walked under the shadow of Lenin's mausoleum, I said softly, "Flora's story has me thinking. I'll bet Akhromeyev, Pugo, and Kruchina didn't commit suicide at all. I'll bet they were murdered."

Roald laughed it off. "What a wild idea," he said.

The next evening we went to visit some friends from the Space Research Institute. The table, as usual, was groaning with a wide array of food and drinks. Everyone was talking at once, it seemed, and the pitch of the conversation got louder and more frantic as the evening went on. Like all Moscow gatherings then, the dinner rocked with gossip about the coup and Gorbachev's role in it.

Suddenly Roald said loudly, "Wait, wait, wait! Susan has a theory. She thinks that Akhromeyev, Pugo, and Kruchina didn't commit suicide. She thinks they were murdered."

Everyone started to talk at once. "Of course!" someone said. "You don't think anyone would jump from a *five*-story window, do you? If Kruchina wanted to commit suicide, he'd have jumped from higher up."

Another concurred. "A good soldier would never hang himself. Traitors are hanged. Akhromeyev was an officer, and an officer would only use his handgun."

To Roald's astonishment, most of the party agreed with my casually advanced theory. As we were to discover in the next few weeks, the murder hypothesis was, in fact, widely entertained.

I'd never seen or heard a more open exchange of viewpoints in Moscow than on that night, but just below the surface, with each fantastic exchange of rumors, one could detect worry. Fear had not been entirely buried with the dead: people talked about how the plotters had diverted Western food aid to military garrisons, for distribution during the "coming winter," a phrase people still used with trepidation. "And by the way, did you hear that the coup plotters also refurbished several gulags?" someone would say in hushed horror. Occasionally someone would brag, with a tremble in his voice, that his name had been on the plotters' list of one hundred enemies.

Yuri Ryzhov, a man whom I had gotten to know well over the previous few years, confirmed the feeling. "Those of us who went to the White House didn't focus on how real the danger was while we were in the middle of things, but when it was over many of us went into a kind of shock. Shock that we had come so close . . ."

This handsome man with silvery gray hair was an unexcitable and sober person whom I had always admired for his sensible approach. He had become one of the most important people in the country right after this abortive coup: he had been tapped to sit on a Defense Reorganization Commission and appointed to sit on the Commission to Reorganize the KGB. *

Yuri was mostly quiet that evening as the noise of the room grew louder and louder. The party continued to reel with theories about the events, and I leaned over and quietly asked him what he thought about the murder theory. In his careful low-key way, even he expressed doubts about the official suicide versions.

When the party eventually dispersed and we stood outside in the cool evening air, my head buzzed from the confusion, the smoke, and the vodka.

---

* Later, when Yeltsin replaced many of the people who had served during the transition, Ryzhov was sent to Paris as Russian ambassador to France.

Ryzhov and I hugged and said goodbye, and I added, "Look after yourself."

"It's too late for that," he replied, with melancholy realism.

Several nights later we were comfortably seated in a cozy room some-where distant from the city center. A protégé of Baklanov's talked in in-credulous terms about what had overcome his boss. A moderate man, our friend probably supported the Yeltsin government, but it didn't stop him from wondering out loud what had gone wrong.

Suddenly someone said in a high excited voice that Secretary of State Baker was on television. Our hostess leaned over and turned up the volume. Baker was visiting Moscow, and for some reason there was a televised exchange of gifts: Gorbachev gave Baker a videotape of his public statement from "captivity" in the Crimea, and Baker gave Gorbachev the flag that had flown over the U.S. capitol on August 21, the day the coup collapsed.

The room was silent. I could see that my host and hostess were stunned. Then the wife, a modest middle-aged woman, turned to me and asked simply, "Why didn't you Americans give *Yeltsin* the flag? He was the one who faced down the tanks. He risked his life. Why Gorbachev?"

I had no answer. But I was embarrassed by the U.S. government's in-sensitivity, and impressed at how clearly this woman, whose husband worked in the complex, knew that with the coup a historic chapter had been closed.

Everyone knew it except "you Americans."

In September, with the failed coup behind Russia, there came renewed speculation that Roald would become politically involved again. He had earlier rejected the notion of running for president of the Academy of Sciences. "I could never have been the president of the Academy. I don't have a Russian name," he explained to me. But after the August events, several friends asked Roald if he would consider taking a high-level job in Yeltsin's government. It wasn't an official approach but the hopeful idea of a few friends who hated to see Roald sitting in between two chairs. They didn't understand that the aborted coup attempt not only effectively put an end to the old system but ushered in an era of new ethnic awareness and a new insistence, on the part of the republics, on asserting control over their own destinies. By Christmas 1991, the Soviet Union was no more. And Roald, as an ethnic Tatar, from now on would always be that: a non-Russian.

The other non-Russian nationalities also understood these dynamics.

The post-coup period was one of astonishing fluidity, with the republics, and the autonomous republics and regions, left scrambling to take advantage of whatever openings they could find. Within weeks, declarations of independence had blossomed in every corner of the Soviet Union, and rumors already had it that Ukraine, in fear that Gorbachev and Yeltsin were forming some powerful new tandem, was on the verge of closing its borders.

During the last days of the Congress of People's Deputies, as they debated and implemented their self-dissolution, Roald arranged a seat for me in the visitors' gallery. One day, in between sessions, we got a good look at Vladimir Zhirinovsky, who'd elbowed his way into the Palace of Congresses and was holding forth in the lobby. At first he attracted only a handful of listeners, but before we'd gone, more than seventy-five people had come to hear him rant, wild-eyed, about the dangerous step the Congress was taking by dissolving itself.

Despite his and others' admonitions, the first and last Soviet Congress of People's Deputies closed its doors forever.

With Roald's parliamentary business over, we went to Kazan to see his parents and meet with political leaders, on what had been intended as a private visit. During the Congress Yeltsin had asked Galina Starovoitova, his adviser on ethnic issues, to go with Roald and me to Kazan. He had thought that Roald's standing in Tatarstan would help Starovoitova, who wanted to discuss relations between Russia and its sovereignty and independence-minded autonomous republics and regions.

The President of Tatarstan had become controversial because he had supported the State Committee on the State of Emergency in the U.S.S.R., which he did, most probably, because he believed that the "autonomous" republics would thereby have been given republic status, more sovereignty than they could hope for under the simple umbrella of the Russian federation. But with the coup's failure, he was now in some trouble, both from the Yeltsin forces and from Tatarstan's progressive elite.

We planned to take the night sleeper, and before leaving for the station, Roald went to check out of the hotel. The floor lady, who had discovered that I was American, was clearly upset that I had shared a room with a Soviet deputy. (To confirm that we were in fact together, one night she had unlocked the door and barged in on us around midnight. Roald had been in the bathroom brushing his teeth and I was sitting up in bed with nothing much on.) That evening, when Roald went to leave his key, she threatened to tell the authorities that he had been sleeping with a "foreign woman."

"I am sure they will be glad to know that we are still together," Roald said coolly. "She is my wife."

We met Galina Starovoitova at the train station and had a light evening snack with her in our compartment before we all turned in for a few hours of sleep.

The next morning we arrived in Kazan to bright sunshine. Waiting for us at the station were many of the republic's high-ranking officials, and we went straight, by motorcade, to visit President Shaimeyev. Roald and I saw almost immediately that there was very little common ground between the Tatars and the Russians. Ethnic perspectives and assumptions had become vastly different in the post-coup days.

The next day, at a final press conference, reporters asked Galina many difficult questions. Despite her efforts at conciliation, the gap between the two camps remained. Suddenly one of the reporters turned to me: "What would you say if the people of Tatarstan elected your husband as President of the Republic?"

At a total loss for words I answered, "I'm ready."

As we were to discover in the coming months, my two words (what was I supposed to say?) were enough to create a fairly sizable debate in Tatarstan, and beyond, about the chance of Roald's return to his republic. Comments appeared in newspapers in Kazan and Moscow; they were even conveyed to me by the Russian Embassy in Washington. And Roald received many telephone calls and appeals from other Tatars. I told Roald seriously that I would support his returning to Tatarstan to run for President if it was something that he really wanted to do. But Roald rejected the idea. "How could I represent the Tatar people when I can't even speak the native language?"

Although my reply to the reporter's question had opened the way for a great deal of speculation about Sagdeev's possible return, it also pried open a piece of Roald. In the now unknown of the former U.S.S.R., he would have to ask himself: If I am not Soviet, who am I? If I am not Russian, then what does it mean to carry a Russian passport? If I do so, does that make me any less Tatar? We knew that the answers to these questions would be a long time coming. It would take the collapse of the Soviet empire and the sheer passage of time before they could form and take shape.

Moscow, like Kazan, was spinning from the late August events. That's why Roald and I were so distressed by our visit to the United States Embassy.

He needed to have his U.S. entry visa reissued, a process he had been told in Washington would take only three days.

Increased emigration made doing business at the Embassy nearly impossible. In order to have his visa processed, we had to set out without breakfast, a shower, or a car, to cue up at 6:00 in the morning. We were due to return to the United States only five days hence. Roald had classes at the University of Maryland to teach and I had to get back to business and launch my daughters in school.

When Roald's turn finally came to see the consular official, after more than an hour's wait, I could tell by the look in his eyes that something was very wrong. "She says it will take two weeks to get the visa."

"But the State Department said that it would take only three days," I protested.

"They did, but this woman says two weeks."

I went up to the window, where a pleasant dark-haired woman sat. Very courteously I explained that there must be some mistake. I told her the State Department had said it would take only three days and we were already booked to return to the United States.

"Yes, but the State Department probably didn't know that your husband is a physicist. We have different regulations for physicists."

I protested. We had gotten a visa in three days just before our wedding, and the whole Embassy had been *very* aware that Roald was a Soviet physicist. What was the problem now? Didn't they keep a list of people who had already been given background checks and cleared? She looked at me blankly.

"What if this were last month? Would the Embassy let a friend of our country languish when his life might be in jeopardy?" I asked.

She looked a little uncomfortable, but still said nothing.

"You know he is married to me, an American citizen. Do you know that he pays substantial taxes in the United States? I can get our marriage certificate and prove that we are married."

"Listen," the woman said from behind the window. "Two weeks is not long to wait. Whenever a Soviet scientist enters an American laboratory, it is regarded as an export of technology."

"I thought the Cold War was over!" I exclaimed. "But even if it's not, in this case the technology transfer is going in the opposite direction, from him to us! My husband has a class of graduate students waiting for his return."

"I'm sorry. All I can do is send his papers to Washington and wait for his visa to be approved."

I was incredulous at this exchange, but below the surface unsettled and fearful. All the rhetoric at the top about the end of the Cold War was useless. It was only talk if it had not translated itself into any kind of meaningful policy at this level.

After lengthy discussion about the problem, Roald overruled my natural instinct to stay with him until he was given his papers. I didn't want to be separated from him in such a volatile and fluid political situation, especially as the Soviet Union was unraveling before our very eyes. But Roald prevailed on me, stressing that I would do him more good in the United States than in Moscow. At least there I could get someone on the telephone to try to expedite the visa process.

I tried very hard to avoid thinking about our imminent separation and to make the most of our remaining time in the Soviet Union.

The rain was coming down in sheets and I rolled over a number of times, looking at the dial on the clock. My limbs felt heavy and my head ached relentlessly. Finally I fell asleep, as if I were descending into a long, narrow passage.

It was still dark when the buzzer finally went off. We dragged ourselves out of bed and dressed as quickly as we could. Roald gathered up my bags.

The green van was waiting for us at the hotel entrance by the time we came down. We headed off toward the Moscow beltway, still in the showering darkness.

Roald and I sat in gloomy silence. He held my hand, which he squeezed from time to time. I could barely look at him, though; I was miserable and humiliated that his U.S. entry visa had not come through. They were now predicting that approval would take more like *three* weeks.

This was the culmination of all my fears: to be separated from Roald in such an unstable political situation. Who knew whether his Soviet passport would even be recognized by the authorities or the border guards by the time he finally got his U.S. visa and could leave?

I had never thought that visa problems would come from the American side. What if it had been exactly one month before, as it easily could have been? If the coup had been successful, the Embassy's delay could have cost Roald his life.

I squeezed his hand back: "Promise me this will never happen again. Don't make me leave next time."

Roald leaned over and kissed me.

The rain came down harder. The van seemed to struggle through vast pools of water on the road, and the windshield wipers swished in frantic unison.

I returned to the United States in rigid anxiety. I asked a number of people for advice about Roald's situation and made calls to the State Department. They told me that perhaps the paperwork had been misplaced. All we could do was wait.

I talked to Roald every night on the telephone, much as we had done in the days before we were married. He filled the phone lines with all kinds of increasingly wild tales about developments in Moscow.

Everyone was moving quickly to take advantage of the power vacuum. Democratic forces sent their own loyal troops, or police, to seize assets, mostly vast tracts of prime Moscow real estate. Although some of their targets had belonged to the Communist Party, not all of them had. We knew of at least two properties, renovated and owned by ordinary people, that were threatened with confiscation by city authorities. Roald also told me that he had gone downstairs two days after I left and found that the Academy of National Economy, where he was staying, had been cordoned off by the police and a decree by Mayor Gavrill Popov had been issued, expelling the Academy from the buildings. The property was unconnected to the Communist Party. Nevertheless, the decree claimed it for the mayor, who planned to use it as a university-style business school, where he would be the (paid) president. I imagined Popov deciding which buildings he wanted, like a greedy man in a pastry shop: "I'll have one of those, one of those, and one of those."

It was ironic that this land seizure was orchestrated by people who Washington thought were the indispensable "democrats" who would lead Russia through a period of critical reform. If anything, this short chapter was straight out of the pages of Bolshevik history. "Rob from the Robbers" or "Expropriate from the Expropriators." There was certainly nothing legal or democratic about how such things were handled.

Moscow in those days had become too much. It was clear that large-scale corruption would be one of the most notable features of the "democratic" era. It was almost too painful to think about the disappointment average Russians would feel, understanding almost immediately that for their bravery and willingness to come out of internal exile they had gotten another group of corrupt politicians. The people had made the historic step, while members of their government were still playing the old Soviet Communist power games.

The Russian people deserved more, and for those of us who believed this intensely, corruption in the name of democracy and market economy was sickening. It would have been even more painful if we had known at the time that two years later Russia's first democratically elected President would do, without apology, what the General Secretary of the Communist Party never had the stomach to do, use advanced weaponry against *his* country's own competitively elected parliament.

We waited three agonizing weeks for Roald's paperwork to come through. I could barely suppress my excitement when I saw him appear through the double doors of the customs and baggage department at Dulles. I ran to greet him. We held on to each other tightly. As on the night of my thirty-eighth birthday, we were again decisively reunited. And like the period before, our reunion marked the beginning of a new chapter.

What changed for us that Thursday afternoon of Roald's return? Perhaps what was different was that we had lost the idealistic glow about what the future would bring to the Soviet Union, at least in the short term; the country's transition promised to be chaotic and possibly even bloody. More important, we no longer had any illusions about the "protective" umbrella the United States would automatically provide for us.

The new world order would be increasingly defined along ethnic and religious lines that have a timeless durability that could make any future conflict uglier and more dangerous than anything we'd seen before. Continuing political turmoil in Russia also carried with it the question: Would there again be a crackdown—to bring order to the increasing chaos, the continued processes of disintegration?

That night I woke, fretful and anxious. White lights blinded my vision, fitful images—obscure and elusive—danced in my head. Denied exit visas, empty canisters of gasoline, abandoned cars and trolleys, border guards stern and unrelenting. The tighter I closed my eyes, the more blinding the white nothingness, the more vivid the impressions.

That dream was different from the ones that used to haunt my nights.

In those days I fought with emptiness and separation, engulfed by swirling thoughts about how I would mobilize the Western press to demand that Roald be freed. During the Cold War human rights could be bartered for trade concessions and arms-control progress—even the scheduling of a summit. Not now. With no further need to prove the righteousness of the Western system, the powerless would again be lost, left to carry their struggles for themselves. And we would wrestle, alone, with our drive to return to Russia and our desire to be free and safe.

I rolled over again. "Would you please give me a hug?" I whispered. Without waking up, Roald drew his arms around me and held me. Suddenly I felt chilled by the boldness of what we had done and the presumptions we'd made. But thank God we did! Whatever the uncertainty, whatever might happen, I knew I'd be comforted by Roald's strong arms, which surrounded me.

In our embrace we form the perfect "circle defense."

Epilogue

During the December 1993 campaign for the new Russian parliament, Roald received the dubious distinction of finding himself ranked number 2 on one of the neo-fascist Vladimir Zhirinovsky's lists of enemies. When I asked him how he felt about it, he shrugged. "There is honor in it."

I wondered for a time if this was bravado on Roald's part, but I came to understand that it was really a statement of another kind: after years of worry about our personal safety and our future, we would simply have to let it go. Life cannot be lived in a state of perpetual fear.

Although nothing like the time before it, the years since the coup of 1991 have not been without their dramas. Twice, Roald's passports were unilaterally declared invalid, and we were caught on one of those occasions in Moscow.

Then as the economy continued to decline, disrupted social forces began again to accuse Russians with Western ties of being "agents of influence." Boris Yeltsin and Foreign Minister Andrei Kozyrev, for a while, were among those so cited, for pandering to the West and doing their bidding in the destruction of the Soviet Union and Russia. They were also held responsible for the collapse of the economy through Western-sponsored "shock therapy." This rash of ugliness was directed at us, too. In the late fall of 1992, rumors circulated everywhere in Moscow that Roald and I had gotten a divorce and that I had had a baby out of wedlock. Friends from all over Moscow called us in the United States to clarify the reports. But the rumors failed to die.

Even more surprising, one day near the end of 1993 I received a phone call from a former U.S. government official. He wanted to recount something he "thought I ought to know about": the chairman of Boris Yeltsin's Commission on Conversion had accused me, by name, of being a CIA agent. This was unprecedented: for a visible American to be denounced publicly as being an intelligence agent, in front of a meeting of Russians and Americans.* "He referred to you as Colonel Eisenhower," my acquaintance told me.

Aside from my natural inclination to laugh about "my rank"—"other Eisenhowers were generals," I said lightheartedly—Roald and I wondered if this was part of some effort either to warn us not to return to Russia or to discourage our Russian friends from visiting us in the United States. If that's what it was, we had some reason to believe that it was no longer coming from the military-industrial complex. Ironically, in the intervening time our relations with the old bosses of the Soviet military-industrial establishment (who still had their jobs) had considerably improved. Many who thought Roald had been a traitor in those first years after our marriage slowly began to see him as an ally, an asset in assisting them with privatization and commercial relations with the West. Indeed, Roald was an interlocutor during the early stages of the space station negotiations between NASA and the Russian Space Agency.

While there might have been residual resentment of us among the intelligence community of the space-military sector, the most likely source of those strange attacks was any one of a number of ultra-nationalist groups, which were, and are, behind the renewed effort to find enemies and scapegoats that can explain the decline and disintegration of the Russian Federation. In their minds the subversive forces are clear: the West and restive ethnic groups like the Chechens, the Dagestanis, and the Tatars on the Volga.†

Tragically Boris Yeltsin, who during the Lithuanian crackdown had reasserted the importance of state-building "bottom up," found unapologetic force, not a peace process, the only means for holding the Russian Federation together. In December 1994 he used significant air power and sent 40,000 troops to Grozny, the capital of Chechnya, to reassert Moscow's control. Threats of such action had also been used on Tatarstan before its

---

* Interestingly, it would never have happened during Communist times. The Communists had, whether they would admit it or not, almost awestruck reverence for American first families.
† The Tatar Republic declared its independence from Russia in the post-coup period and confirmed it with a successful endorsement in a 1992 referendum.

humiliating acquiescence to a treaty with Moscow. With the initiation of a war against Chechnya, Yeltsin understood that Russia would need the "image of an enemy" in order to create national unity. Was nothing learned when central power collapsed in Moscow in 1991?

Our emotions today are varied as we watch the resulting turmoil of those failed processes Roald helped to launch. Disappointment, even anguish, are the strongest of those, but fear is no longer part of our daily lives. Although now it has pretty much gone, the feeling of peril has in many ways defined who we are today. And the risk that we took then has paid us priceless dividends. We have emerged stronger and freer, with a clearer picture of our place in the new order. But for many of our colleagues along the way, there have been great losses, and a sadness, perhaps, still lingers. Many people have gone or have scattered—like debris from a terrible crash. Sakharov is dead. Papa is dead. Weisner is dead. Shishlin died, too, of a heart attack. (My, how he hated to see the rewriting of these historic events already under way in Russia: "Gorbachev *never* thought Eastern Europe would be lost," he'd tell us.) Selyunin is dead. Falin is in Germany. Plekhanov is in Canada. Gerasimov is in Pennsylvania, Korotich is in Boston, and Roald's children and grandchildren have left the former Soviet Union and now live near us in Washington. Ivan, Roald's driver, owns and runs a horse farm near Kiev. Of those still in Russia, Osipyan is out of politics, leading a quieter life, again as a scientist. Arbatov has an all but empty institute left, gutted by so many who've gone, and Velikhov does little physics these days—engaged as he is in selling offshore oil. Sergei Ivanov, we were told, took to the bottle and is now unemployed, and someone said that Rumyetsky is now mixed up with the Russian mafia. Baklanov went to prison and was later pardoned. Shevardnadze went from the frying pan into the fire—he's now President of strife-ridden Georgia. But the saddest figure of all is Gorbachev, who has spent these last years going from gathering to gathering, collecting checks, and acknowledging standing ovations for his own failure to meet his objective, the reform of the Communist system. In the end, institutions failed, people betrayed one another, and the relationships within that society are still in dizzying flux.

Unlike the rest of them, Roald and I were lucky. The thin and fragile chain of events went our way, and the choices that many people made in pursuit of their fate brought us to ours. We are together.